Collaborative Collection

DEVELOPMENT

A Practical Guide
for Your Library

■ James Burgett
■ John Haar
■ Linda L. Phillips

American Library Association
Chicago   2004

The paper used in this publication meets the minimum requirements of American National Standard for Information Sciences—Permanence of Paper for Printed Library Materials, ANSI Z39.48-1992. ∞

Library of Congress Cataloging-in-Publication Data
Burgett, James, 1948–
    Collaborative collection development : a practical guide for your library / James Burgett, John Haar, Linda L. Phillips.
        p.   cm.
    Past, present, future — No one said it would be easy : benefits and problems — Fundamentals : the principles of CCD — The state of the art : varieties of CCD practice — Prerequisites : resources required to initiate and sustain CCD — Creating the framework for an effective CCD partnership — CCD documentation and legal agreements — Investing in success : economics of CCD — Outreach : promoting and publicizing CCD — CCD's impact : assessment and evaluation — Sustaining CCD in the local library.
    Includes bibliographical references and index.
    ISBN 0-8389-0881-0 (alk. paper)
    1. Cooperative collection development (Libraries) 2. Collection management (Libraries) 3. Library cooperation. I. Phillips, Linda L. (Linda Lucille), 1947– II. Haar, John M. III. Title.

Z687.15.B87 2004
025.2′1—dc22   2004004817

Printed in the United States of America

08 07 06 05 04   5 4 3 2 1

CONTENTS

FIGURES

ACKNOWLEDGMENTS

The authors thank the University of Tennessee Professional Development Awards Committee for a stipend that provided research assistance, software, and travel support during the writing of this book. Amy Self earned our special gratitude for her bibliographic and clerical assistance. We appreciate the guidance and rigor of our editors at ALA Editions, Marlene Chamberlain and Mary Huchting. Nancy Petersen, head of collection development at the Knox County (Tennessee) Public Library, served as our critical reader. We deeply appreciate her candid suggestions and diligent review of countless revisions. Public librarians who read this book should thank Nancy, too. To our respective partners, Teresa Hensley Burgett, Ann Carey, and Kenneth McFarland, we express a gratitude that goes beyond words for their patience and support.

INTRODUCTION

What profession does not value the power of collaboration in the information age? From medicine to business, a team of people with unique knowledge, skills, and approaches often comes together to tackle significant problems. Building library collections is an enterprise of magnitude worthy of the team approach. Regardless of library size, type, clientele, or parent organization, librarians have unique perspectives to share about acquiring and accessing materials for their users. When libraries have similar missions, organizational structure, and clientele, an even greater potential exists for the stimulus of collaboration.

In 1994, representatives from the University of Kentucky and the University of Tennessee signed an agreement that created the Information Alliance. Vanderbilt University joined the Alliance in 1999. The agreement stated:

> We advocate information access as the key to the pursuit of excellence in all research and development endeavors for our organizations. This agreement represents a formal commitment to collaboration that is central to our individual library goals and objectives. An alliance among these organizations will strengthen library user access to regional resources, and link information experts formally and informally. Three research libraries within a relatively close geographic area, the University of Kentucky, the University of Tennessee, and Vanderbilt University, can enhance their individual collections and services through an ongoing program of collaboration.

As leaders of collection development at these libraries, we are committed to developing relationships and pursuing projects to fulfill the vision that our library directors and campus administrators expressed in the agreement. Over the past decade, we and our predecessors sponsored meetings for subject counterparts at our respective institutions, with the result that some of our colleagues have begun collaborative collection development projects. We have sponsored training workshops with nationally recognized experts. We have designed a serials archive for which each of the three libraries commits to retaining specified journal backfiles so the others may discard theirs, confident that physical access is available from a trusted partner. We have saved money by subscribing to electronic resources as a consortium, and we have combined our purchasing power to negotiate with journal aggregators.

Our preparation for engaging in collaborative collection development (CCD) was random, the cumulative effect of experience with collection building, work with library users, and participation in professional associations. The abundance of literature about CCD confirms that while librarians continue to value cooperation, they lament its many unfulfilled possibilities. From our CCD experiences and our reading of its literature, we conclude that libraries and their clientele have profited from their considerable investments in CCD. We recognize the need for an authoritative, well-organized synthesis of CCD issues that applies to all types of libraries. A guide that approaches CCD systematically will be of use to librarians and administrators who are considering CCD projects in a dynamic print and electronic environment.

The purpose of this book is to bring together in one place the essential components for starting and sustaining a collaborative collection development program. We take a practical approach to the major issues pertinent to CCD for library directors, collection development officers, and subject specialists who want to launch or participate in CCD activities. The first chapter presents a context for CCD that summarizes progress to date and suggests paths for collaboration in the future. A chapter about CCD benefits and barriers offers a rationale for collaborative endeavors, and another chapter defines principles for successful CCD programs, whether traditional or experimental. A chapter on varieties of CCD practice illustrates the broad spectrum of possibilities for using CCD to accomplish local collection development goals. Chapters on creating and sustaining CCD organizational structures suggest specific steps to assure positive results over the long term. A discussion on the economics of a CCD program gives practical ways of considering costs and benefits. Assessment is a natural component of CCD economics, though an elusive issue in any library function. The benchmarking and measurement strategies we describe can guide a practitioner toward appropriate local applications. Other chapters cover promotion, publicity, and legal issues.

The book can be read sequentially or as individual essays on specific topics. We present issues in context, illustrating current practice with examples of projects. The extensive bibliography pulls together key resources for deeper exploration of CCD. Although we cannot offer answers to many of the complex issues embedded in collaboration, we remain optimistic about the potential for CCD. We recognize the risk involved, but we also appreciate the benefits over time. We offer this book as a starting point for those who wish to build, manage, and assess a CCD program. We wish you every success in expanding on the experiences of librarians who embrace collaboration as an essential function in their collection building programs.

COLLABORATIVE COLLECTION DEVELOPMENT
Past, Present, Future

When the late John W. Gardner quipped, "We are all faced with a series of great opportunities—brilliantly disguised as unsolvable problems," surely he was thinking of collaborative collection development (CCD). For decades, librarians have been tantalized by the potential for combining the strengths of their libraries to build collections, union catalogs, delivery services, automation systems, and, most recently, digital libraries. Collaborative projects achieved positive results in the past century in spite of many false starts, faded dreams, and outright failures. Describing CCD progress is elusive because its products are difficult to measure and opinions vary as to the relative success of CCD programs. Yet, the benefits of innumerable collaborative projects, particularly those sponsored by the research library community, cannot be disputed. Even though many CCD projects have not met librarians' expectations, CCD in the aggregate has demonstrated tangible progress. A standard collection development textbook by G. Edward Evans places CCD in the professional canon of librarianship.[1] Devoting an entire chapter to the subject, Evans succinctly summarizes CCD types, benefits, barriers, issues, and program examples and provides a brief, if somewhat dark, introduction for those considering a CCD venture. The bibliography contains representative sources about CCD programs in academic, school, special, and public libraries.

Formal programs of collaboration have become a matter of broader and more urgent interest among libraries of all types and sizes as means of controlling erosion in the quality of collections and services. The flat budgets, materials cost inflation, and prospective space shortages of the past few decades are especially compelling incentives for libraries to employ collaborative collection development and management. Fortunately, a robust technology environment is exceptionally supportive for CCD, offering potential solutions to some long-standing difficulties with collaboration. The future for CCD seems brighter in the electronic age.

THE IMPACT OF TECHNOLOGY

The digital world has only begun to change the ways that people find and use information. Librarians and their clients have eagerly embraced new digital technologies, discovering global information from their workstations. Investments in electronic resources have put powerful and comprehensive commercial full-text databases on the desktop in the library, office, and home. Library catalogs now include links to freely accessible websites selected by librarians. And, libraries are making their unique and valuable print materials accessible to the world through ambitious digitizing projects. Increasingly, the local library collection provides convenient access to resources held anywhere in the world.

It is small wonder that collection development and management practices are changing as information resources proliferate in digital form. Before the 1970s, collection development emphasized acquisition of resources, but in the past three decades, a shift has occurred toward enabling *user access* to resources held locally and elsewhere, as the number of published materials exceeds library purchasing power and shelving capacity.[2] Technological advances have vastly streamlined the content selection process. Sophisticated approval, subscription, and licensing options now complement traditional practices for collection building. Libraries are buying more access to electronic resources, with less emphasis on local ownership. Where traditional collection development practices focused on selecting individual items from among numerous choices, in the electronic environment librarians often choose aggregated resources. This trend requires less time than selecting individual items and portends that collection development librarians will devote more attention to other issues in the future.[3]

Collection Development and Collection Management

Still, print and other formats represent the vast majority of content in library collections. Considerable ingenuity is required to purchase and store print as the electronic portion of the budget grows and as library buildings approach capacity. Librarians now give more attention to collection management along with selection in order to get the best value from their investments in materials owned and accessed. Collection management functions, such as those in figure 1-1, represent the range of activities necessary for making information content easily accessible to current and future users.

In its broadest sense, then, CCD is a collection management activity. All the tasks in figure 1-1 lend themselves to collaboration, if the results are shared across libraries. Collaboration is one strategy that helps libraries use limited funds to take best advantage of the tantalizing array of information resources that continue to appear on the market in spite of the reduced buying power in today's economic environment. CCD employs collection management strategies on behalf of two or more libraries to enhance the breadth and depth of shared

FIGURE 1-1 *Twenty-First-Century Collection Management Activities*

- Compare local holdings with titles available on a subject to inform new selections.
- Track and analyze use data to decide whether to add or withdraw multiple copies.
- Conduct retention review to cull out-of-scope, little-used, or outdated materials.
- Select and transfer low-use materials with potential research value to high-density storage facilities.
- Analyze collection condition and apply appropriate preservation treatments.
- Select and digitize materials for access and preservation.

collections. Although the benefits of CCD (limiting unnecessary duplication, saving space, controlling costs) seem evident, developing and maintaining a viable CCD program is demanding. Familiarity with some landmarks in CCD history, an understanding of CCD principles, and knowledge of techniques for implementing and sustaining CCD programs will prepare librarians and administrators for confronting seemingly unsolvable problems. To assist those who will develop and lead CCD programs, the following chapters weave a discussion of theoretical issues with models of successful collaboration.

This chapter defines terms associated with CCD, describes key developments in the history of CCD, and summarizes the major issues facing CCD practitioners. The literature of CCD contains an abundance of books and articles about rationale, program descriptions, theoretical models, and problems. Figure 1-2 highlights resources that provide a quick survey of CCD for those with limited time to delve into background reading. With such resources to provide context and this guide to supply principles and strategies, a practitioner should be well prepared to launch and sustain a CCD program.

CCD: COOPERATION WITH A HUMAN DIMENSION

An early but generally accepted definition of *cooperative collection development* is "cooperation, coordination, or sharing in the development and management of collections by two or more libraries entering into an agreement for this purpose."[4] Some cooperative collection development agreements focus on the reduction of overlap, particularly for expensive, specialized materials. Other projects (possibly among the same group of partners) seek to expand resources and may require that a pool of money be created for new purchases. Our use of the phrase *collaborative collection development (CCD)* implies cooperation with a human dimension.[5] The phrase reflects the perspective that librarian attitudes and commitment are central to launching and sustaining successful programs of shared collection development. Thus, we define *collaborative collection development* as multiple libraries coordinating the development and management of their collections with the goal of building broader, more useful combined collections than any library in the group could build individually. When two or more libraries commit to work together systematically on any of numerous and diverse collection development and management projects, they

FIGURE 1-2 *CCD-Express: A Quick Survey of Resources*

Branin, Joseph J. "Shifting Boundaries: Managing Research Library Collections at the Beginning of the Twenty-First Century." *Collection Management* 23, no. 4 (1998): 1–17.

Evans, G. Edward (with the assistance of Margaret R. Zarnosky). "Cooperative Collection Development and Resource Sharing." In *Developing Library and Information Center Collections.* 4th ed., 454–87. Englewood, CO: Libraries Unlimited, 2000.

Harloe, Bart, ed. *Guide to Cooperative Collection Development.* Chicago: American Library Association, 1994.

Hewitt, Joe A., and John S. Shipman. "Cooperative Collection Development among Research Libraries in the Age of Networking: Report of a Survey of ARL Libraries." *Advances in Library Automation and Networking* 1 (1987): 189–232.

International Coalition of Library Consortia (ICOLC). "About the International Coalition of Library Consortia." http://www.library.yale.edu/consortia/ (accessed May 13, 2003).

Johnson, Peggy, and Bonnie MacEwan, eds. *Collection Management and Development: Issues in an Electronic Era. Proceedings of the Advanced Collection Management and Development Institute, Chicago, Illinois, March 26–28, 1993.* Chicago: American Library Association, 1994.

Kachel, Debra E. *Collection Assessment and Management for School Libraries: Preparing for Cooperative Collection Development.* Westport, CT: Greenwood, 1997.

Olson, Georgine N., and Barbara McFadden Allen, eds. *Cooperative Collection Management: The Conspectus Approach.* New York: Neal-Schuman, 1994.

Shreeves, Edward. "Is There a Future for Cooperative Collection Development in the Digital Age?" *Library Trends* 45, no. 3 (Winter 1997): 373–90.

Weber, David C. "A Century of Cooperative Programs among Academic Libraries." *College and Research Libraries* 37, no. 3 (May 1976): 205–21.

are engaging in CCD. CCD may foster access to resources in all formats, print and digital, or it may focus on a single area, such as access to a suite of databases. Libraries may participate in CCD programs to extend the scope and depth of their collections or to address specific problems, such as shortage of shelving space.

Why Collaborate?

Why collaborate on building collections? Through local collection development programs, libraries purchase materials likely to be needed by their clientele. Exponential information growth and insufficient library purchasing power in recent decades have dictated that no library can afford to acquire, manage, and store everything published, nor everything possibly needed by its users. Confronted with this reality, large research libraries launched some of the first formal cooperative programs in an attempt to assure that everything published would be acquired by one of them. Many other collaborative programs have less ambitious but similar goals of purchasing materials in complementary areas to reduce duplication and expand the breadth of resources available for their users.

Libraries also collaborate to gain convenient access to materials that may be outside the scope of the local collection, but are occasionally needed by the local clientele. Multitype cooperatives that include public, academic, and special libraries (or combinations of these) provide their users access to collections containing popular reading, scholarly works, and specialized materials (such as medical or religious) that an individual library might not ordinarily purchase.

There are political incentives for cooperation, too. Library funding agencies appreciate the wise use of resources. Because the costs of CCD are not readily apparent, administrators are more likely to recognize potential benefits and overlook the costs. However, if a funding agent provides special funds or preferential treatment to support collaboration, a savvy librarian will take advantage of such opportunities to expand resources, human and material, on behalf of the library's users.

Effective CCD depends on a symbiotic relationship among three library functions—bibliographic access, interlibrary lending, and collection development. *Bibliographic access* enables library users to discover available resources, often through union catalogs that list the holdings of a group of libraries. *Interlibrary lending* or *ILL* (and, sometimes, on-site borrowing) assures that materials needed by users at partner institutions can be requested and delivered. The *collection-building* portion of the triad focuses on acquiring future resources, the means to guarantee that needed materials will be owned by one of the partner libraries. Materials held by a partner library are only useful to the group if clientele can discover the existence of an item and borrow it when needed. Therefore, collection development in the collaborative context depends on easy access to the catalogs of group members and efficient document delivery.

RESOURCE SHARING: INFRASTRUCTURE FOR CCD

CCD offers a systematic approach to building collections among the partners in a group. The terms *resource sharing, network, bibliographic utility*, and *consortium* frequently arise in discussions about CCD. In a narrow sense, *resource sharing* refers to "bibliographic access and delivery of one library's materials to other libraries in an agreement or a consortium or network."[6] A *network* links libraries through shared bibliographic utilities.[7] A *bibliographic utility*, such as OCLC or RLG, provides online access to the holdings of participating libraries, along with such services as shared cataloging, interlibrary loan, and group purchasing.[8] OCLC regional bibliographic utilities—such as NELI-NET (New England), SOLINET (Southeast), AMIGOS Services, Inc. (Southwest), Western Service Center (Northwest), WILS (Wisconsin), MINITEX (Minnesota and the Dakotas), and ILLINET (Illinois)—provide local attention to libraries of all types and sizes in a geographic area.

Finally, a *consortium* refers to "a community of two or more libraries that have formally agreed to coordinate, cooperate in, or consolidate certain functions. Consortia may be formed according to geographic area, functional type, format, or subject."[9] Other names for groups formed to share resources include *alliance, collaborative, cooperative, digital library*, and *program*. With similar goals and functions, such organizations provide a framework and a group name that represents the institutions pooling a portion of their assets to enhance resources for their local clientele. Assets may consist of cash contributed through membership dues, collection materials, subject or technological expertise, equipment, political influence, and administrative oversight. Consortia services include combinations of cataloging service, subject expertise, materials selection, materials processing, subscription services, and group purchasing at a discount.

Libraries typically participate in more than one resource-sharing group. A school library may belong to a multitype statewide network in addition to a city or county consortium. Large academic libraries participate in local and statewide groups and pay thousands of dollars for membership in national research support groups, such as the Center for Research Libraries (CRL), whose mission includes resource sharing along with other initiatives.

Resource-sharing programs supplement local collections by extending access to content or other resources owned by libraries or organizations that have formed a group. CCD enhances resource sharing by organizing collection management toward an aggregate consortial collection that serves local clienteles. When librarians engage in CCD, they often do so within the framework of an existing network or consortium. Or, they form a new partnership that defines the relationships among the members of their organization as a basis for structuring projects and representing the collaboration to clientele and vendors. CCD happens at the intersection of collection management and resource sharing.

LANDMARKS IN CCD EVOLUTION

Collaborative by nature, librarians for centuries have devised ways to share individual collections. Library historians describe examples of cooperation in medieval libraries. Predecessors of today's CCD programs, however, had their roots in the compilation of catalog holdings in the nineteenth century.[10] Discussions of local lending arrangements have been documented as early as 1851, and formal cooperative cataloging ventures date at least to 1876.[11]

Research Library Initiatives

Joint acquisitions efforts among large research libraries in the early twentieth century expanded collaboration beyond shared cataloging and interlibrary lending. In 1913–14, on behalf of Harvard University, Brown University, Northwestern University, the John Crerar Library, and the American Antiquarian Society, Walter Lichtenstein, library director at Northwestern, purchased nine thousand volumes along with newspapers and manuscripts on a buying trip to South America.[12] In the early 1930s, the University of North Carolina (UNC) and Duke University received a grant to create a joint catalog and divide book collecting subject areas.[13] A relationship that continues today, the program began with the vision of university presidents and the commitment of library directors to create viable programs where no models existed. University librarians Robert Downs (UNC) and Harvie Branscomb (Duke) and their staffs set goals and developed principles of cooperation. They successfully garnered faculty support and secured outside funding for materials acquisition and retrospective conversion of bibliographic records. North Carolina State University later joined the UNC–Chapel Hill and Duke collaboration, and, in 1980, the libraries formed the Triangle Research Libraries Network (TRLN). The group grew to include North Carolina Central University and continues to build on the enviable convergence of opportunity, support, and results apparent in this long-standing affiliation. TRLN librarians have added thousands of resources to their collections and have shared professional knowledge in formal and informal discussions on such issues as serials cost inflation, subject liaison, and materials delivery. Geographic proximity of the libraries, top administrative support, and grant funding are among the factors that engage staff enthusiasm and collaboration.

National Scholarly/Bibliographic Support Groups

National scholarly and bibliographic support associations, particularly the Association of Research Libraries, the Center for Research Libraries, the Library of Congress, OCLC, and the Research Libraries Group, have provided significant leadership for collaboration since the early twentieth century.

Association of Research Libraries (ARL)

In 1932, the directors of 42 large research libraries established the Association of Research Libraries (ARL) to develop the resources and usefulness of research collections in North American libraries. The organization now includes 124 major research institutions.[14] ARL's initiatives encompass scholarly communication, library assessment, and library management. Several programs support collection development.

Center for Research Libraries (CRL)

In 1949, ten academic libraries formed the Midwest Inter-Library Center, forerunner of the Center for Research Libraries (CRL).[15] Supported through membership fees and grants, CRL engages in cooperative collection projects to support scholarly research, including the acquisition of specialized scholarly materials for loan to members. CRL sponsored national conferences on collaborative collection development for its members in 1999 and 2002, with outcomes that included action items explored by working groups.

Library of Congress (LC)

Given its cultural presence as the largest library in the world, the Library of Congress (LC) is a leading contributor in building and managing research collections. The role of the Library of Congress in supporting numerous cooperative programs is discussed later in this chapter.

OCLC

OCLC was incorporated as the Ohio College Library Center in 1967 for the purpose of shared cataloging. Today, OCLC, a not-for-profit membership organization, and its regional affiliates serve 43,559 libraries in eighty-six countries and territories around the world.[16] OCLC offers cataloging, databases, group purchasing, and preservation services as well as an active research and development section that addresses information issues of concern to all types and sizes of libraries. Interlibrary loan service, a cornerstone of resource sharing in academic and public libraries, became much more robust when, in 1979, OCLC launched an interlibrary loan module using library holding symbols in OCLC cataloging records as the basis for placing requests. These machine-readable catalog records provided an easily accessible bibliographic description of materials at other libraries and added precision to identifying libraries that might lend a needed item. Standards and guidelines developed by interlibrary loan practitioners built an effective, albeit slow, process for sharing library collections. Continual improvements to the OCLC interlibrary loan service have streamlined requests and interlibrary financial transactions, while expedited delivery through courier and online transmission has dramatically reduced the time a user must wait after placing a request.

Research Libraries Group (RLG)

In 1974, Harvard, Yale, and Columbia University libraries and the New York Public Library formed the Research Libraries Group to share resources, staff expertise, and operations. Now a not-for-profit membership organization of over 160 universities, national libraries, archives, historical societies, and other institutions with research collections, RLG has developed the RLIN (Research Libraries Information Network) bibliographic utility, information databases, software, and online systems that enable cooperative solutions to acquisition, delivery, and preservation of information.[17] Many products and services are available to members and nonmembers.

The collective energy of these national groups has contributed tremendously to the quality of collections available to the research library community and to the development of programs that support and promote CCD.

National and International CCD Programs

Prominent library directors leading the national associations have worked toward grand visions for CCD over several decades. Some of the resulting programs focused on international area studies, systematically adding scholarly materials to collections primarily located in only the largest research libraries. Fortunately, the collections developed through these programs are available to the international community of scholars through interlibrary lending and on-site access.

The Farmington Plan

One historic endeavor was the Farmington Plan, an ambitious experiment in the coordinated purchase of foreign materials. Sponsored by the Association of Research Libraries from the 1940s to the early 1970s, the Farmington Plan organized member libraries to collectively acquire a copy of every foreign book of potential interest to U.S. scholars. Although in 1965 alone, fifty-two research libraries acquired more than 22,419 volumes, the Farmington Plan gradually lost momentum and evolved into other projects.[18] The plan was officially terminated in December 1972 for reasons that included administrative and logistical problems, increased use of blanket ordering services, reduced acquisition budgets of the participants, and inception of the Library of Congress National Program for Acquisitions and Cataloging (NPAC).[19]

National Program for Acquisitions and Cataloging (NPAC)

With a mission similar to that of the Farmington Plan, NPAC endeavored to acquire and catalog in a timely way all valuable scholarly materials published throughout the world. NPAC, funded through the Higher Education Act of 1965, opened its first office in London in 1966 and expanded to thirteen overseas offices by 1971.[20] The Library of Congress now maintains regional offices in Brazil, Egypt, India, Indonesia, Kenya, and Pakistan for collective acquisition efforts in more than sixty countries. The offices acquire, catalog, preserve, and distribute library materials for the Library of Congress and the 106 institutions, primarily academic research libraries, that participate in the program.

Global Resources Program

Also devoted to improving access to international research resources is the Global Resources Program, a CCD program established in 1997 by ARL and the Association of American Universities (AAU) with funding from the Andrew W. Mellon Foundation. Seed money is used to acquire resources from Africa, Germany, Japan, Latin America, South Asia, and Southeast Asia. The program is envisioned to transcend mere acquisition by developing a better understanding of the materials needed by scholars and the ways that libraries can provide access to them, including the recruitment and training of future area specialists.[21]

CCD Tools

Other national programs resulted in CCD processes and tools that librarians in more modest-sized libraries can use to develop local collections and support CCD. In the late 1970s and early 1980s, RLG and ARL, with help from various American Library Association committees, developed the Conspectus and the North American Collections Inventory Project (NCIP), enabling librarians to describe their collections according to shared definitions and guidelines. RLG's Conspectus uses a numeric scale of 0–5 (representing a range from no holdings to comprehensive collecting) to show a library's existing collection strength, current collecting intensity, and goals for future collecting, all according to LC class numbers.[22] ARL's Office of Management Studies led the development of the NCIP that provided the framework and documentation for libraries to implement the Conspectus by contributing data to an online inventory of collections according to shared definitions and guidelines.[23]

Although reliant on the judgment of individual librarians, the Conspectus provided a snapshot of collection strengths and offered valuable insights about local collections. Considerable discussion in the library literature outlines benefits and liabilities of the Conspectus as well as examples of applications in all types and sizes of libraries. Whatever the reasons—its subjectivity, complicated methodology, or political disinterest in cooperation—the Conspectus has not achieved its intended vision to be the foundation for CCD among research libraries. However, it is still available for librarians to assess collections. Now called the WLN Conspectus, "the conspectus approach" software is available from OCLC as a component of its Automated Collection Assessment and Analysis Services.[24]

A less subjective collection measure was the National Shelflist Count, established by the American Library Association in 1973 to measure the number of titles by LC class among participating libraries. It was the forerunner of today's North American Title Count (NATC) administered by ALA's Association for Library Collections and Technical Services.[25] NATC numerical data, primarily contributed by academic libraries, are valuable for comparing collection size, offering a complement to the Conspectus focus on collection content. For 688 Library of Congress (LC) and National Library of Medicine (NLM) call number ranges, NATC contains tables that enumerate and analyze the number of classified titles (regardless of format) held by participating U.S. and Canadian libraries. Twelve counts have been conducted since its inception; participants increased from seventeen in 1973 to fifty-five in 2001. Any library can use the NATC database to measure collections and use the relational data in single- and multiple-institution settings. NATC is valuable for CCD partners who want to compare collections, coordinate a new program, and evaluate results. A useful first step for librarians who are getting acquainted with CCD counterparts is to assess their local collections using the Conspectus and NATC.

MULTITYPE CONSORTIA

Although the largest research libraries have collaborated on national and international scales, the majority of libraries are more likely to participate in local, state, and regional alliances. From 1930 to 1960, cooperative projects emerged at a rate of about one per year; from 1960 forward, the rate of new projects increased dramatically, with eighteen formed in 1970 alone.[26] Attesting to the growth and diversity of formal collaboration, the 2002–2003 edition of *American Library Directory* lists more than 440 active networks, consortia, and other cooperative library organizations in the United States and Canada whose members are libraries of all sizes and types. Two of the earliest consortia were MINITEX, the Minnesota Interlibrary Telecommunications Exchange, and ILLINET, the Illinois Library and Information Network, both established during the 1960s. Their stories are representative of the multitype (composed of academic, public, and special libraries) cooperative agencies that have emerged across the country over the past forty years.[27] Common to consortia such as these were centralized processing, delivery services, photocopying, reciprocal borrowing, and automation services, including production of union lists. Some consortia had centralized headquarters with staff. However, a 1972 study of academic library consortia reported that activities related to CCD were limited, possibly because cooperatives gave higher priority to less-expensive initiatives with more immediate results.[28]

An exception is the Network of Alabama Academic Libraries (NAAL), established in 1984 to coordinate resource sharing among public and private institutions offering graduate education.[29] NAAL's Cooperative Collection Development Committee created a framework for a statewide cooperative collection development program that outlined each participant's responsibilities and secured state funding. Funded by the Alabama Commission on Higher Education (ACHE) and the participating libraries, NAAL members have obtained access to several databases of common interest, with each member paying its share of the total cost negotiated by ACHE. The consortium recently received a grant from the Institute for Library and Museum Services to digitize state historical treasures, continuing CCD in the digital arena.[30]

Many statewide networks formed more recently have had CCD as an incentive, particularly for shared access to databases. A 1996 special issue of *Library Hi Tech* featured network developments in forty-six states, including background on hundreds of consortia, such as the well-known OhioLINK, GALILEO, and the Committee on Institutional Cooperation (CIC), that thrive today.[31] The International Coalition of Library Consortia (ICOLC), formed in 1997 to facilitate discussion among consortia on issues of common interest, now has over 150 members, another signal of the library network's vitality in the digital age. With links to member websites, the ICOLC web pages give useful examples of consortium organizational details and scope of service. Also valuable to librarians contemplating CCD partnerships are ICOLC statements on such current issues as statistical measures of web-based resources and preferred practices for selection and purchase of electronic information. The ICOLC website connects to Library Consortia Documents Online, a collection of primary source documents on the governance and administration of library consortia and cooperatives. The ICOLC website also contains illustrations for starting or evaluating CCD programs, a bonanza of possibilities for CCD through a network.[32]

Today's library networks have demonstrated great success in sharing access to electronic resources. They complement print-based CCD projects sponsored by groups of libraries within and across networks around the world; examples are highlighted throughout this guide. Collaboration in the realm of print is beginning to converge on developing print archives that would preserve the paper versions of journals in publishers' online collections. Because the print collection occupies prime library real estate and will receive less use in the future, libraries can collaborate on storing a limited number of print copies for the common good.

SCHOOL, SPECIAL, AND PUBLIC LIBRARY CCD

The many documented examples of CCD throughout the world, including those in public, special, and school libraries, confirm that collaboration has appeal in diverse communities. A project supported by the Library Services and Construction Act (LSCA) among four public libraries in rural east-central Illinois demonstrated that CCD can be successful among libraries of all types and sizes. When participants cooperated in seeking solutions to limited funds and lack of materials and resources, the result was better, more cost-effective service to the community.[33] Collection assessment projects conducted jointly by public libraries in Illinois, Nebraska, Alaska, and other states reflect a similar commitment to collaboration; a common theme among the programs was their use of the Conspectus to compare collection strengths as a first step toward setting goals.[34]

Exemplifying CCD in the subject area of law, six libraries formed the Whatcom County [Washington] Legal Materials Group for the express purpose of strengthening collections.[35] The group, composed of two special, two public, and two academic libraries, received grant funds to acquire print materials and database access. Participants produced a brochure publicizing their services and demonstrated service improvements through formal evaluation.

For school libraries, the most likely CCD partners may be public libraries. Such was the case for public schools in California that were awarded special collection development funds from the state.[36] The schools relied on professionals from public libraries to help select and provide access to new materials, evidence of the emerging trend that a valuable CCD commodity is human expertise. CCD practitioners can learn from projects such as these that reflect productive and relatively unpublicized relationships among libraries within various consortia.

Recognizing the importance of the human element in successful programs, the preceding projects affirm a theme in the literature on cooperative collection development: collaborative collection projects succeed or fail because of attitude, trust, and communication among CCD participants. CCD practitioners can learn from projects such as these that reflect productive and relatively unpublicized relationships among libraries within various consortia.

CCD FOR THE FUTURE

Cooperative projects now exist among libraries of similar type or size as well as across library sizes, types, and geographic regions. CCD activities range from well-funded formal programs to informal recognition of the differences in collection focus among resource-sharing partners. Although many have written about the limited success of CCD programs, library consortia are thriving, new collaborative ventures continue to emerge, and the professional literature abounds with program descriptions. Because results are difficult to quantify and costs are often intangible, debate continues about the practicality and cost-effectiveness of CCD programs. Many CCD initiatives have quietly faded away for a variety of reasons—lack of leadership, failure of counterparts at partner institutions to embrace the goals of the program, lack of clarity in goals, and difficulty in measuring results.

In 1983, Joe Hewitt and John Shipman surveyed ninety ARL members to document current CCD activities and to identify enabling factors as well as barriers in actual practice. Their landmark study covered CCD program scope and content, geographic distribution, and reasons for collaboration, and included opinions of collection development practitioners.[37] The researchers learned that the most common program activities included sharing information about expensive purchases, coordinating journals selection, and making joint purchases. Problems cited by librarians focused on program organization and procedures for implementation. ARL libraries placed high value on the *idea* of CCD, but actually implementing a program was fraught with difficulty. The researchers concluded that CCD was not a mainstream activity in research libraries and that establishing a CCD program was too demanding for most, given the perceived benefit.

Local Access to Global Collections

Today's collection management environment is dramatically different from the period surveyed by Hewitt and Shipman. The phrase *local access to global collections* describes contemporary trends in publishing and collection management.[38] Library collections now include access to valuable information located on servers around the world. Many libraries select and catalog resources that are freely available on the Internet to integrate these materials with their local holdings. Universities have begun to explore the concept of local institutional repositories where researchers post scholarly work, such as theses and dissertations, articles published in refereed journals, and technical reports, on local computers linked to the Internet. This increased interest in expanding access has generated a campaign to encourage scholars to share their work freely, including peer-reviewed journal articles, preprints, preliminary findings, and data sets.[39] Collaboration will be essential for the open access movement to succeed. Assuring that all disciplines are represented somewhere in the world could become a CCD initiative.

Trends such as these incorporate CCD values, offering a bridge between the last decades of the twentieth century and the future digital world. Although library collections are still predominately print-based, the enthusiasm of users for all things electronic and the explosion of web-accessible resources, both commercial and free, will inevitably influence CCD opportunities and practices.

Online services have indirectly fulfilled many traditional CCD goals. Citation and full-text databases, connections to catalogs that quickly reveal resources available at other libraries, and freely available websites offer local clientele a virtual universe of resources. Future CCD programs can build on these achievements. Dual print and electronic library collections present myriad issues on which traditional

CCD principles and innovative practices can come together. Perhaps librarians of the future will spend less time building collections; in fact, collaborative models developed for print collections in the twentieth century may not be relevant much longer.[40] As print and electronic systems merge, librarians may become content managers rather than selectors.[41] National libraries and associations will continue their leadership in digitizing print collections to preserve and expand access to the research treasures of the world. Librarians will select and incorporate global resources of interest to their clientele into local collections. Library partnerships will focus on finding the best ways to meet local information needs. Formal collaboration may involve sharing subject expertise, solving specialized library functional problems, and creating web pages.[42] The digital world has just begun to change communication and learning. As librarians and their clients ponder the consequences of local access to global collections, it is inevitable that collaboration patterns will change.

A New Golden Age

What lies ahead for collaborative collection development? The library community could be on the brink of a new golden age for resource sharing. Collaborative collection development and management can bolster services that are eroding through funding limitations. Funding agents recognize the benefits of collaborative collection development and applaud librarians' efforts to limit unnecessary duplication, save space, and reduce costs through collaboration. The current technological environment promotes communication among CCD partners, supporting good ideas with the means for success. Prospects seem unlimited for all kinds of collaboration.

Implementing and maintaining a viable collaborative program are demanding. Although each CCD experience adds to our cumulative understanding, much remains to be tried and the results shared. Numerous books and articles describe the obstacles to moving beyond the culture of a self-sufficient local collection. However, a library collection that consists of items held locally along with resources accessed globally calls for a more interdependent approach to collection building. One of the values that informed the development of our Information Alliance was to create a framework that would transcend the people involved at any given time.[43] Recognizing that the process of CCD moves slowly, we recommend setting measurable goals and creating as simple an organization as possible. Have patience, persevere, and recognize that the long-term benefits will be worth the effort. The words of Hugh Atkinson have been a touchstone for us: "We should not be afraid to fail. We will never have absolute guarantees of success, and it is only through attempting to provide better library service that we will in fact improve our libraries and their services."[44]

NOTES

1. G. Edward Evans, with the assistance of Margaret R. Zarnosky, "Cooperative Collection Development and Resource Sharing," in *Developing Library and Information Center Collections,* 4th ed. (Englewood, CO: Libraries Unlimited, 2000), 454–87.

2. Joseph J. Branin, "Shifting Boundaries: Managing Research Library Collections at the Beginning of the Twenty-First Century," *Collection Management* 23, no. 4 (1998): 5.

3. Ross Atkinson, "Access, Ownership, and the Future of Collection Development," *Collection Management and Development: Issues in an Electronic Era. Proceedings of the Advanced Collection Management and Development Institute, Chicago, Illinois, March 26–28, 1993,* ed. Peggy Johnson and Bonnie MacEwan, 92–109 (Chicago: American Library Association, 1994).

4. Paul H. Mosher and Marcia Pankake, "A Guide to Coordinated and Cooperative Collection Development," *Library Resources and Technical Services* 27, no. 4 (October–December 1983): 420.

5. Paul H. Mosher, "Cooperative Collection Development Equals Collaborative Interdependence," *Collection Building* 9, no. 3/4 (1989): 30.

6. Mosher and Pankake, "Guide," 420.

7. Ibid.

8. OCLC, http://www.oclc.org/ (accessed May 13, 2003); RLG, http://www.rlg.org/ (accessed May 12, 2003).

9. Bart Harloe, ed., *Guide to Cooperative Collection Development* (Chicago: American Library Association, 1994), 22.

10. Joe W. Kraus, "Prologue to Library Cooperation," *Library Trends* 24, no. 2 (October 1975): 169.

11. David C. Weber, "A Century of Cooperative Programs among Academic Libraries," *College and Research Libraries* 37, no. 3 (May 1976): 205–21.

12. Ibid., 207.

13. Patricia Buck Dominguez and Luke Swindler, "Cooperative Collection Development at the Research Triangle University Libraries: A Model for the Nation," *College and Research Libraries* 54, no. 6 (November 1993): 470–96.

14. Lee Anne George and Julia Blixrud, comps., *Celebrating Seventy Years of the Association of Research Libraries, 1932–2002* (Washington, DC: Association of Research Libraries, 2002).

15. CRL, http://www.crl.edu/ (accessed November 5, 2003).

16. "About OCLC," http://www.oclc.org/about/ (accessed May 3, 2003).

17. RLG, http://www.rlg.org/ (accessed May 12, 2003).

18. Weber, "Century," 209.

19. Abner J. Gaines, "Farmington Plan," in *Encyclopedia of Library History,* ed. Wayne A. Wiegand and Donald G. Davis (New York and London: Garland Publishing, 1994), 193.

20. John Y. Cole, "Library of Congress. Washington, D.C., USA," in *Encyclopedia of Library History,* ed. Wayne A. Wiegand and Donald G. Davis (New York and London: Garland Publishing, 1994), 379.

21. Deborah L. Jakubs, "The AAU/ARL Global Resources Program: Both Macrocosm and Microcosm," *ARL: A Bimonthly Report on Research Library Issues and Actions from ARL, CNI, and SPARC,* no. 206 (October 1999); Association of Research Libraries, "AAU/ARL Global Resources Program," http://www.arl.org /collect/grp/grp.html (accessed May 3, 2003).

22. Nancy E. Gwinn and Paul H. Mosher, "Coordinating Collection Development: The RLG Conspectus," *College and Research Libraries* 44, no. 3 (March 1983): 128–40.

23. Jutta Reed-Scott, *Manual for the North American Inventory of Research Library Collections,* rev. ed. (Washington, DC: Association of Research Libraries, 1988).

24. OCLC Lacey Product Center, Automated Collection and Analysis Services, http://www.oclc.org/western/products/aca/conspect.htm (accessed May 2, 2003).

25. Association for Library Collections and Technical Services, ALCTS CMDS North American Title Count, http://www.ala.org/Content/NavigationMenu/ ALCTS/Publications6/Catalog/Collection_Management1/2001_North_American _Title_Count.htm (accessed November 5, 2003).

26. Weber, "Century," 210.

27. Michael J. LaCroix, "MINITEX and ILLINET: Two Library Networks," *Occasional Papers* (University of Illinois at Urbana-Champaign. Graduate School of Library and Information Science) 178 (May 1987): 1–42.

28. Ruth J. Patrick, *Guidelines for Library Cooperation: Development of Academic Library Consortia* (Santa Monica, CA: System Development Corporation, 1972), 172.

29. Sue O. Medina, "The Evolution of Cooperative Collection Development in Alabama Academic Libraries," *College and Research Libraries* 53, no. 1 (January 1992): 7–19.

30. Network of Alabama Academic Libraries (NAAL), http://www.ache.state .al.us/NAAL/ (accessed May 13, 2003).

31. C. Edward Wall and Donald Riggs, eds., "State of the State Reports: Statewide Library Automation, Connectivity, and Resource Access Initiatives," *Library Hi Tech* 14, no. 2/3 (1996): 1–352. See also OhioLINK, http://www.ohiolink.edu (accessed May 13, 2003); GALILEO, http://www.galileo.peachnet.edu (accessed May 13, 2003); and CIC, http://www.cic.uiuc.edu/ (accessed June 26, 2003).

32. ICOLC, http://www.library.yale.edu/ consortia/ (accessed May 13, 2003).

33. Ruth Shasteen, "Cooperative Collection Management among Four Rural Libraries," in *Cooperative Collection Management: The Conspectus Approach*, ed. Georgine N. Olson and Barbara McFadden Allen, 99 (New York: Neal-Schuman, 1994).

34. Georgine N. Olson and Barbara McFadden Allen, eds., *Cooperative Collection Management: The Conspectus Approach* (New York: Neal-Schuman, 1994).

35. Robert Lopresti, "Sharing the Law: A Cooperative Legal Materials Project," *Advances in Library Resource Sharing* 3 (1992): 17–27.

36. Blanche Woolls, "Public Library—School Library Cooperation; a View from the Past with a Prediction for the Future," *Journal of Youth Services in Libraries* 14, no. 3 (Spring 2001): 8–10.

37. Joe A. Hewitt and John S. Shipman, "Cooperative Collection Development among Research Libraries in the Age of Networking: Report of a Survey of ARL Libraries," *Advances in Library Automation and Networking* 1 (1987): 189–232.

38. Branin, "Shifting Boundaries," 2.

39. Association of Research Libraries, "Issues in Scholarly Communication: Open Access," http://www.arl.org/scomm/open_access/ index.html (accessed May 14, 2003).

40. Edward Shreeves, "Is There a Future for Cooperative Collection Development in the Digital Age?" *Library Trends* 45, no. 3 (Winter 1997): 373–90.

41. John M. Budd and Bart M. Harloe, "Collection Development and Scholarly Communication in the 21st Century: From Collection Management to Content Management," in *Collection Management for the 21st Century: A Handbook for Librarians*, ed. G. E. Gorman and Ruth H. Miller, 3–25 (Westport, CT and London: Greenwood, 1997).

42. Shreeves, "Future," 388.

43. Information Alliance, http://www.lib.utk.edu/~alliance/ (accessed June 12, 2003).

44. Hugh C. Atkinson, "Atkinson on Networks," *American Libraries* 18, no. 6 (June 1987): 439.

2

NO ONE SAID
IT WOULD BE EASY
Barriers and Benefits

Collaborative collection development is probably the most discussed and least practiced concept in all of collection management and development. Whatever its frequency of employment, no one can dispute that it is the subject of intensive, if not excessive, deliberation and analysis. The literature is replete with articles (our bibliography is only a sampling) examining conceptual underpinnings and reporting case studies of CCD. Conferences on the topic sell out; programs fill auditoriums beyond capacity.

Even if CCD is practiced more than we might realize, it would still be fair to say that a disturbing imbalance exists between the volume of rhetoric and the level of activity. In fact, a thorough study of the topic makes it difficult to avoid the suspicion that discussion is too frequently a surrogate for action. This global phenomenon also plays out locally. Although detailed preparation is indispensable to successful collaboration, those who manage CCD projects can attest that endless dialogue and overly meticulous planning are often dilatory weapons in the hands of those who would rather not participate.

CCD continues to fascinate librarians despite our reluctance to implement it. We find it tantalizing in its possibilities but see the road to its fulfillment cluttered with obstacles and pitfalls. Most of the problems cited here are drawn from literature written not by opponents of CCD, but by its advocates. Even those who are firmly committed to the concept acknowledge that it is difficult to achieve. In fact, effective collaboration may well be impossible to attain without boldly confronting the many potential obstructions before making a commitment.

These concerns range from the emotional to the eminently rational. Some may seem trivial, while others cut directly to the core of our value system and challenge time-honored precepts of library service. But all are vitally important to those, from institutional administrators to working librarians, who raise them, and all therefore carry the power to undercut CCD projects. Collaboration, as a human enterprise, totally depends for its success upon the goodwill of its participants. Thus, CCD managers should seriously address the objections of those they rely on to support and practice collaborative programs. They should also be mindful that none of the most often cited barriers is insurmountable, especially if negotiated in the context of the desirable outcomes of CCD described later in this chapter.

The four major obstacles to collaboration are the sacrifice of autonomy, risk aversion, organizational complexities, and financial disincentives. Figure 2-1 includes questions addressed in the following sections.

SACRIFICE OF AUTONOMY

CCD is almost universally accepted as a wonderful idea in theory. But the first obstacle is that distributed collection building inevitably compromises each participating library's freedom to develop collections independently without concern for overlap or duplication with other libraries. Although our vision may be global, our focus must be local, and any process that restrains our freedom to act unilaterally to serve local needs is one that deserves careful scrutiny.

It is no coincidence that the proliferation of library consortia in the 1990s paralleled the emergence of web-based digital resources. Participating in consortia enables libraries to acquire electronic materials at a lower cost than they would pay individually (sometimes, in fact, they pay nothing at all). What makes this transaction uniquely appealing is that each participant receives a "copy" of a product that it desires to offer locally. Each can provide any consortium-acquired resource to its patrons immediately upon demand. Consortial pur-

| FIGURE 2-1 | *Concerns to Address When Considering CCD* |

▓ Sacrifice of Autonomy
   Will patrons suffer if my library collects at a lower intensity in
      some fields?
   Should we spend local funds on materials to be used by patrons of
      other libraries?
   Will administrators perceive CCD as a waste of financial resources?

▓ Risk Aversion
   What happens if partners do not live up to their commitments or
      withdraw?
   Will my library lend more to other libraries than it receives from
      them?
   Can I rely on selectors at other libraries to build collections for my
      patrons?
   Will my library be obligated to build collections our patrons don't
      need?

▓ Organizational Complexities
   Will my library find compatible partners?
   Can we develop a clear and equitable workload for all the libraries
      in the consortium?

▓ Financial Disincentives
   Will the cost of organizing and administering CCD outweigh the
      benefits of collaboration?
   Is it possible to measure CCD costs and benefits?

chasing of electronic resources is the ultimate win-win situation. Every consortium member, in effect, acquires every electronic tool for itself at a discount and sacrifices nothing.

When collaborative purchasing is print-based, however, this dynamic changes completely. Savings accrue not from bulk purchases of multiple copies of print materials, but from the purchase of single copies of each work to be held at dispersed locations and shared among the members. Collaborative schemes require member libraries to relinquish the convenience of locating all these print items in their own collections in exchange for participating in an effort to broaden the group's aggregate collecting strength. No matter what the library gains, the attention of its governing body, its staff, and possibly its users will inevitably be drawn to what it gives up.

Few libraries are genuinely independent. Most report to a higher administrative entity, be it a college, school system, or local government, upon which they depend for financial support. Yet wherever they fit in an overarching structure of governance, they ordinarily retain a wide measure of autonomy that they guard tenaciously. This autonomy is, in librarians' world view, synonymous with our freedom of action to develop collections and services targeted to local needs. Even when we acknowledge that our budgets are wholly inadequate to address these needs effectively, we may feel that any remedy that diminishes our autonomy comes at too high a price.

Though CCD is actually an exercise in reciprocity, it can appear to be an act of dependency and altruism that runs counter to powerful institutional tendencies toward self-reliance, self-sufficiency, and competition. In large academic libraries, CCD forces reexamination of a myth, still prevalent in collection building practice if not in rhetoric, that it is possible and desirable—indeed, a mark of prestige— to build comprehensive collections unilaterally.[1] In libraries of all types and sizes, it violates a time-honored imperative that local money should be spent only on local needs and never for resources not needed locally.[2]

Institutional administrators, especially, may not be warmly receptive to proposals that their libraries acquire materials specifically for the purpose of sharing them with other libraries. Moreover, entering into a compact that, whatever its benefits, obligates us *not* to acquire materials our patrons may desire cuts to the core of our service-oriented sensibilities. We are not comfortable telling patrons that there are conscious gaps in our collection because we have agreed that another library take responsibility for a discipline.[3] Nor do we find it easy to justify document delivery, no matter how rapid, as a viable alternative to the convenience of finding items tucked away on our shelves.

Some uncomfortable trade-offs are inevitable in a carefully planned scheme of collaborative collection building and resource sharing. But librarians and library users may find them more palatable by focusing on the real choices at hand in the austere economic environment of contemporary collection development. We no longer have the luxury (if we ever did) of filling all local needs through local acquisition. Even in the largest libraries, comprehensive collection building has long since been exposed as the myth it always was, and smaller libraries find it increasingly difficult to fulfill their more modest aims of crafting collections to serve the immediate information demands of their constituencies.

Reduced purchasing power and the concomitant growth of inter-library loan activity make it clear that every library already operates in a web of dependent relationships to round out its collections. Our real choice is to coordinate acquisitions or to continue to practice the fragmented culture of autonomous collection building. We can purchase ever-smaller segments of the materials we consider essential and gamble that other libraries have serendipitously acquired the items that we could not afford—and that we can borrow them within a reasonable time. Or, we can engage other libraries in a joint collection development program to increase the probability that these items can be readily identified and quickly supplied. We can choose to have our freedom of action reduced by CCD, where we exercise control, or eroded by a fiscal contraction that is beyond our control.

RISK AVERSION

When a library enters into a CCD agreement, it ordinarily pledges to build collections in designated categories at a depth sufficient to supply more than basic-level resources for the users of every library in the consortium. To meet its obligations to the consortium, the library will reallocate funds to reduce its rate of acquisition in other categories where it relies upon a partner library's collection to provide resources for its patrons. If librarians plan carefully, reductions will occur in areas that are peripheral to local interests, and the library will maintain core collections even where it downsizes. Unavoidably, however, the library will intentionally impair its ability to respond to local information demands in some subjects or formats with materials in its own collection. Librarians and users will have to trust another library, over which they have no operational control, to capably build and maintain the collections they have determined not to build. This act of trust is at the heart of the CCD bargain. As in any relationship, trust entails a leap of faith, a calculated risk that a partner will fulfill its commitments. In this case, the risk is all the more acute because the obligations at issue are usually not legally binding. Lack of trust presents the most significant psychological barrier to a library's participation in CCD.

Every library in a CCD program places trust not only in partner libraries' administrations and staffs, but also in their parent organizations and funding agencies. Even if goodwill prevails among the participating libraries, some may encounter external difficulties, such as economic setbacks, that could force alteration of their prior commitments to the consortium. New library or institutional administrators may be less attracted to collaborative endeavors than were their predecessors.[4] In the worst-case scenario, a participant may pull out of the group, leaving the remaining members with collection gaps that have widened over years of intentional neglect and with nowhere to turn within the consortium for immediate help.

Other CCD risks can stem from fundamental differences in the sizes and missions of consortial partners, particularly in multitype cooperatives. These disparities lead to fears among larger libraries that their ratio of contributions to receipts may be unjustifiably large.[5] University librarians, for instance, might view CCD as little more than a means of funneling resources acquired at dear cost to municipalities or small colleges who failed to invest adequately in their libraries. Relations with institutional administrators and patrons could suffer from a perception that a library inconveniences its primary users by lending its materials too generously to other libraries.

Persistent questions rooted in traditional collection development values reflect the risks taken by libraries that invest in CCD. Will selectors distanced from a library's users in location and organizational context be able to anticipate these users' needs discerningly? Will a bibliographer at a large public university be mindful of the specialized research interests of faculty at a small private institution? Will a librarian who acquires materials for a suburban public library be conversant with the reading habits of an inner-city branch's clientele? Collections built for multiple libraries could become so generic that most members of the consortium are no longer well served.

Fulfilling consortial obligations could weaken collections in areas at the center of a library's local collection policy. Commitments to acquire materials at an intensive level in some subjects may limit funding for other subjects of key local interest.[6] The same commitments might lock a library into building intensively in areas that decline in importance as its user population changes and patron needs evolve. An agreement that once enabled a library to build collections where it wanted to be strongest could, after years of faculty turnover, curricular revision, or demographic shifts, become a counterproductive drag on its ability to respond to new information demands.[7] One reason the Farmington Plan disintegrated was its inability to adapt to the changing priorities of its member institutions.[8]

Libraries joining a CCD project should clearly understand that they are entering into a risky venture. It should be equally clear, however, that conventional collection development has become a high-risk exercise in stretching declining buying power to meet expanding demands. Collaboration does not mean abandoning the safe and sure for a precarious journey into the unknown. Rather, it means tempering a practice that is increasingly unsustainable with a no less uncertain but potentially more secure alternative that acknowledges risk but is vested in systematic plans.

ORGANIZATIONAL COMPLEXITIES

Collaborative collection development can take many forms. A basic, easily achievable project might be an ad hoc agreement among a few libraries to purchase and share segments of an expensive microform set. More sophisticated partnerships might attempt to coordinate serials cancellation. Even more elaborate is the creation of a distributed last copy repository. The most highly developed model of CCD, that which attracts most of our rhetorical attention, is a detailed work plan that assigns responsibility for building intensive print collections in clearly defined categories (subjects, languages, or formats, for instance) to cooperating libraries. Where a program fits on the scale of complexity from informal agreement to highly structured consortium determines the level of difficulty its participants will encounter in planning and sustaining collaboration. And the greater the degree of this difficulty, the more discouraging the prospect of CCD becomes. Problems in identifying suitable partners, delineating a clear and equitable distribution of labor, and measuring costs and benefits are the chief impediments to converting the often glib talk about CCD into action.

Alliances formed among libraries of similar sizes, budgets, and institutional missions tend to offer the greatest prospects for successful collaborative collection building. Though multitype cooperatives for resource sharing and purchasing digital materials operate effectively in many regions, print-based CCD can be challenging for consortia that include, for example, large academic libraries, college libraries, and public libraries, each with distinct and even divergent collection-building agendas. Thus, libraries contemplating CCD programs are inclined to seek organizationally compatible libraries as potential partners, a task that can often be quite difficult. This problem is likely to afflict large research libraries most acutely, if only because there are far more small libraries than large ones.

Hewitt and Shipman found that for ARL libraries the lack of suitable regional partners was a major impediment to participation in print-based CCD. Many reported dissatisfaction with their experience in local or state consortia predominately composed of non-ARL libraries. They preferred to join other ARL members in geographic proximity and with similar commitments to developing research-level collections.[9] The Triangle Research Libraries Network (TRLN), often cited as the prototype of research library cooperation, works because these factors are clearly present. Smaller academic libraries and public libraries may find it easier to identify prospective partners because medium- to small-sized libraries are more numerous and more frequently characterized by favorable geography and mission compatibility. But they will have to contend with other barriers related to organizational structure and governance.

Many libraries responding to the Hewitt-Shipman survey also cited "lack of comparable collection development structure" as a significant problem in operating CCD programs.[10] CCD is functionally a people-to-people endeavor achieved through regular contacts among collection development practitioners. True collaboration takes place only if those who build collections can communicate with their counterparts about collections issues as they arise. If one library organizes selection responsibilities by subject while another organizes by language, for instance, selectors may not match well enough to collaborate effectively. Libraries who organize their collection development operation on a traditional hierarchical model may not pair ideally with those who take a team approach to management.

Procedural variations can also hinder progress. Libraries who manage serials selection and deselection by committee may have difficulty coordinating subscriptions with libraries whose bibliographers can independently acquire and cancel serials. Even differences in classification systems can impair the creation of a consortial conspectus.[11]

Structural and operational inconsistencies can complicate the creation of a collaborative schema that is fiscally, organizationally, and politically viable. Delineating each library's collecting responsibilities, an exercise in which precision is crucial, could break down over an inability to define subject terms in a lingua franca intelligible to all parties. Academic libraries often define subjects in terms consistent with their parent institutions' localized and idiosyncratic curricula, and one library's understanding of the intellectual landscape of a discipline may differ radically from another's. The increasingly interdisciplinary nature of research and instruction can challenge those attempting to identify discrete collecting areas to apportion among consortial partners.[12] Where does psychology intersect with educational psychology or psychiatry? Will the focus of women's studies be the same at each institution? When all can reach consensus on describing a subject, disagreements may arise about defining what is core, to be collected by every library in the group, and what is peripheral, to be acquired only by the library charged with building a research-level collection for the collaborative.[13]

When partnering libraries' financial assets vary widely, disparities in their acquisition commitments will surely result. Large libraries, reflecting that they are net lenders by a wide margin and that the consortium's workload is unevenly distributed, will have to work through their suspicions that the smaller partners are exploiting them.[14] Reservations may also arise with the discovery that not all participating libraries are equally efficient in their operations, leading to resentment that some partners are not pulling their fair share of the collaborative load.[15]

FINANCIAL DISINCENTIVES

Libraries that enlist in CCD ventures with the objective of reducing their acquisitions expenditures are likely to find that sharing collections will not adequately compensate for a downsized materials budget. CCD is not a cost-cutting measure. It implies that collection spending will be curtailed in some areas but increased in others. It is a tool that groups of libraries can employ to pool and thereby conserve their financial resources and inflation-eroded buying power to cope with the rapidly escalating expenses of building and managing collections of information resources for their clienteles. Because sound fiscal management is a paramount goal of CCD, libraries must constantly weigh the costs of cooperation against the potential return on their investment. If the operational infrastructure of CCD costs more than the benefit of having other libraries supply materials to our patrons, the worth of the entire exercise must be questioned.

The support system for CCD can become a considerable financial investment for participating libraries. Partners must create or expand upon conspectus data and develop methods of sharing on-order information.[16] A reliable and efficient document delivery program is essential. Building a distributed serials archive or coordinating subscriptions can became a labor-intensive process of identifying titles, shipping volumes to the archive, establishing bibliographic control, and maintaining a transaction record. Travel funding for meetings and workshops, even the value of librarians' time spent in contact with their counterparts, are quasi-hidden costs that must be contemplated.[17] If collaborative programs encompass collection building, document delivery, serials coordination, sharing of expertise, and other activities, partners may feel it necessary to create an umbrella organization to manage the enterprise, further driving up expenses. And, as a consortium grows in size and complexity, legal, political, and economic issues may come to dominate the decision-making process.[18]

Complicating any economic analysis is the absence of a generally accepted model for measuring the costs and benefits of CCD (though we will address some methodologies in chapter 8). Measurement cannot begin without data, however, and consortial participants should reach consensus at the outset on data-gathering protocols that will provide relevant, coherent information for evaluating the effectiveness of their programs.[19]

The costs and managerial challenges of print-based CCD may prompt libraries to reconsider its intrinsic value, especially in light of current legal and technological developments. Copyright legislation aimed at restricting information sharing could further limit our fair use rights to copy materials. More significantly, the explosive growth of electronic information causes some to question whether libraries should dedicate the time and money to organize elaborate print-based CCD programs. At the very least, they suggest, these programs should be concentrated in areas where digitization is least likely to have a major impact in the near future.[20]

THE CASE FOR CCD

Why, despite so many impediments, does CCD remain a compelling and widely advocated idea? The answer goes straight to the relentless budgetary pressure of runaway materials costs, pressure that has afflicted libraries for almost two decades and shows no signs of abating. During this period of fiscal retrenchment and curtailed acquisitions, no other concept has offered brighter promise for preserving the richness and depth of collections at large libraries, expanding collections services at smaller libraries, and containing costs for everyone.

CCD proceeds from the premise that in a constrained economic climate, libraries can no longer expect to build superior or even adequate collections independently. If each library proceeds unilaterally as inflation forces it to acquire ever smaller portions of the published universe, it risks unnecessarily duplicating many little-used materials that its patrons could borrow from other collections. Conversely, it may fail to acquire many other items not readily available elsewhere. By coordinating acquisitions, libraries can maximize their aggregate purchasing power even as their individual financial fortunes decline. They can better position themselves to build broad-based collections by identifying resources that need to be held by only one or perhaps a few contributors and provided to others through document delivery. Each contributor can continue to acquire core resources for its clientele while redirecting its remaining funding toward intensive purchasing in predetermined fields. It will share materials in these fields with consortial partners and rely on the partners to build and share intensive collections in other fields.

At a time when well-developed CCD programs remain more the exception than the rule, there is abundant evidence of the corrosive impact of inflation on library purchasing power. Excessive materials pricing has become so entrenched in the library economy that it now seems part of the status quo. Even a brief survey of the fiscal damage provides a cautionary glimpse of the grim future that is highly probable if we complacently continue to practice independent collection development.

As commercial interests came to dominate the publication of scientific serials, the cost of periodicals in science, technology, and medicine—fields in which journals are the primary vehicle for transmitting research results—rapidly outstripped both the general inflation rate and the growth rate of subscribing libraries' budgets. Academic libraries responded by reducing monograph spending and canceling subscriptions, measures that were fiscally responsible and economically unavoidable, but destructive to their ability to meet the information needs of their communities. Successive years of double-digit cost increases produced further cutbacks in periodical and monograph acquisitions. Compounding the strain on collections budgets were the expanding number of print publications and, more recently, the appearance and rapid proliferation of expensive electronic resources.

Libraries now find themselves trapped in a vicious spiral: the more they spend, the less they receive. Between 1986 and 2000, members of the Association of Research Libraries saw their cost per serial rise by 226 percent and their serial expenditures increase by 192 percent. Even though they had spent over 12 percent more each year for serials, on average, they purchased 7 percent fewer serial titles at the end of the period than at the beginning. At the same time, monograph prices increased by 66 percent, while expenditures rose only 48 percent, resulting in a net decline in monograph purchasing of 17 percent. The consumer price index increased by 57 percent during the period.[21]

By the late 1990s, efforts were under way to moderate materials price inflation. The Scholarly Publishing and Academic Resources Coalition (SPARC), an ARL project, began in 1998 to partner with publishers of moderately priced scientific periodicals to compete with titles published by major for-profit enterprises. Preprint servers, on which scientists can post articles before publication in freely accessible open archives, provided an alternative to dissemination of research results by commercially produced journals. But underlying inflationary trends remained stubbornly in place, and libraries began the twenty-first century as they ended the twentieth, trying to manage collections with financial resources that cannot keep pace with the cost of information.

This fiscal erosion means that individual library collections are not and cannot be as rich in variety or depth as before. Whatever a library's size, it is probably less able (without extraordinary budget increases) to provide information resources locally for its clientele. On a global scale, the diversity of libraries' aggregate collection is threatened. U.S. academic libraries are unable to acquire international publications comprehensively.[22] Fewer dollars can be dedicated to the careful selection and purchase of unique and nonmainstream materials, meaning that collections are becoming more homogenized and less distinctive.[23] The unmistakable lesson is that business as usual is an increasingly untenable economic strategy that undercuts our mission. By continuing to buy separately, we will each buy much less. And, if we do not coordinate, we will probably duplicate each other much more.

CCD was not conceived as a stratagem for saving money by decreasing spending on collections. It is, rather, a device in which libraries coalesce and manage their collective budgets to contend with the withering effects of inflation that none can resist individually. Despite the difficulties of organizing and operating collaborative programs, no alternative can match their capacity for arresting the worst outcomes of the pay-more-buy-less spiral. The financial discipline and careful planning they encourage can also mitigate the consequences of stagnant or declining library incomes caused by recessions or other economic setbacks.[24]

Though CCD appeals to librarians primarily as a coping strategy for rampant materials cost escalation, to see it purely as a defensive effort is to unnecessarily limit its scope and underestimate its possibilities. The core concept of CCD carries the potential for grand schemes of collection building presently beyond the means of all but the most well-financed libraries. Large research libraries can envision a collaboratively built megacollection that encompasses resources held regionally, nationally, or even internationally. If a consortial collection held, at least in theory, all subjects at all levels, then it could be said to be truly comprehensive, a designation often misapplied to local collections in conspectus projects.[25] A comprehensive international collection may be emerging, built haphazardly through the uncoordinated efforts of libraries across the world. It remains for libraries to develop it through planned collaborative selection and to build links among access tools.[26]

If this vision is too fanciful for most libraries, viable CCD programs also open the door to a multitude of less breathtaking but eminently practical benefits. Cooperatively built collections, even among small libraries, will be characterized by more breadth and depth than those built autonomously by a single library. Paired with serviceable bibliographic access and a speedy and reliable document delivery system, combined collections can offer each library's clientele a significantly increased chance of locating and retrieving needed materials more quickly than through traditional interlibrary loan. In an age when Internet bookstores have raised the public's level of service expectations, speed is much more than a trivial attribute. Patrons of libraries engaged in CCD may occasionally find needed titles elsewhere because of consortial priorities. But with judicious planning, far more instances should occur in which titles formerly accessible only after weeks of waiting will be relatively close at hand. Even if a library finds itself to be a net lender to consortial partners, the service and promotional value of items rapidly found and delivered should compensate for the imbalance of resource sharing.

Immediate access to resources previously available only at considerable time and distance is an obvious advantage, but successful CCD ventures can embolden participants to explore more extended collaborative collection management endeavors. Coordinated preservation programs can eliminate the costly redundancy of restoring rarely used materials.[27] Joint cancellation and weeding projects, though a challenge to manage, help minimize the impact of deselection by increasing the chances that at least one copy or one current volume of formerly duplicated items will continue to be available within a consortium.[28] Shared storage of low-demand monographs and serial backfiles can enable partner libraries to withdraw duplicates of items in the consortial repository, confident that these materials can be quickly supplied when requested. By conserving shelf space in this way, each library in the group increases its physical capacity to accommodate collection growth and defers the expense of constructing new buildings or acquiring off-site storage facilities.

Productive cooperation in collection development and management cultivates a collaborative ethic that extends into other library activities. Libraries that coordinate collection building might create a parallel program to distribute the workload of digital reference services. They may find that they can apportion some job responsibilities across multiple institutions on the model of shared collections. Perhaps every library in a group need not recruit bibliographers or catalogers skilled in the same foreign language. It could be more efficient for each library to hire experts in a different language and have them each select or catalog for several libraries. Multilibrary staff development initiatives, exchange programs, and internships can all motivate staff members throughout the consortium to increase their knowledge and skill levels by learning from each other. Publication projects (like this one) can grow from interaction among counterparts within the partnership.[29] Librarians from multiple organizations can work with researchers and publishers to experiment with new forms of digital publication that serve the economic interests and protect the intellectual property rights of all parties.[30] One author speculates that in the future, collection development librarians may find that the most important resource they have to share, with users and each other, is their expertise.[31] Figure 2-2 presents a summary of the potential benefits of CCD.

CONCLUSION

Planning and executing CCD is far from a simple matter, and one does not have to look hard to find reasons not to attempt it. Most of the problems addressed in this chapter are imposing, and all should be confronted forthrightly in each project's design phase, but none is insoluble. Achieving and maintaining collaboration that truly works for all partners are time-consuming, organizationally complex, managerially demanding, and heavily charged with fiscal consequences.

FIGURE 2-2	*Why Participate in CCD?*

- CCD offers the best hope of responding to rampant growth in the number and cost of library materials.

- Libraries can only build comprehensive collections collaboratively, not individually.

- CCD can provide fast, reliable service to patrons who need materials not in their local library's collection.

- CCD leads the way to collaborative preservation, deselection, and storage programs.

- CCD encourages a cooperative ethic that can lead to increased staff efficiency and expertise.

In other words, CCD is characterized by descriptive terms that we frequently and appropriately apply to traditional collection development. The decision to participate in a collaborative enterprise should turn not on the difficulties of implementation, but on a thorough consideration of the value of current practices and a clear assessment of the potential benefits of change.

A key issue is whether conventional collection development is still responsive to an information environment that has evolved so radically in the recent past. Publication in all forms continues to expand, and conglomerates intent on building information monopolies increasingly dominate the publishing industry. Digital publication has forever altered methods of intellectual inquiry and patterns of disseminating knowledge. Materials costs continually rise at a rate double or triple that of the cost of living. Libraries have adjusted to these elemental changes principally through creating consortia to coordinate joint purchasing of electronic products. Although this has been an imaginative and generally successful tactic, it offers only partial relief from the host of challenges that confront us. We have yet to fundamentally rethink our independent approach to building and managing print collections, where we continue to invest most of our time and money. To consider the worth of CCD is to ask whether staying the course is a strategically sound collection development methodology for navigating a profoundly changed landscape.

NOTES

1. Mosher, "Cooperative Collection Development," 29 (see chap. 1, n. 5).

2. Ross Atkinson, "Rationality and Realpolitik: Prospects for Cooperative Collection Development in an Increasingly Networked Environment," in *Scholarship in the New Information Environment: Proceedings from an RLG Symposium Held May 1–3, 1995, at Harvard University*, ed. Carol Hughes, 29 (Mountain View, CA: Research Libraries Group, 1996).

3. Deborah L. Jakubs quoted in Milton T. Wolf, "Cooperative Collection Management: Online Discussion," *Collection Management* 23, no. 4 (1998): 62.

4. Robert P. Holley, "Cooperative Collection Development: Yesterday, Today, and Tomorrow," *Collection Management* 23, no. 4 (1998): 27.

5. Holley, "Cooperative Collection Development," 25; Evans, "Cooperative Collection Development," 458.

6. Ross Atkinson, "Preservation and Collection Development: Toward a Political Synthesis," *Journal of Academic Librarianship* 16, no. 2 (May 1990): 100.

7. Holley, "Cooperative Collection Development," 26; Barbara Maass, "The New Mythology: Co-operative Collection Development," *Canadian Library Journal* 46, no. 1 (February 1989): 27.

8. Evans, "Cooperative Collection Development," 454.

9. Hewitt and Shipman, "Cooperative Collection Development," 198–99.

10. Ibid., 221.

11. Evans, "Cooperative Collection Development," 466.

12. Holley, "Cooperative Collection Development," 26.

13. Shreeves, "Future," 377.

14. Ross Atkinson, "Preservation," 100; Harloe, *Guide*, 4.

15. Evans, "Cooperative Collection Development," 458.

16. Barbara McFadden Allen, "Consortia and Collections: Achieving a Balance between Local Action and Collaborative Interest," *Journal of Library Administration* 28, no. 4 (1999): 89.

17. Holley, "Cooperative Collection Development," 27.

18. Evans, "Cooperative Collection Development," 457.

19. Harloe, *Guide*, 5.

20. Shreeves, "Future," 383, 387.

21. Martha Kyrillidou and Mark Young, *ARL Statistics 1999–2000: A Compilation of Statistics from the One Hundred and Twenty-Two Members of the Association of Research Libraries* (Washington, DC: Association of Research Libraries, 2001), 9–10.

22. Anna H. Perrault, "The Printed Book: Still in Need of CCD," *Collection Management* 24, no. 1/2 (2000): 130.

23. Milton T. Wolf and Marjorie E. Bloss, "The Whole Is Greater than the Sum of Its Parts," *Collection Management* 24, no. 1/2 (2000): 110.

24. Harloe, *Guide*, 3.

25. Ross Atkinson, "Preservation," 100.

26. Harold Billings, "Shared Collection Building: Constructing the 21st Century Relational Research Library," *Journal of Library Administration* 31, no. 2 (2000): 4–5.

27. Mosher and Pankake, "Guide," 421; Harloe, *Guide*, 4.

28. Mosher and Pankake, "Guide," 421.

29. Harloe, *Guide*, 4.

30. Allen, "Consortia and Collections," 90.

31. Shreeves, "Future," 373.

FUNDAMENTALS
The Principles of CCD

$\mathbf{A}$ll collaborative collection development programs, regardless of size or type, operate with a set of working principles. The principles are encoded in the statements, or sometimes the unspoken assumptions, that announce the CCD endeavor, justify its existence, define its purpose, articulate anticipated outcomes, and suggest or specify general measures for reviewing and evaluating the project. Principles are mental images that incite and govern behavior, the policies that beget procedures. Because CCD is complex, its principles encompass a wide range of disparate issues, including accountability, performance, and timelines. The principles governing CCD establish a framework for addressing local needs and goals, ensuring that CCD projects figure into the local planning process. They underscore the human component of cooperative activities and reinforce the fact that CCD represents just one approach to increasing user access to resources.[1]

The importance of clarifying core CCD principles cannot be overestimated. If CCD is a form of outsourcing, the imperative becomes all the more important that CCD vision statements, the written embodiment of underlying principles, be approached with the same concentrated care and serious deliberation as other commitments of time, energy, and financial resources. If we accept the premise that much CCD is done through the "backdoor," that is, libraries relying on neighboring libraries to collect in certain areas, the need to externalize and formalize such tacit arrangements becomes all the more pressing. But what principles underlie cooperative projects of the types that libraries typically engage in? What principles govern the installation and maintenance of these cooperative endeavors? What are the expectations of those engaged in collaborative activities? What outcomes do they anticipate? Why are they in it? What are they in it for?

The sheer amount of literature devoted to CCD reflects the widespread agreement on the need for the enterprise. Scattered throughout this literature are references to the principles that guide CCD. This chapter synthesizes the most important of these and groups them into categories. Principles do not exist in isolation. They express multiple, interrelated concerns. It may prove useful and convenient to look at some of the principles that are repeatedly mentioned in the literature through the perspective of the community most affected. This chapter will look at one group of principles in some detail. These key principles governing CCD projects are user-centered, library-centered, and project-centered. The chapter will also briefly enumerate a series of complementary concepts underlying the key principles and representing fundamental elements to be incorporated into CCD documents.

USER-CENTERED PRINCIPLES

It is a truism in the library profession that libraries and the collections they house exist to serve their users. Library professionals have long asserted that one rationale for collection development has been to enable libraries to fulfill a "dispensing role," that is, to assemble those resources users want where they want to access them.[2] To fulfill this function, traditional libraries attempted to build comprehensive local collections, often through competitive and opportunistic acquisition. More recently, however, the myth of self-sufficiency has given way to a more practical and realistic point of view that the user is better served through cooperation, not competition.[3] Libraries themselves have perhaps long known this, but now the insight is dawning on a wider public, the very legislative agencies that dispense funding for state-assisted libraries. In 1998, Minnesota, for example, allocated additional money to state colleges and universities along with the mandate that these funds be managed cooperatively.[4] It is not surprising, then, that CCD has been described as the strategy of the twenty-first century.[5]

The user-centered principle that forms the cornerstone of CCD states: *Users will be provided access to a broader range of information resources of potential use without jeopardizing the integrity of the local holdings or reducing user access to heavily used materials.* Virtually all CCD projects described in the literature express or imply that increased access to resources is a desired outcome. Many documents from institutions with CCD projects contain some reference to expanding access for users. A goal of the Boston Library Consortium's Agreement on Collection Responsibilities in Asian Business and Economics is to "increase the range of monographic materials on the subject of Asian Business and Economics available to patrons of the libraries in the Boston Library Consortium."[6] Likewise, the mission documents of the Latin America North East Libraries Consortium (LANE) express a strong commitment to maintain or enhance the "consortium collection" for the benefit of users.[7] The principle of increased access can be put into practice in a number of ways. Shared electronic subscriptions, big-ticket purchases of microfilm collections, and divided collecting responsibilities are among the more common approaches.

In an ideal situation, users, not librarians, should build collections. This precept applies to CCD projects as well. The challenge thus becomes how to involve the user directly in CCD activities. And at what point? If direct involvement of users is ultimately not feasible in the strictest sense, CCD project planners must ensure that user points of view are accurately and forcefully represented in the design, implementation, and management of CCD projects. Involving patrons may be the weak link in the CCD planning process, but inclusion must remain a primary goal if the project is to find acceptance among those it is intended to serve. User resistance to CCD projects can be decreased—and cooperation with patrons, library boards, and funding agencies increased—if CCD librarians can demonstrate that users play a crucial role in fashioning a plan intended to benefit patrons who use the collection.[8] Libraries must establish and maintain strong, effective channels of communication with users. They must redouble their efforts when contemplating CCD projects.

In the absence of user participation, the librarian becomes the user's advocate. Those involved in providing library services, and particularly those tasked with CCD responsibilities, must constantly research how users seek and use information. A corollary to user advocacy in CCD projects addresses the need for user education. Certainly, users need be informed about CCD projects, ideally in the planning phase, and then kept up to date after implementation of the project. But user education must go beyond publicity, beyond simply letting users know that new resources are available. On the one hand, users must be thoroughly trained in the use of new products to which the library will have access as a result of CCD. Just as importantly, users must be made aware that some of the resources available to them come courtesy of CCD agreements. That is, the role of CCD as an instrument of building collections must be persuasively communicated to users. Through training and education, patrons become independent users in the broadest possible sense.[9] Figure 3-1 summarizes the user-centered principles of CCD.

FIGURE 3-1 *User-Centered Principles*

User-Centered CCD

- strives to increase users' access to information

- attempts to engage users in building consortial collections

- trains users in individual resources and educates them about the information marketplace

---

LIBRARY-CENTERED PRINCIPLES

In CCD endeavors, a number of principles relate to the organization itself. Like the users of a library who benefit from the principle of broader access resulting from CCD, the participating library should derive some benefit through participation in CCD activities.

First, *CCD projects should allow the library to optimize its financial resources.* Indeed, financial concerns are the driving force of CCD. The decline in purchasing power with the concomitant increase in the number and prices of items published is a well-documented state of affairs. CCD is one strategy for coping with rising costs and reducing the risks of missing essential research materials.[10] Projects that distribute collecting responsibilities, and thereby distribute collection development costs, are based on this principle. By joining forces,

CCD participants can leverage their funds and cover a wider spectrum of the information universe. Libraries can optimize funds through CCD, but this does not mean that expenditures are reduced, only that they are realigned or redirected within a larger context. The successful optimization of financial resources strikes a balance between costs and benefits. As libraries redistribute costs while increasing benefits, they achieve economic efficiency.[11] The interrelationship of CCD costs and benefits is expressed as value. An individual library can measure the value of a product, project, or program only in relation to local needs and aspirations.

Second, *CCD can address space and storage challenges confronting many libraries.* Fiscal responsibility includes the library's use of its physical facilities. The serials archive of the Information Alliance, for example, was designed not only to preserve a print repository of journals duplicated among the three institutions, but also to better use the limited space within the respective libraries.[12] The trend toward joint storage facilities to gain extended shelf space also illustrates this situation. One study using data from the nine campuses of the University of California estimated that two-thirds of those libraries' operating budgets and physical space is allocated to assembling and processing collections.[13] Given the huge investment in collection assembly, maintenance, and storage, whatever means the library uses to optimize the unit cost of information offers a potential payoff for the library in both dollars and goodwill.

Third, *libraries should recognize that CCD projects maximize personnel resources in many ways.* CCD is not just about material resources. We often neglect the value of people, in terms of both costs and benefits, perhaps because expenditures of human resources are more difficult to quantify than are other aspects of CCD. Although the cost savings on a shared subscription to an electronic database can be readily calculated, the expense associated with the time and expertise of a librarian to master and provide instruction in the databases is multidimensional and almost defies precise quantification.

CCD projects often challenge participants to acquire new expertise. CCD also encourages them to develop new methods for working in a collaborative environment. It encourages them to review and amend existing assumptions about the effectiveness, efficiency, and levels of service at their local institution. The influence of CCD-inspired critical thinking patterns on other areas in the library can be beneficial across the board, not just within the context of the CCD project.

In addition to sharing responsibility for building collections, CCD projects can focus on sharing personnel and their expertise. Examples of this include a cooperative reduction of cataloging backlogs in Slavic and East European languages and distribution of responsibility for cataloging Southeast Asian materials among ten major universities.[14] Collaboration increases human capital when staff members gain new knowledge that benefits their institution, users, and collections.

Fourth, *CCD projects increase symbolic capital and enhance the perception of the library as cultural institution.* In the CCD context, the perceived value of the library is likely to increase in proportion to the number of unique resources to which it can provide access. Traditionally, collections have played a symbolic role—the larger the collection, the greater the status and prestige of the owning institution.[15] Through CCD, libraries become relational; that is, individual institutions become part of a greater whole and thereby multiply the number of resources available to users.[16] In the networked environment, each library relates to others to provide local users access to global resources. Geography is no longer a primary organizing principle for libraries. In the absence of physical barriers, the challenge to libraries is to find new methods of informing users about the extended, distributed collections available through participation in consortial programs.[17]

Finally, *CCD mitigates the homogeneity of many library collections by providing the framework for individual libraries to focus on unique materials.* Research suggests that similar libraries tend to develop similar collections.[18] This is a drawback of local collection development, in which emphasis is rightly placed in core collections to the neglect of more esoteric materials. However, by encouraging local focus on unique materials, CCD enlarges the reputation of the library for providing resources when and where they are needed. The government-funded Minnesota project, for example, achieves this outcome. Organizers recognized that some duplication among their collections was desirable, but they established a goal of reducing duplication and increasing the number of unique titles in the system. With the incentive to diversify that CCD provided, several libraries made a concerted effort to acquire books held nowhere else in the state.[19]

By creating relationships among libraries and producing more diverse collections, CCD offers a means of expanding the symbolic role of the library by redefining *collection* and *library* at the same time. CCD activities establish the essential unity and interconnectedness of all libraries. When one library benefits, the generic library as an institution serving the common good also benefits. This symbolic principle deemphasizes the library as physical place, re-creating it as an information space.[20] Figure 3-2 summarizes the library-centered principles of CCD.

FIGURE 3-2	*Library-Centered Principles*

Library-Centered CCD

- enables libraries to optimize financial resources

- enables libraries to address space and storage challenges

- encourages libraries to maximize staff potential

- contributes to the symbolic function of libraries

- provides a framework for acquiring unique materials

PROJECT-CENTERED PRINCIPLES

The projects libraries undertake for the common good have an inherent value that transcends their immediate utility to core clients and participating libraries. While maintaining a focus on the needs of local users, project-oriented principles allow an institution to more broadly define its mission within the larger information community. More often, CCD projects governed by these principles have long-range payoffs and fit the profile of collecting for the ages.

CCD projects that focus on creating community value are based on the principle of cooperation for the common good. In many respects, the Germanists' project of the Information Alliance at the University of Kentucky, the University of Tennessee, and Vanderbilt University falls into this category.[21] This project distributes collecting responsibility for modern German-language authors among the three institutions. All three continue to collect core authors, but noncore authors (from the point of view of the local collections) are now, for the first time, receiving attention. As a result, more unique holdings are available to all the users of all the participating libraries, independent of the immediate use value of the holdings to local patrons. The Germanist bibliographers intend to offer expanded access to their on-campus users, but a major philosophical appeal, and the significant justification of the project, transcends the borders of the three campuses to include the anticipated needs of German studies regionally and even nationally.

A more expansive, more formalized example is the Books-Not-Bought In Ohio (NBIO) project that unites OhioLINK libraries and book vendor YBP Library Services. By reporting titles not purchased by any OhioLINK library, this innovative collaboration is to provide for systematic collection of titles that may have otherwise slipped through the cracks. This paradigm shift creates allies out of previously independent, though interdependent, segments of the information cycle and ultimately enables each to gain "a sense of common purpose, capable of creating far greater and enduring value than either of the constituents could imagine if left to operate individually."[22] With technological and psychological obstacles overcome, the NBIO project now offers the potential for expanding this innovative solution to a broader community.

Some CCD activities are invoked and justified by the times, the sum of factors at a particular historical juncture. These mitigating factors include the political environment, the state of technology, and institutional definitions and duties. In short, certain times call certain types of CCD projects into existence. Successful projects are the appropriate response to the challenge or opportunity presented by a certain historical intersection. For example, many libraries traditionally sought gifts of information materials or pursued exchange opportunities. Whole departments were created to manage gifts and exchange activities. This long-running CCD solution to a particular challenge was a product of the time in which it originated, a time in which mail was the only option for acquiring much of this often esoteric material. The NBIO project came about in a far different climate. It became a reality only after the technology required to implement it had evolved. Time will tell if this innovative CCD approach acquires the broader applicability that will make it a long-term solution similar to long-lived gifts and exchange programs. Figure 3-3 summarizes the project-centered principles of CCD.

FIGURE 3-3   *Project-Centered Principles*

Project-Centered CCD

- pursues projects for their own merit

- champions projects in response to developments in the information environment

- advances the common good in conjunction with meeting local needs

INCORPORATING CCD PRINCIPLES INTO DOCUMENTATION

CCD documents, especially those that translate the CCD vision into practice, must concern themselves with principles that govern the implementation and day-to-day performance of the project. These principles require documents that address concerns that have long plagued cooperative work and continue to jeopardize its success. In the following paragraphs, we offer sets of paired principles as organizing points for constructing CCD governance documents.

Foremost are the principles of *executability* and *sustainability*, which encompass financial, human, tactical, and logistical dimensions. Of primary concern is whether the proposed CCD activity is realistic and practical. Can the plan actually be executed? Begin with an assessment of the environment in which the plan will operate: Are the participating institutions matched within the framework of the proposed cooperation? Has each identified benefits and assessed and accepted the risks? Sustainability, the ability of the project to operate over time, depends on such factors as funding, complexity, the degree of oversight and leadership.

The twin principles of *responsibility* and *accountability* must also be incorporated into a CCD document. A project must be designed, implemented, and managed by people who have the skills, background, and resources to make it a priority and a success. Because they bear the responsibility for ensuring that the project progresses, they must be granted the authority to listen and respond to the concerns of participants, make course adjustments as necessary, and scale the project to the level of participants' commitment. Likewise, those individuals must be accountable to the higher authority that has given the charge and provided the support for the CCD objective. That higher authority, be it the library administrations of participating institutions or a task force that has defined the mission, must develop evaluation and assessment measures for the project. Both groups, those responsible and those to whom they report, must define the terms and expectations of the project in a manner that ensures accountability, but does not stymie managerial responsibility.

Project managers should articulate the principles of *comprehensibility* and *communicability* by asking whether the rationale and justification for the project can be readily understood by those not involved in its design. Can project objectives and outcomes be understood without intervention and constant explanation by managers? CCD projects must be politically acceptable to their communities of interest. For example, if the donor of restricted funds has specified that they be used for a particular subject area, reducing acquisitions in this area to fulfill collaborative agreements may not be politically astute. The principles must communicate the CCD vision to multiple audiences, such as administrators, library staff, and users. The principles must also address issues of education in the broadest sense, informing local users how they benefit from distributed collections and instructing them in the use of cooperative products.

Finally, the principles of *flexibility* and *adaptability* must be incorporated into the documents that initiate and govern CCD endeavors. These two principles ensure that policies and procedures are codified in a way that does not straitjacket the project or prevent its evolution in response to experience. Flexibility ensures that CCD documents provide options for meeting the goals of the project. Adaptability, on the other hand, provides for mechanisms that allow the project, after periodic review, to respond to changes in information and institutional environments. Such changes might include the introduction of new technologies, the appearance of new formats, or shifts in disciplinary and mission focuses.

CONCLUSION

In this chapter, we have reviewed some key principles governing CCD activities, highlighting user-centered principles, library-centered principles, and project-centered principles. User-centered principles focus on providing greater access to more information sources for users, engaging them in building a cooperative collection, and educating them in the multiple aspects of the CCD endeavor. Library-centered principles detail how CCD allows libraries to optimize financial resources, maximize personnel resources, and increase the symbolic capital of the library as an institution. Project-centered principles suggest that some CCD projects possess intrinsic value, while others benefit an audience beyond the members of an individual consortium.

Principles of executability and sustainability, comprehensibility and communicability, responsibility and accountability, and flexibility and adaptability should be incorporated into CCD documents. In the end, all CCD activity is about creating value not only for the users of information, but also for the institution that mediates and manages access on their behalf.[23] Established at the start of the enterprise, the principles discussed here will ensure that the CCD program creates value. This value will be reflected in the enriched array of information resources available to users and in the improved management of institutional assets available to the library. Creating value follows naturally from the exercise of sound principles. For this reason, take time at the beginning to clarify the key principles underlying your CCD project. Its success depends on establishing these principles and letting them guide you to the desired results.

NOTES

1. Remarks by Barbara McFadden Allen as summarized in: Peggy Johnson, "Symposium on Cooperative Collection Development: A Report," *Library Acquisitions: Practice and Theory* 20, no. 2 (1996): 158.

2. Michael Buckland, *Redesigning Library Services: A Manifesto* (Chicago: American Library Association, 1992), 55.

3. Paul Mosher, "Collaborative Collection Development in an Era of Financial Limitations," *Australian Academic and Research Libraries* 20 (March 1989): 9.

4. Diane Richards, "Making One Size Fit All: Minnesota State Colleges and Universities Manage a Legislative Mandate for Cooperative Collection Development," *Library Collections, Acquisitions, and Technical Services* 25, no. 1 (Spring 2001): 93–112.

5. Robert Martin, opening presentation at the New Dynamics and Economics of Cooperative Collection Development Conference hosted by the Center for Research Libraries at the Aberdeen Woods Conference Center, Atlanta, GA, November 8–10, 2002.

6. George J. Soete, comp., *Collaborative Collections Management Programs in ARL Libraries,* SPEC Kit 235 (Washington, DC: Association of Research Libraries, Office of Leadership and Management Services, 1998), 29.

7. Ibid., 42.

8. Johnson, "Symposium," 158.

9. Buckland, *Redesigning*, 65 ff.

10. James Burgett, John Haar, and Linda Phillips, "The Persistence of Print in a Digital World: Three ARL Libraries Confront an Enduring Issue," in *Crossing the Divide: Proceedings of the Tenth National Conference of the Association of College and Research Libraries, March 15–18, 2001, Denver Colorado,* ed. Hugh A. Thompson, 77 (Chicago: Association of College and Research Libraries, 2001).

11. Donald B. Simpson, "Library Consortia and Access to Information: Costs and Cost Justification," *Journal of Library Administration* 12, no. 3 (1990): 89.

12. Burgett, Haar, and Phillips, "Persistence of Print," 78–79.

13. Buckland, *Redesigning*, 55.

14. Jacqueline Byrd, "A Cooperative Cataloging Proposal for Slavic and East European Languages and the Languages of the Former Soviet Union," *Cataloging and Classification Quarterly* 17, no. 1/2 (1993): 87–96; and Fe Susan Go, "Is

Cooperative Cataloging Realistic? Thoughts of a Southeast Asian Bibliographer," *Cataloging and Classification Quarterly* 17, no. 1/2 (1993): 169–79.

15. Buckland, *Redesigning*, 56.

16. Billings, "Shared Collection Building," 3–14.

17. Wendy Pradt Lougee, *Diffuse Libraries: Emergent Roles for the Research Library in the Digital Age* (Washington, DC: Council on Library and Information Resources, 2002), 19.

18. Perrault, "Printed Book," 119–36.

19. Richards, "One Size," 13.

20. Lougee, *Diffuse Libraries*, 19.

21. Burgett, Haar, and Phillips, "Persistence of Print," 78.

22. Julia A. Gammon and Michael Zeoli, "Practical Cooperative Collecting for Consortia: Books-Not-Bought in Ohio," presented at the New Dynamics and Economics of Cooperative Collection Development Conference hosted by the Center for Research Libraries at the Aberdeen Woods Conference Center, Atlanta, GA, November 8–10, 2002, http://www.crl.edu/awcc2002/GammonZeoliPaper.pdf (accessed November 6, 2003).

23. Martin, opening presentation.

CHAPTER

4

THE STATE OF THE ART
Varieties of CCD Practice

Determining how broadly—to say nothing of how effectively—libraries practice collaborative collection development is at best an imprecise exercise. There is no widely accepted output measure for CCD comparable to collection and expenditure statistics sponsored by the Association of Research Libraries, the Association of College and Research Libraries, or the Public Library Association. Fortunately, a survey conducted under the auspices of the Center for Research Libraries (CRL) provides us with a snapshot of active CCD projects at the outset of the twenty-first century.

CURRENT CCD ACTIVITY

In the fall of 2001, a CRL workgroup surveyed consortia and networks internationally to develop a "map" of current CCD projects. The map's purpose is to acquaint librarians contemplating CCD participation with the range of collaborative possibilities. Eighty-nine projects submitted responses, and the resulting map, while representing a self-selected sample, illustrates the span, variety, and potential of current endeavors. It also offers an opportunity to assess the state of contemporary collaboration.[1]

Age: For most participating libraries, CCD is a relatively recent undertaking. Fully 72 percent of the reported projects began in the 1990s, confirmation of the emergence of electronic database–purchasing consortia during the decade. Those projects in which print-based activities are major components tend to have been in operation longer. Although 52 percent of them began in the 1990s, 33 percent date their origin before 1980.

Geographical Distribution: The geographical distribution of the U.S. projects is wide but very uneven. The Midwest is home to the most (36 percent), the Southeast the second most (22 percent). Only 13 percent are located in the Northeast, 3 percent in the Southwest, and 7 percent in the West. CCD is predominately a regional activity; no more than 19 percent of the projects can be considered multiregional or national. State-based projects, many initiated through government funding, are prevalent. Fifty-six percent of the projects report all their participants located in one state. Even where state mandates are not at issue, libraries are inclined to seek partners in fairly compact geographic zones. In 75 percent of the projects, all participants are located in no more than two states, in almost all cases contiguous. Where print-based activities are paramount, it appears that mutual interest is somewhat more determinative than proximity. Only 45 percent of these projects are based in a single state.

Operating agreements: Over half the projects (54 percent) operate through formal working agreements, including charters or instruments of incorporation. Thirty-five percent consider themselves the product of informal arrangements among participating libraries.

Funding: Whether consortia are chartered or not, collaboration is a heavily self-supported endeavor. Although many groups report multiple funding arrangements, 75 percent of all projects receive funding from member institutions. Twenty-eight percent receive government funding, and 23 percent have obtained grant funding.

Composition: If the survey responses accurately reflect collaborative participation by type of library, CCD is primarily an endeavor of academic libraries. In only one project do public libraries comprise all the members, and very few multitype projects responded. Large academic libraries participate more frequently than smaller academics. Many state-based consortia include both large and medium-to-small academic libraries, but few cooperative ventures consist exclusively of medium-to-small academics.

Subjects and Formats: Because most consortia acquire multidisciplinary electronic resources or collect print materials in area studies that include several disciplines, no subjects emerged as preferred areas of collaborative focus. Format preferences are, however, quite clear. Seventy-five percent of the projects engage in activities related to electronic resources, while 54 percent incorporate one or more print-related endeavors. Other formats attract considerably less consortial attention: microform, 33 percent; video, 21 percent; audio, 18 percent.

Focus: The survey left no doubt of the degree to which the acquisition of digital resources has become a powerful generator of library collaboration. Sixty percent of the projects broker the shared purchase of electronic products. A comparatively small 33 percent participate in the coordinated selection or purchase of monographs (print or electronic), 38 percent in the coordinated selection or purchase of serials, and 30 percent in the coordinated selection or purchase of other materials. Ten percent are building joint print serial archives; 16 percent are working toward the joint storage of print materials, and 12 percent toward the joint storage of nonprint materials.

ELECTRONIC CCD

Purchasing digital products has become the most widely practiced form of collaborative collection development in a remarkably short time, essentially within the past decade. Such purchasing is popular because it produces noticeable and immediate outcomes, all of them positive, and is largely free of the thorniest problems that have long made print-based CCD so challenging to organize and sustain. It is, in fact, a fundamentally different exercise than collaborative print acquisition.

When libraries coordinate their print collection building, a primary goal is to reduce duplication of resources. When they jointly purchase an electronic resource, however, duplication becomes their objective. In some cases, such as electronic journal collections, each library may obtain a somewhat different mix of product segments, but generally, all participants receive a product that is identical in most respects to that acquired by their consortial partners. They share the acquired materials simultaneously in real time, not sequentially through document delivery mechanisms.

Financial incentives also play out differently in print and electronic collaboration. Libraries that cooperatively build print collections should not expect to realize reductions either in the cost of individual titles or in their acquisitions spending. The advantage of shared print collecting lies in using the consortium's total budget to buy a set of unique resources that no member could afford separately. The chief reason libraries combine to purchase electronic products, however, is to reduce the cost of the products. By merging their buying power and offering vendors multiple sales in a single transaction, participating libraries pay a share of the total cost that is less than they would pay if they purchased the product individually.

In these core differences lie both the attraction of electronic collaboration and the explanation for its explosive growth. Libraries who share the cost of digital products do not have to make hard decisions about what they will cease collecting or formulate a collaborative collection development policy with multiple partners. Nor do they have to convince staff, patrons, and administrators of the advantages of cooperation when the chief advantage, cost reduction, is evident. The only contentious issues they may have to navigate are developing formulas for cost sharing and determining who will take the lead in negotiating with vendors.

Another advantage of electronic CCD is that libraries can employ it to compensate for undersized print collections. A group of libraries in South Africa, for instance, formed a consortium that acquired electronic databases partly as a means of overcoming generations of inequitable resource allocation under the apartheid system.[2]

Libraries participate in electronic CCD in a variety of organizational models, from ad hoc consortia that form solely to purchase one product to incorporated agencies that manage the acquisition, licensing, and billing for elaborate collections of databases and electronic journal aggregations. At the informal end of the spectrum, two or more libraries may approach a vendor and negotiate a discounted price for a group purchase. Each library pays separately and with its own funds. Libraries may pay identical amounts or disproportional shares based on the size of their user populations. Because the group is unstructured, its membership may fluctuate as different groups of libraries join to acquire different products, creating impermanent alliances of convenience based on immediate interests. These loose organizations place a special burden on their lead negotiators, who have to strike deals acceptable both to the vendor and their multiple constituents.

The 1990s witnessed the development of highly organized consortia, many of which include an administrative staff to handle negotiation with vendors. Membership is usually more formalized, and libraries often belong to more than one consortium. In one model, member libraries choose whether to participate in each deal and pay a share of the cost. Library staff members are relieved of the responsibility for negotiation, and, in return, the library may pay the consortium a surcharge for its administrative costs. In an alternate model, the consortium is funded by a government agency, usually a state, to pay for digital products supplied to all members. Some statewide consortia combine models, with member libraries paying for some databases and the consortium paying for others.

Most electronic financial transactions are leases rather than purchases. Consequently, librarians, whether they represent consortia or individual library members, have had to develop the arcane skill of negotiating license agreements that govern how each library can provide a database to its users and how each user can use the database. More formalized consortia may have an advantage over ad hoc library groupings in licensing because their staff members, through repeated efforts or formal training, have acquired a knowledge of contract law and negotiation techniques to best protect their patrons' opportunity to use databases without unreasonable restrictions.

TRADITIONAL CCD:
ONE-TIME SHARED PURCHASES

The number of libraries engaged in cooperative electronic acquisition far exceeds the number involved in collaborative programs to build collections of print materials, microforms, or other formats. Yet "traditional" CCD retains its ability to attract interest as library buying power continues to decline. Although over half the projects responding to the CRL survey indicate some print-based interest or activity, a close review of project descriptions and follow-up interviews reveals that far fewer incorporate a viable print component. Slightly over one-third of the eighty-nine reported projects engage in the cooperative selection of print resources or the cooperative storage of print materials. Of this group, 71 percent coordinate monograph selection, 65 percent serial selection. Although initiating and sustaining print-based cooperation is clearly more demanding than forming and operating database-purchasing consortia, the map illustrates that print-based CCD is, if not exactly thriving, certainly alive, well, and even rich with opportunities for those able to stay the course and build viable programs.

The least complex form of nonelectronic CCD, a form relatively easy to implement, is the one-time or occasional cooperative purchase of expensive items where multiple libraries share the cost and agree to share the materials. Multivolume print sets or large microform collections best lend themselves to this approach. Individual libraries may find such resources too costly to acquire or determine that, although they provide important information, their potential usage is too low to warrant their expense. Smaller public and school libraries can buy one copy of an expensive reference source to serve an entire district.[3] Sometimes a series of purchases can be grouped into an ad hoc one-time project. A group of academic libraries formed the Intensive Cuban Collecting Group to coordinate the acquisition of several hundred Cuban serials and declared their work complete when they had established a shared collection.[4] In all cases, shared purchase and access is a cost-effective tool that permits participating libraries to acquire highly priced materials, which they might otherwise have to forgo, at a substantial discount. It also tends to be non-controversial because it involves materials that participating libraries would generally not purchase independently.

Shared so-called big-ticket purchases are a relatively low-risk way for libraries to enjoy some of the budgetary and collection-enhancing advantages of CCD. But even these seemingly simple ad hoc transactions carry ongoing obligations that each participant needs to consider. First, the purchasing libraries must agree on which library or libraries will hold the purchased materials (some microform collections can be segmented among multiple sites). Because shared purchases work only when coupled with shared access, the holding library or libraries must agree to lend the materials to all partners, even if the items fall into such categories as reference sources or microfilm sets that may ordinarily be excluded from interlibrary loan. Moreover, even if the purchase is a one-time project, the access should be permanent. Libraries that contribute to the purchase should add records to their local catalogs, even for segments that they do not hold, with information on how patrons can obtain the items. Likewise, all the libraries need to maintain a record of the purchase.

One of the most appealing aspects of ad hoc big-ticket purchases is that they can build interlibrary confidence and a cooperative spirit that can lead to more elaborate collaborative collections ventures. Ad hoc purchasing was one of the first successes of the Triangle Research Libraries Network and helped establish a cooperative mentality that made further joint activities possible.[5]

PROGRAMMED ACQUISITIONS

Although one-time purchases are a useful tool, CCD agreements with the most lasting impact are those that commit libraries to long-term collection building agendas. These arrangements may include programmed big-ticket acquisitions, monograph selection, management of serial collections, or other coordinated activities. Libraries that have implemented these projects have successfully employed a number of models for decision making, ranging from the highly centralized to the broadly distributed.

Centralized Model

One of the oldest models is that of a member-funded central agency that purchases materials on behalf of its members or coordinates their collaborative purchasing programs. This approach is closely identified with the research library community because its best-known exemplar is the Center for Research Libraries (CRL). CRL began in 1949 as a joint venture of several midwestern research libraries to cooperatively store little-used materials from their collections and to coordinate a program of cooperative acquisition of highly specialized materials.[6] Today its membership numbers approximately 170 libraries in the United States and Canada.

CRL's basic program is essentially a series of ad hoc big-ticket purchases. Member institutions pay annual dues that fund acquisitions (and other administrative costs). In return, members may propose that the center purchase expensive research materials. Proposals are put to a vote of the membership. Purchased materials are held at the center in Chicago, accessible through the center's catalog, and are circulated to member libraries upon request for use by their patrons. CRL also operates several ongoing acquisition programs in such areas as foreign dissertations, foreign government documents, and international newspapers. Members set policy for these activities but do not vote on each acquisition. The same is true for programs (each requiring separate membership) to microfilm government publications, journals, newspapers, and personal papers from Africa, Latin America, the Middle East, Asia, and Eastern Europe.

Since its inception, CRL has illustrated the value of basic CCD principles. Many items are so esoteric that one copy can adequately serve many libraries with large user populations. Because of this fact, comparatively well-financed libraries can benefit from the economy of shared purchase and access.

Centralized repositories offer advantages to their members in relieving them of decisions about who will purchase and who will store cooperatively selected materials. They can also free members of the need to reserve precious shelf space for little-used resources. On the other hand, centralized agencies are an expensive CCD tool. Members pay not only for purchased materials, but also for buildings, maintenance, and staffing.

Distributed Model

Decentralized models avoid much of the overhead cost, and they are far more widely practiced. Participating libraries assume responsibility for collecting in assigned areas, and they house the materials they acquire. Yet even ventures in decentralized cooperative acquisition and storage can feature centralized administration. Such was the case of perhaps the earliest national CCD project, the Farmington Plan.

The Farmington Plan: The plan, conceived by the Library of Congress and sponsored by the Association of Research Libraries, began in 1948 as an effort to increase holdings of foreign research materials in American libraries. Each of sixty participating libraries agreed to purchase materials published in over 120 assigned countries throughout the world. To provide bibliographic access, member libraries supplied catalog cards for materials acquired through the plan to the National Union Catalog, and members made the materials available for interlibrary loan. The plan ended in 1972.

The Farmington Plan's salient feature was its systematized approach to collecting. Defining each library's responsibility by country (or by LC class within selected countries) established a clear division of labor and minimized opportunities for overlap. Many contemporary CCD projects emulate the Farmington formula of using geography as the basis for selection assignments. But this attribute could not prevent other negative factors from causing the plan's demise. Post mortems have offered many explanations for the participating libraries' decision to terminate the plan, from poor oversight to changes in acquisition tools to budgetary problems. The Farmington Plan is generally viewed today as a noble failure, but this assessment may be unfair. It lasted twenty-four years, significantly expanded research library holdings of international publications in the postwar era, and disbanded when economic circumstances and library business practices rendered it unnecessary. CCD programs do not always need to be permanent to be successful.

Public Law 480 Program: Another short-lived, mid-twentieth-century collaborative project combined centralized administration with distributed storage. Like Farmington, it sought to increase the holdings of international publications at American research libraries. The Public Law 480 program, named after its enabling legislation, began in 1962. Using public funds (actually foreign currencies obtained through the sale of surplus agricultural products), the Library of Congress acquired materials chiefly from the Middle East and South Asia and distributed them to participating libraries.

State Incentives: In the recent past, state governments have provided incentives, in the form of funding and governance, for libraries to participate in distributed programs. For example, in the early 1990s, the Network of Alabama Academic Libraries awarded grants to member libraries that submitted proposals to strengthen their research-level collections in defined subject areas.[7] The grants were designed to serve a statewide agenda, enhancing library support for research, through building local collections.

Characteristics of Current Distributed Projects

Most decentralized CCD projects are self-governing organizations in which participating libraries negotiate distributed collecting responsibilities and each member pays for and houses materials it acquires as part of its consortial obligation. Decision making for selection and budgeting is situated at the local level. Participants ordinarily commit themselves to cataloging the materials they purchase and providing online access to their catalog records through a consortial union catalog or links to member library catalogs. They also agree to share materials in their collections with other member libraries on a priority basis, often through expedited document delivery mechanisms, such as courier services or express mail. They may share among themselves specialized materials that they would not routinely lend to other libraries, like microforms or videos.

Experience indicates that distributed collecting works best among libraries of similar size and mission. It is certainly possible for multitype libraries (academic, public, corporate) to find enough common ground to develop a cooperative program. In fact, it may be that such consortia are unusual not because they cannot work, but because they are rarely attempted. Librarians tend to associate most frequently with other librarians from similar organizations: academic librarians interact professionally with other academic librarians, public librarians with other public librarians. The comfort level and familiarity we find with our colleagues doubtlessly goes a long way toward determining whom we first approach with CCD proposals.

Geographic proximity is not an absolute prerequisite for collaboration, but forming a consortium within a state or region is likely to be less demanding than organizing a multistate or national project. Although many of the earliest CCD efforts were national in scope, regional projects now predominate. Familiarity doubtlessly plays a part here, too, but so do more practical matters. Creating a rapid document delivery network and scheduling meetings of administrators or selectors, for instance, are generally easier when participants are not widely separated by distance. Interregional or national consortia may be stronger if they start as smaller regional endeavors that gradually build outward.

Whatever its membership or geographic distribution, a CCD project must have some sort of common understanding among its members concerning each library's responsibility for building a portion of the consortial collection. The understanding may be a collection policy statement or an informal working agreement, but it must articulate, in terms clear to all parties, every member's assigned collection-building obligation. Libraries can assume responsibility for subjects, geographic areas, languages, formats, or any other characteristic that is, by mutual agreement, a meaningful point of demarcation.

The areas of responsibility can be as broad or narrow as participants wish, as the following examples show:

> In the Information Alliance (University of Kentucky, University of Tennessee, Vanderbilt University), German literature selectors determined that none of the three libraries collected systematically beyond the top tier of best-known German authors. They then decided that each library would assume responsibility for collecting works by and about authors assigned to them from a list of contemporary German-language writers.
>
> The University of Michigan (UM) and Michigan State University (MSU) cooperate in building Eastern European resources in

the humanities and social sciences. UM is responsible for the Balkans, while MSU collects materials on the Baltic States.

The University of Michigan and Indiana University have joined for almost twenty years in a similar project in Slavic collection development. Indiana focuses on Georgia and Slovenia, while Michigan concentrates on Armenia and Bosnia-Herzegovina.

The Tri-College University Libraries (Concordia College, Minnesota State University, and North Dakota State University) divide responsibility for collecting items reviewed in *Choice*.

Four rural public libraries in east-central Illinois agreed to develop one or more subject areas at a strength sufficient to serve the needs of the entire group.[8]

A consortium of public, school, college, hospital, and military libraries located in Wayne County, North Carolina, negotiates informal agreements to alternately purchase expensive reference sets.[9]

Area studies appear to form the surest path to success in collaborative print collection development, at least among large academic libraries. Incentives for cooperation may be stronger in these fields because building intensive multidisciplinary collections covering all of Latin America, Eastern Europe, or South Asia is beyond the means of even the most well-financed libraries. Prospects for reaching agreement on collecting responsibilities are doubtlessly strengthened in focus areas that lend themselves to organization by country, language, or material type. The Triangle Research Libraries discovered early in their collaborative history that dividing collecting responsibilities geographically worked well for all parties.[10] Duke and North Carolina have long shared in developing research-level collections on Latin America; each acquires specialized resources from assigned countries. On a broader scale, twenty-eight libraries across the country participating in the Global Resources Program, sponsored by the Association of American Universities and the Association of Research Libraries, have agreed to collect Latin American materials related to designated countries, regions, or subjects.[11]

Government documents is another area in which opportunities for cooperation readily present themselves. Geography, subject, format, or issuing agency could form the basis for a distributed depository profile.[12] Smaller libraries lacking area studies collections might consider building shared documents collections as a good CCD beginning point.

Although a clear division of responsibilities is essential for CCD projects to operate effectively, most successful consortia do not attempt to rigidly enforce schemes for shared collection building. Participants usually define their areas of responsibility somewhat loosely to create flexibility in selection. Likewise, few consortia require a firm budgetary commitment from their members, permitting each participant to adjust its level of commitment to changing local financial conditions.

Combined Model

Some consortia combine distributed acquisition and storage with centralized selection. In this model, multiple libraries can take advantage of the subject or language expertise of a single selector, who may work independently or on the staff of one member library. The selector chooses materials to be purchased and housed by each member library within the parameters of each library's assigned area of responsibility and budgetary allocation. The Scottish Consortium for Chinese Studies, for example, employs a librarian to serve both Edinburgh and Glasgow Universities in this capacity. The University of Arizona and Arizona State University have shared the services of a Slavic studies bibliographer. The Triangle Research Libraries employ a single bibliographer to select materials and provide faculty and student liaison in South Asian studies for four institutions.[13]

UNSTRUCTURED CCD

A variation on decentralized CCD is a less-structured confederation in which libraries each pursue collection building independently without any obligation to acquire assigned subjects, languages, or geographic areas for the consortium. Yet they operate in the knowledge of their partners' collection policies and attempt to complement each other's collections and avoid duplicating materials that they consider noncore resources for their clienteles. They can also rely on their partners to build and share collections in subjects, languages, or geographic areas in which they do not collect intensively.

This *complementary approach* is obviously much less coordinated than one in which partners agree on a plan that carefully defines how they will divide collecting responsibilities.[14] It carries a high degree of risk that partners will overduplicate some portions of their aggregate collections and overlook gaps in other portions. On the other hand, it is much less taxing to negotiate and administer than are standard CCD agreements, and participants need not feel that they have sacrificed their autonomy to build collections in areas they view as important. Nor is any library required to pledge a budgetary contribution to the project.

To be most effective, this approach might be employed when two or more libraries recognize that their collections already complement each other in certain categories and agree to work together to maintain this serendipitous relationship. The Michigan–Michigan State project in Eastern European collections began in this way.[15] Even where this symbiosis does not necessarily exist, forming a complementary relationship could cultivate a sense of common purpose among libraries that could lead to more formal working agreements.

An imaginative variation on complementary CCD is the *consortial approval plan* developed by OhioLINK. Although participating OhioLINK libraries work under the umbrella of a contract negotiated by the consortium, they retain their autonomy to create profiles specific to their needs. The collaborative hook exists in their ability to view other OhioLINK libraries' profiles and book receipts through a consortial link in their vendor's (YBP) database. They can voluntarily adjust their profiles or make acceptance or rejection decisions on particular titles in the knowledge of their partners' acquisitions. OhioLINK's shared catalog and document delivery service provide assurance that items held at partner libraries are bibliographically identifiable and physically accessible. OhioLINK librarians adopted the consortial approval plan following years of stalled progress on other CCD initiatives and after examining evidence of a steadily growing homogenization of their aggregate collection.[16]

COLLABORATIVE SERIALS MANAGEMENT

Collaboration need not always entail selection of electronic or print resources. Collection management projects supplement selection programs in some consortia and are the primary form of cooperative activity in many others. These projects most often encompass the cancellation and retention of serials.

Coordinated serials cancellation suggests itself as a response to budgetary pressures, though there is no evidence that libraries have widely employed it. Multiple libraries often find themselves undertaking cancellation projects at the same time. This can happen most often among publicly supported libraries within a state and whose budgets grow or diminish at the same rate. By sharing information about titles under consideration for cancellation, they can avoid duplicating each other's decisions. If they can agree to have at least one library retain a subscription to titles canceled by the others, they can blunt the most severe impact of cancellation projects. The agreement assures all members of the group that there will be a reliable source to supply articles from serials they cancel. A shared catalog and expedited document delivery can make the arrangement even more attractive.

The proliferation of consortial licensing arrangements for publisher-based electronic journal packages has introduced a variation on the theme of serials coordination. Frequently, the terms of these licenses stipulate that if a single library in the consortium subscribes to any journal in the package, all libraries in the group acquire electronic access to the journal. This provision creates an incentive for the libraries to reduce the overlap among their print subscriptions in order to increase the number of electronic journals available to the group. Libraries may cancel most print subscriptions to journals that are held by multiple members and, in turn, add print subscriptions to journals not held by any member of the consortium. The more unique print subscriptions, the greater the number of electronic journals that can be offered to patrons of the consortial libraries. Licenses may impose some limits on this activity, but it is an eminently rational means of enlarging each library's serial collection through collaborative collection management.

SHARED ARCHIVES

Another form of collaboration in print serials management is a joint serial archive. As libraries find themselves increasingly stressed to house their growing print collections, a shared serial archive permits them to simultaneously enjoy the space-saving advantages of weeding and the reassuring retention of serial backfiles. Canceled or ceased serial titles are prime candidates for shared archives. The Information Alliance has formed a shared archive of ceased titles or those canceled by one or more of its members. Each of the members agrees to hold the backfiles of selected periodicals and serve as the library of record for the consortium, meaning that it will not discard the backfiles without consulting its partners. The library of record obtains volumes from the other libraries as needed to make the consortial backfile of each periodical as extensive as possible. Thus, each library can feel free to withdraw its backfile of a periodical in the archive (unless it is the library of record) and reclaim valuable shelf space.

A shared archive can also be a preservation tool. The National Plan for Australian Newspapers, a project of the National Library of Australia and the country's seven state libraries, endeavors to locate, acquire, preserve, and make accessible all newspapers ever published in Australia. Once it identifies a newspaper, the project works to preserve an original print copy in an Australian library. The libraries also microfilm the papers.

Libraries have discovered that shared archives are a cost-effective means of preserving print backfiles of serials widely held in electronic form. As electronic journals displace print, retaining print backfiles becomes more a matter of preserving a copy of record than providing resources that users wish to consult. A group of cooperating libraries can share the preservation copy. The Southeastern Pennsylvania Consortium for Higher Education, a collaborative of eight college libraries, created a joint "last copy" depository for print or microfilm copies of titles in the JSTOR Arts and Sciences I collection. Members transferred volumes to designated libraries to create a single consortial backfile and were then free to withdraw unneeded volumes. The Center for Research Libraries has established a similar program to retain a preservation backfile of JSTOR journals for its members.

Shared archives work best when their holdings are bibliographically accessible through the catalogs of the participating libraries or a consortial catalog. In this way, both libraries and patrons can readily identify the location of volumes and issues they wish to consult. An expedited consortial document delivery program is also an important feature that permits users to obtain desired articles quickly.

Creating and maintaining an archive can be challenging. Staff members of participating libraries will have to work through their reservations about giving serial volumes to other libraries and discarding their own holdings. Identifying serial titles to nominate for the archive may not always be straightforward, and maintaining a record of exactly which serials are in the archive is an ongoing need. Yet the benefits of saving storage space and reducing duplicative preservation investments make shared archives worthy of serious consideration.

Conserving space also motivates libraries to create consortial storage facilities for lesser-used monographs as well as serials:

> The Washington Research Library Consortium operates a shared off-site storage facility that serves seven libraries.
>
> The Southwest Regional Depository provides a storage facility serving Miami University, the University of Cincinnati, Wright State University, and Central State University.
>
> Five academic libraries in Amherst, Massachusetts, administer a shared storage facility, a converted Air Force bunker. They withdraw duplicate copies, and four of the five libraries cede ownership and control of stored materials to the depository itself.[17]

Building or acquiring a single facility to serve multiple libraries is considerably less expensive than each library acquiring and staffing a separate facility. Shared archiving enables partnering libraries to eliminate multiple copies of low-demand monographs and establish "last copy" repositories.

Libraries frequently create and store digital archives on a cooperative basis, as the following examples show:

> The Florida Center for Library Automation is assisting libraries in creating digital collections of historical, environmental, and cultural materials.
>
> PANDORA, a consortium of Australian libraries, is establishing a shared archive of Australian online publications.
>
> The Kansas State Historical Society and the University of Kansas Library are jointly digitizing primary source materials in their archives relating to territorial Kansas. The documents reside at a website designed to serve secondary schools.
>
> The Library of Congress is partnering with a group of American and Russian libraries and museums to create Meeting of Frontiers, a bilingual multimedia library relating the exploration and settlement of the American West and the simultaneous exploration and settlement of Siberia and the Russian Far East.

These endeavors enable cooperating institutions to merge their sometimes disparate archival materials into a coherent digital collection while sharing the costs of converting, preserving, and protecting electronic data.

COLLECTIONS-RELATED PROGRAMS

Other collaborative endeavors may fall outside the strict definition of collection development or management, but they seek to broaden access to classes of materials. The *Global Resources Program* focuses on cooperative actions to improve access to international research materials. The program's regional projects relate to Europe, Asia, Africa, and Latin America. They include digital archiving, but several of them entail the creation of union lists of hard-to-find resources, tables of contents of journals that are neither widely held nor indexed, and document delivery agreements with overseas libraries.[18] Although these initiatives target large research libraries and feature international cooperation, they employ strategies that could be equally useful for college or public libraries in expanding access to fugitive local or regional publications.

Preservation is another collection-related area ripe for cooperation. We described earlier how shared archives can assure that last copies of low-use monographs or serials can be preserved, but libraries can also realize economies by collaborating on preservation projects unrelated to other endeavors. The *Brittle* program, founded at the University of Kansas, includes over sixty member libraries. Members intending to make preservation photocopies submit their selected titles to an electronic discussion list. Other members have the option of requesting copies for themselves at reduced prices.[19]

Clearly, CCD can take many forms. Every project, however, has in common the vision of its participating libraries and their commitment to take risks and invest their corporate energies to achieve the benefits of cooperation.

NOTES

1. For a full description of survey findings, see John Haar, "Report of Working Group to Map Current Cooperative Collection Development Projects," presented at the New Dynamics and Economics of Cooperative Collection Development Conference hosted by the Center for Research Libraries at the Aberdeen Woods Conference Center, Atlanta, GA, November 8–10, 2002, http://www.crl.edu/awcc2002/Project%20Mapping%20WG%20Report.pdf (accessed November 7, 2003).

2. Heather M. Edwards, "South Africa's GAELIC: The Gauteng and Environs Library Consortium," *Information Technology and Libraries* 18, no. 3 (September 1999): 123.

3. Kachel, *Collection Assessment*, 84.

4. Dan C. Hazen, "Cooperative Collection Development: Compelling Theory, Inconsequential Results?" in *Collection Management for the 21st Century: A Handbook for Librarians*, ed. G. E. Gorman and Ruth H. Miller, 269 (Westport, CT and London: Greenwood, 1997).

5. Dominguez and Swindler, "Cooperative Collection Development," 474.

6. Linda A. Naru, "The Role of the Center for Research Libraries in the History and Future of Cooperative Collection Development," *Collection Management* 23 (1998): 49–50.

7. Medina, "Evolution," 12–13.

8. Shasteen, "Cooperative Collection Management," 98.

9. Diane D. Kester and Shirley T. Jones, "The Birth and Growth of Library Resource Sharing in Wayne County," *North Carolina Libraries* 53, no. 3 (Fall 1995): 118.

10. Dominguez and Swindler, "Cooperative Collection Development," 487.

11. Deborah L. Jakubs, "The AAU/ARL Global Resources Program at a Crossroads: Achievements, Best Practices, New Challenges, and Next Steps," Association of Research Libraries, 2002, http://www.arl.org/collect/grp/crossroads .html (accessed November 7, 2003).

12. Dominguez and Swindler, "Cooperative Collection Development," 487.

13. Christian E. Filstrup, Jordan M. Scepanski, and Tony K. Stewart, "An Experiment in Cooperative Collection Development: South Asia Vernaculars among the Research Triangle Universities," *Collection Management* 24, no. 1/2 (2000): 101.

14. Ross Atkinson, "Preservation," 100.

15. Alan Pollard (University of Michigan Library) in discussion with John Haar, June 21, 2002.

16. Carol Pitts Diedrichs, "Designing and Implementing a Consortial Approval Plan: The OhioLINK Experience," *Collection Management* 24 (2000): 18–20.

17. Willis E. Bridegam, "A Collaborative Approach to Collection Storage: The Five-College Library Depository," 2001, http://www.clir.org/pubs/reports/ pub97/contents.html (accessed November 7, 2003).

18. Jakubs, "Global Resources."

19. Bradley L. Schaffner, "Specialized Cooperative Efforts in Collection Development: An Analysis of Three Slavic Programs," *Collection Management* 24, no. 3/4 (2000): 266–67.

PREREQUISITES
Resources Required to Initiate and Sustain CCD

Some CCD projects, such as joint purchases of expensive materials, are impromptu, one-time efforts that require little preparation. Although successful ad hoc projects may lead to more permanent interlibrary relationships, they do not in themselves imply further commitments from any participant. But when a library decides to enter into an ongoing CCD *program*, it effectively takes on long-term obligations that engage its administration, its staff, and even its patrons in an entirely new paradigm of collection development, resource sharing, and public service.

Obviously such a decision should not be undertaken without thorough consideration of its consequences. Equally important is a complete evaluation of whether the library possesses all the resources needed for entry into a CCD program and, if not, whether it is prepared to make the economic, managerial, and technological investments to acquire them. This chapter describes the core components, from leadership posture to technical infrastructure, that a library will need to draw upon as it begins and sustains a CCD relationship.

VISIONARY LEADERSHIP

The vital resource for CCD success is a library administration committed to the concepts of shared collection building and reciprocal access. If CCD is to realize its potential for enlarging patrons' information options, administrators must be prepared to articulate its benefits to staff and users. Leaders must promote its advantages, energize staff members, and—most important—stay the course and keep their focus. Mere acquiescence will not suffice. Nor will an enthusiasm that wanes when the next big thing comes along. CCD leadership must be steady and resolute. If a library's leaders are not convinced that collaboration is worth a considerable investment of time and energy to initiate, they should not begin the process.

CCD is in many respects a radical departure from traditional norms of collection development and library service, one that challenges time-honored precepts of library autonomy and self-sufficiency. While some members of the library's staff and patron community might embrace the concept as a promising innovation, others may respond with indifference or hostility. CCD cannot succeed in the absence of a broad supportive consensus among those who must put it into practice, and visionary leaders must build this consensus. It is neither necessary nor realistic for them to generate universal enthusiasm, but it is critical for them to encourage those who are receptive and to convince doubters to at least suspend their skepticism until they can fairly judge the results of change.

Sustained administrative support is a characteristic common to almost all productive collaborative programs. Following its 1999 CCD conference, the Center for Research Libraries charged a working group to explore best practices for maintaining cooperative endeavors. The group reported a direct relationship between upper administrative commitment and CCD success. A CCD program has its best chance of prospering when the impetus to establish it comes from high up the administrative ladder.[1] Directors and other leaders can underscore CCD's importance by positioning it as part of their library's strategic vision. More importantly, they can provide funding, staff, and other resources to help fledgling projects get started and take hold. This type of administrative backing was critical in creating the Statewide California Electronic Library Consortium, for example.[2] Administrative encouragement must work at both the conceptual and operational levels.[3] Leaders need to provide the intellectual stimulus for CCD as well as practical guidance to move projects past the inevitable financial and procedural obstacles.

The manner of an administrator's endorsement of CCD is all-important. Collaboration is almost certain to fail if a director's backing begins and ends with an order to make it happen. By definition, CCD is an eminently human enterprise that can be viable only if library staff members who select materials and provide public service buy into the concept and make it an integral part of their routines. If they accept CCD in principle, staff members are most likely to promote its advantages to users wholeheartedly. Thus, leaders should think in terms of nurturing a local culture that is accepting of CCD and willing to employ it. They must make the case—carefully, convincingly, and repeatedly—that traditional collection development practice, no matter how effective, can be improved upon and be made more responsive to patrons' information needs, and that CCD represents an opportunity to supplement local acquisition with a broader, richer shared collection. Figure 5-1 illustrates how visionary leaders can muster arguments and evidence that demonstrate where the present model falls short and how collaboration leads to better service.

As they work to build support, administrators must also make it clear to staff that CCD is an institutional imperative. Nothing will increase chances for success more than widespread staff acceptance of

---

FIGURE 5-1   *Make the Case for CCD*

- Analyze collection overlap with other libraries, and question whether noncore resources need to be held in multiple locations in the same region.

- Provide examples of other materials not held in the region, and promote the benefits of trading some excessive overlap for improved access to such items.

- Demonstrate how inflation erodes buying power and inhibits each library's ability to continue to build local collections of the same depth and breadth that characterized holdings acquired years earlier.

- Explain how new technologies for bibliographic access and data transmission might be employed to enable users to quickly identify and obtain resources that were once difficult to find.

the concept. Knowledge that innovation is welcome, in fact expected, by upper management can go a long way toward overcoming inertia and wearing down resistance. Once it moves beyond initial confidence-building projects, cooperation cannot remain a voluntary exercise of the risk-takers in an organization. Everyone must participate.

Leaders should supplement the intellectual case for CCD by offering practical support to build and maintain cooperation. Assistance in the form of funding or staffing can demonstrate the administrative commitment to CCD and reemphasize its importance to the organization. This tangible support can help those charged with implementing CCD to work through the inevitable problems of establishing relationships with new partner libraries. Figure 5-2 suggests small investments to stimulate CCD programs.

CCD is an exercise in coordination and collaboration. Directors of partner libraries should consult with each other about strategies for promoting CCD to their staffs and patrons. Their consultation sets a noticeable example and models the kind of behavior they seek to encourage. It also enables them to exchange ideas about crafting justifications for shared collection building and to compare notes on effective methods of jump-starting projects with gestures of practical support.

All the work that administrators do to get CCD programs off the ground may well be wasted if they do not hold fast to their commitment and provide long-term, unwavering support. They will almost certainly need to persevere through a variety of unexpected problems: departures of counterpart administrators and the necessity of

---

FIGURE 5-2 *Investments in CCD*

- Grant release time for collection development staff to attend retreats or brainstorming sessions to identify areas that could benefit most from collaborative endeavors.

- Fund selectors to visit partner libraries and meet their counterparts.

- Allot administrative staff time to prepare background studies, collection assessments, and other documentation to inform project planners.

- Award incentive grants of supplemental materials funds for bibliographers who arrange workable cooperative projects with their counterparts at other libraries.

bringing replacements up to speed; disagreements among selectors about areas of responsibility; foot-dragging by obstinate holdouts. Skeptics may see these events as reasons for abandoning the program, so leaders will need to be tenacious, remain positive, and keep everyone focused on goals. They must insist that CCD remain an organizational priority and be willing to invest considerable time in its implementation.

INTEGRATED BIBLIOGRAPHIC ACCESS

A robust technological infrastructure is not an absolute prerequisite for CCD, but its presence provides an unequaled promotional and functional resource for collaborative programs. Integrated online catalogs, informative websites, and automated interlibrary loan request forms are tools that can help libraries fully realize the potential of coordinated collection building and exhibit the utility of CCD to their users.

No utility can favorably impact CCD more than an integrated public access catalog that displays the holdings of all libraries in a consortium. Fortunately, vendors have developed several new products that merge data from the catalogs of multiple libraries. An immediate advantage is that patrons can see for themselves the value of bibliographic access to an expanded set of information resources. Viewing the holdings of consortial libraries is a powerfully persuasive demonstration of the benefits of collaboration. Enhancing catalog records of items in partner collections with a link to an interlibrary loan (ILL) form or circulation request places users in direct control of resource sharing. Once they experience the gratification of selecting and obtaining a needed book or article from another library, it will be all the easier to convince them—and reluctant staff members—of the usefulness of coordinating resource acquisition with other libraries to further broaden their range of choices.

Ideally, the integrated catalog should serve as each library's primary public access catalog so that patrons can use a single tool to search both the holdings of their own library and those of its partners. If the integrated catalog software is not adequately developed to provide all the requisite features of a local catalog, it can still be a useful accessory. In this case, it is all-important to make it a prominent link on the library's home page with a clear explanation of its function.

The economic implications of acquiring and operating an integrated catalog are, obviously, considerable. See chapter 8 for further discussion of economic issues. The catalog utility itself is a major investment, and skilled staff to install and maintain it must be in place. Whether to undertake the expense is a decision for each library to make in the context of its ability to pay and the value it places on resource sharing and coordinated collection development. The cost of integrated bibliographic access, like any investment, can best be weighed in terms of its potential payoff.

The catalog may not always be a wholly new cost. Periodic upgrades for online catalogs are now part of the cost of doing business, and the integrated tool might be purchased as part of a normal replacement cycle. One way to control the costs of bibliographic access is to treat the access tools as consortial acquisitions. Just as multiple libraries can reduce their individual costs for databases through group purchasing, they can negotiate savings by jointly procuring a catalog utility. Hosting the utility at a single site can decrease development and maintenance expenses through eliminating hardware duplication and redundant staff. Staffing can be another shared expense; the model of shared bibliographers can be applied to information technology specialists who could rotate among multiple libraries.

EXPEDITED DOCUMENT DELIVERY

CCD is an empty exercise without a well-developed resource-sharing capability. Pairing an efficient document delivery system with an integrated catalog provides the means to transform collaborative collection development from theory into a working tool that builds and manages multiple library collections to increase patrons' ready access to information.

As we mentioned earlier, an interlibrary loan (ILL) link within the catalog record display is a highly desirable feature. Equally important is what happens after patrons click the "submit" button. Traditional staff-mediated interlibrary loan can suffice, but the strength of consortial relationships really hits home with users if materials borrowed from partner libraries move on a faster track than other ILL requests. Amazon.com and other customer-oriented online retailers have raised user expectations for rapid delivery of products. Libraries would do well to demonstrate to patrons that obtaining books from consortial partners is easy and involves only minor delays.

Priority Processing

If ILL staff must process all interlibrary borrowing requests, it is nonetheless possible to build consortial priorities into the workflow. Requests submitted through the integrated consortial catalog, for instance, can receive the highest processing priority. For other requests, partner libraries should be at the top of the lending string for items they hold. On the other end of the transaction, lending requests received from partner libraries should also carry priority status for fulfillment. These steps assure that patrons seeking materials in the collaborative collection receive them as quickly as possible. This valuable promotional device goes a long way to reassure skeptics and counterbalance misgivings about CCD's collection-building trade-offs, which we discussed in chapter 2.

Using technology to reduce or eliminate staff intervention can increase the speed of interlibrary borrowing transactions. Integrated catalogs can now be teamed with peer-to-peer resource sharing software that enables libraries' automated systems to communicate with each other to initiate interlibrary loans. Authorized users of one library in a consortium can be authenticated by a partner library's system and permitted to borrow items directly from the partner's collection. Thus, when a patron at Library A searches the consortial catalog, identifies an item held by Library B, and places an interlibrary loan request, the ILL staff at Library A need not review or authorize the transaction. The request goes straight to Library B's system, which checks to see if the patron is authorized to borrow at Library A. Once the system establishes authorization, it charges the item to the patron.

Interlibrary loan becomes interlibrary circulation, freeing ILL staff to concentrate on nonconsortial requests. The borrowing transaction, because it did not have to wait in a queue for staff mediation, takes little more time than a circulation transaction in a single library. Moreover, the process itself symbolizes the links between libraries, illustrates yet again the efficacy of cooperation, and forms a major building block in the support structure for CCD. In fact, an interlibrary circulation capability is frequently a distinguishing characteristic of the most successful collaborative programs.[4]

Speedy Transport

Of course, processing interlibrary borrowing requests with dispatch only partly addresses the need for speedy resource sharing. The other part of the equation is how quickly a library can transport the borrowed materials to a waiting patron at another library. Reducing the time between the patron's placement of a request and receipt of materials is a key consideration in developing a CCD-friendly service environment. Surface mail was the preferred method of transport in the past, but today a multitude of speedier alternatives exist. For nonreturnable items, such as articles, fax or digital transmission can outperform mail delivery by several days. Digital library-to-library delivery tools, such as ARL's ARIEL, can be paired with other utilities to send electronic copies directly to a borrower's office or home computer, further reducing turnaround times. For books, libraries can consider using express mail for items sent to other members in the consortium. Better yet is a courier service. Libraries can pool their own vehicles to deliver materials on a regular schedule, or they can outsource the service to a commercial courier. Illinois, for instance, has provided a statewide network of vans for over a decade.[5]

Reciprocal Borrowing

Resource sharing need not always be a matter of delivering materials to patrons. Establishing reciprocal borrowing privileges enables patrons registered at one library to charge out materials from other libraries in a consortium. Libraries in the Triangle Research Libraries Network (TRLN) have offered this service for over fifteen years.[6] OCLC sponsors a similar program for faculty at participating academic institutions. Permitting users to browse the stacks of partner libraries and identify the materials they need is sometimes more helpful than delivering documents.

Cost Considerations

Just as an integrated catalog is a cost center, so too is expedited resource sharing and document delivery. As always, each library must judge for itself whether to make the added investments based on its budget and the value it places on the enhanced services the investments produce. Most libraries decided long ago, for instance, that interlibrary loan brought user benefits significant enough to be worth the cost in personnel, postage, and telecommunications. Resource sharing joined with an active CCD program may increase ILL demand to the point that increased staffing will be necessary. Acquiring software to reduce staff mediation of requests may counterbalance this pressure to some extent, but these tools also come at a premium. Replacing surface mail with express mail and digital delivery tools represents another expense consideration. Courier costs vary depending on whether the service is in-house or outsourced, the volume of delivery, number of delivery points, distance, and other factors. Libraries should expect to pay more for couriers than they pay for mail.

One way to measure the value of these expenses is to compare the delivery cost per item to the average cost of items in the library's collection. If the item type is monographs, for example, a simple method is to contrast the cost of shipping each book by express mail or courier with the average purchase price of books. A more inclusive comparison matches the total cost of each delivery transaction, including ILL staffing, software, mail, or courier, against total purchase cost, including purchase price, shipping and handling, and acquisitions and cataloging staffing.

Transforming ILL

The measures discussed in the preceding sections reinforce to patrons and staff that items in the consortial collection are, if not quite the equal of items in the local collection, a close second in terms of ready identification and expedited availability. CCD is much easier to implement and promote when everyone is assured that materials collected by partner libraries are easy to find and obtain.

Consortia need not feel limited to sharing only items that have traditionally been loaned between libraries. If collections are opened fully to patrons of consortial libraries, materials such as large book sets, multireel microfilm collections, videos, and DVDs can be loaned, even for extended periods, to collaborating institutions. Why should multiple libraries go to the expense of purchasing expensive but little-used resources of this kind when they can make use of their integrated catalogs and document delivery mechanisms to offer a single copy to everyone in their combined patron pool?

Once a consortium has an integrated catalog and enhanced document delivery program in place, it has an infrastructure capable of supporting the introduction of collaborative collection development. But the infrastructure can play only a supporting role. As always, the most critical success factor is people.

SUPPORTIVE COLLECTION DEVELOPMENT ENVIRONMENT

As noted earlier, committed and consistent leadership is probably the best predictor of CCD sustainability. But this leadership should not reside solely at the top of an organization. Those charged with responsibility for administering a library's collection development program, whether they reside in middle or upper management, are also in a position to wield a determinative influence on the course of CCD planning and execution. CCD can function in a variety of organizational settings, but its prospects improve when someone, be it a director, an associate director, a team leader, a coordinator, or other responsible party, is unambiguously tasked with directing the library's participation in collaborative collections activities. Ideally, the CCD manager should be the staff member with primary responsibility for local collections programs to synchronize collection building at the local and consortial levels.

Collection development officers obviously need to buy into the culture of CCD themselves so that they can convince others to do so. They also need to be vested with sufficient autonomy and authority, subject to upper administrative review, to make management decisions about functional matters, such as the division of labor and the structure of CCD projects. Their ability to move projects forward may be strengthened if they have direct supervisory responsibility for collection development practitioners. If this is not consistent with the library's organizational model, they can be effective in coordinator or team leader roles. In either case, their ability to make persuasive arguments and cultivate support will be a more useful asset than the power to issue orders.

Most importantly, the collection development officer must preside over a viable local collection development program. Before a library can consider entering into a collaborative collection-building arrangement, it must have an established collection development operation of its own. This implies a budget line for collections that is allocated by discipline, genre, material type, or other characteristics that will accommodate reserving and tracking funds for consortial acquisitions. It also means a staff, large or small, full-time or part-time, charged with responsibility for selecting materials and managing collections. These selectors must know the information needs of the library's clientele in order to make informed decisions about which materials to hold locally and which to obtain through cooperative agreements.

Heads of collection development will face the challenge of cultivating a corporate mindset supportive of CCD. They will have to find a balance between providing clear and steady direction and offering sufficient latitude. Selectors should feel comfortable in a consortial environment and free to develop their own collaborative methodologies. A positive staff attitude means everything. Cooperation imposed from above will very likely encounter resistance rather than receptiveness.[7]

For CCD to work, everyone involved must accept a new paradigm. Collection development will have to connote an idea far more inclusive than the act of selecting materials for a particular library. The library's collection must come to be defined not only by what the library owns itself, but also by what it can readily access from partner libraries.[8] Thus, the work collection development staff members do to build collaborative collections becomes as important as their efforts to develop local holdings. CCD must be not a niche activity, but a core activity.

Collection development officers need to find ways to instill confidence that CCD is a long-term relationship among libraries. If staff members suspect it to be nothing more than the latest management fad, their skepticism will be hard to breach, and they will never cultivate the trust in other libraries that is a core part of the process. Personal relationships build library relationships. Bringing together the people who must cooperatively build and manage multiple library collections moves CCD out of the realm of cold theory and gives it a human face. Projects that seem implausible in the abstract can become conceivable, even desirable, when peers meet and discover common interests and shared goals.

When selectors from partner libraries get together, either electronically or in person, collection development officers should establish an ambiance, provide a sense of direction, and get out of the way. It may help to remind everyone of why the libraries became involved in a CCD program. Perhaps it was to build a broader aggregate collection, or develop deeper subject collections at each library, or formulate a cooperative storage plan. Whatever the combination of motivations, everyone should begin the process prepared with the same knowledge and aware of a shared vision. Only then can they begin to convert vision to reality. At the outset, identify low-cost, low-commitment projects to build the trust and confidence needed for more elaborate undertakings in the future. Chapter 6 includes suggestions for these kinds of introductory ventures.

The cost of confidence building is generally limited to staff travel and communication. One meeting may not be enough; regular follow-ups are necessary to expand upon initial contacts. Nonetheless, in most cases (unless the partner libraries are located outside a reasonable driving distance), these are minimal investments in what, with persistent leadership, should become an enduring association.

MANAGEMENT INFORMATION TOOLS

If they are to plan intelligently, collection development officers and selectors need an array of information about each other's collections—their strengths, weaknesses, gaps, and overlap. These data can identify promising possibilities and greatest needs for collaboration. Data also provide another means of convincing doubters of what can be gained through collaboration.

Budget Allocations

An allocated collections budget is basic for any collection development program, and it is a core tool for CCD participation. Each library should have a plan for spending collections money, no matter how much or how little, so that it can appropriate and track its contributions to consortial acquisitions. Do not be reluctant to share budget documentation with partners. Comparisons of allocations can often lead to identification of areas of affinity, where multiple libraries are building collections of similar strength. Conversely, budgets may reveal other areas where libraries can complement each other's acquisitions (for example, we'll build in computer science, where we've allocated major funding, if you'll build in statistics, where you're concentrating your funds).

Where libraries have collections budgets of varying sizes, budget documents can help determine contributions in proportion to ability to pay. Even small libraries have areas of budgetary emphasis. They can target these areas as their consortial responsibility, permitting others to reduce funding in the same categories.

Collection Development Policies

Policies, another collection development staple, add substance to budget statements. Well-written policies describe the programs or interests each library's collection serves and the kinds of resources the library intends to acquire in support of each program or interest. Sharing collection policies with partners can be another useful means of discovering targets of cooperation. Members of CARL (Colorado Alliance of Research Libraries) created a uniform format for their policies to facilitate cross-library comparisons.[9] Writing or standardizing collection policies is a potential consortial project in itself.

Conspectus Data

The Conspectus is another invaluable comparative tool. Libraries in a collaborative relationship often apply the Conspectus methodology before embarking on CCD. No other tool better measures and expresses collection strengths and the library's goals for collection building. Exchanging Conspectus data is potentially the most informative means for consortial partners to learn about each other's collections. If the participating libraries lack up-to-date Conspectus results or if their results are organized in incompatible formats, developing a group conspectus could be a useful beginning project for the consortium (see chapter 6). The combined data are an instrument that describes the joint collection in a lingua franca that all participants can understand.[10]

Shelflist Counts

While the Conspectus addresses the quality of a collection, shelflist counts are purely quantitative measures. Yet they, too, can be helpful comparative instruments that reveal each library's areas of collecting emphasis. When all libraries in the consortium use the same classification system, it is particularly informative if each library segments its count by a standard set of subclasses. For larger libraries, the North American Title Count offers a model of this kind.

Customized Collection Assessment

There are a number of ways to evaluate specialized portions of collections. Libraries should conduct joint evaluations to pinpoint areas of redundancy and identify common needs. Literature selectors can develop belles lettres lists and compare each library's holdings of works by and about each author. In the sciences, lists of periodical subscriptions can establish each library's strengths. In all fields, serial holdings reports may suggest how each library could contribute to a joint backfile archive. Checking standard bibliographies against catalogs is another way to identify options for collaborative collecting. Circulation statistics and interlibrary loan data provide information about collection use and patterns of demand.[11] Even lists of materials currently on order can illustrate patterns of overduplication.

The costs of compiling this information are chiefly staff-centered. Policy writing and collection evaluation can be time-consuming and labor-intensive. Libraries with well-managed collection development programs should employ most of these analytical tools for local self-assessment even if they have no cooperative aspirations. Virtually all the data they gather to share with partners should be highly useful internally.

Collection management information is intrinsically valuable outside the framework of CCD. Even if your library never succeeds in establishing a viable long-term collection-building partnership with other libraries, the investments in preparing for CCD will produce a better library. You will know more about your collection, have a clear plan for rationally allocating financial resources to develop your collection, and be better able to identify materials at distant locations that you can quickly deliver to your patrons. Figure 5-3 summarizes the attributes that will help ensure success in CCD.

FIGURE 5-3   *Is Your Library Ready for CCD?*

These attributes characterize libraries most likely to enjoy successful CCD experiences:

Leaders committed to CCD for the long term who promote the concept and provide sustained intellectual and practical support

Catalogs that display holdings of all consortial partners and enable users to make online interlibrary loan requests

Expedited document delivery capability for items requested from partner libraries

A viable local collection development program headed by a staff member who works to build a CCD-friendly culture

A commitment to compile and share information, such as budgets, collection policies, Conspectus data, shelflist counts, and assessment results, that identifies areas of consortial collaboration and reciprocation

NOTES

1. Cynthia Shelton et al., "Best Practices in Cooperative Collection Development: A Report Prepared by the CRL Working Group on Best Practices," presented at the New Dynamics and Economics of Cooperative Collection Development Conference hosted by the Center for Research Libraries at the Aberdeen Woods Conference Center, Atlanta, GA, November 8–10, 2002, http://www.crl.edu/awcc2002/BESTPRACTICESRPTrev.pdf (accessed November 7, 2003).

2. Ibid., 4.

3. Harloe, *Guide*, 2.

4. Shelton, "Best Practices," 15.

5. Doris Rahe Brown, "Cooperative Collection Development: The Illinois Experience," in *Collection Management for the 1990s: Proceedings of the Midwest Collection Management and Development Institute, University of Illinois at Chicago, August 17–20, 1989*, 145–46 (Chicago: American Library Association, 1993).

6. Julie Blume Nye, "A New Vision for Resource Sharing: TRLN Document Delivery Project," *North Carolina Libraries* 53, no. 3 (Fall 1995): 100.

7. Harloe, *Guide*, 2.

8. Ibid.

9. Donnice Cochenour and Joel S. Rutstein, "A CARL Model for Cooperative Collection Development in a Regional Consortium," *Collection Building* 12, no. 1/2 (1993): 37–38.

10. Harloe, *Guide*, 11.

11. Karen Krueger, "A System Level Coordinated Cooperative Collection Development Model for Illinois," in *Coordinating Cooperative Collection Development: A National Perspective*, ed. Wilson Luquire, 57–58 (New York: Haworth, 1986).

STRATEGY
Creating the Framework for an Effective CCD Partnership

Given the diversity of collaboration models currently in practice, a library administrator contemplating CCD may blanch at the panorama of possibilities and the energy required to begin a new program. Fortunately, the components of a CCD framework incorporate strategies that are already familiar to every library manager:

- Start small.
- Don't expect the program to debut as a finished product.
- Build upon modest successes that you promote aggressively.
- Anticipate and address potential logistical barriers.

A successful CCD program framework formally expresses a vision and relationship among partners while it informally accommodates continual change in the environment. This chapter considers six vital elements in a CCD framework: selecting a partner, creating a mission statement and goals, achieving results, publicizing accomplishments, assessing progress, and developing mechanisms to sustain the partnership. These elements can be applied to program development whether the project extends an existing collaboration or involves an entirely new set of participants. The principles, benefits, barriers, and models covered in earlier chapters demonstrate the need for CCD organizational structures that serve diverse project goals and methods. Developing a CCD framework that is both productive and sustainable can address some historic barriers.[1] The framework will influence relationships among participants, their organizations, and the CCD partnership.

A first step toward developing a CCD framework is to consider the needs of your library clientele. Libraries participate in cooperatives to enhance the quality of services for their users. Base your decisions about partners and goals on characteristics of successful cooperative ventures, such as those in figure 6-1.

While considering the potential value of a CCD endeavor for your library users, recognize intangible or indirect costs and benefits. For example, suppose that your clientele frequently wait several weeks to get copies of current fiction at your library. You and other librarians in your geographic region could design a project like the collaboration among four public libraries in east-central Illinois that resulted in faster access to a larger collection.[2] The partners analyzed their local collections, wrote collection development policies, divided responsibility for developing subject strengths, and relied on the

FIGURE 6-1	*Characteristics of Successful Cooperative Ventures*

- The collaboration offers benefits for all participants.
- Each partner contributes resources to the program.
- Although each library gives up some autonomy for the benefit of the collaboration, each supports effective leadership and receives an opportunity to participate in governance.
- Consortium accomplishments result in better, faster, easier, and more comprehensive access to resources needed by each library's patrons.
- The partnership enables each library to achieve local goals.
- Members of the consortium trust one another. Trust is essential.
- Cooperation has the potential to thrive at local, regional, national, and international levels, and across these boundaries.
- Members do not expect CCD to reduce overall acquisitions expenditures.

shared catalog already available to them through a local consortium. The project resulted in expedited materials delivery, external funding, a group plan for more judicious use of collection funds to support targeted subject areas, and much deeper familiarity with local collections.

Librarians have started CCD programs to increase the number of titles available for users, to reallocate materials expenditures to purchase more unique items, to improve access to existing resources, and to reduce the costs of collection maintenance by collaborating on such projects as weeding, storage, and preservation. Begin by listing needs in your own community that could be addressed through CCD and use this as your point of reference while considering the options available for collaboration. Let your community environment and information needs guide decisions about a CCD framework.

SELECTING PARTNERS

Chances are that your library belongs to one or more information networks and that you have informal cooperative ties with local libraries. Surveys suggest that if you are involved in a CCD project, its focus most likely is on shared access to electronic databases. Given the varieties of collaboration possible for building collections, consider potential partners outside the expected relationships. Consider, for example, whether a potential partner library should be similar to yours in mission and scope. The 2002 CRL survey described in chapter 4 confirms that the vast majority of libraries involved with CCD are academic and that libraries with a similar mission and scope, such as ARL libraries, have the longest history of successful collaboration. A classic example of this is the Triangle Research Libraries Latin American project.[3] Other documented programs in which the partners have much in common include those of the University of Arizona and Arizona State University, the Five Colleges of Ohio, and the New England Law Library Consortium.[4] A compelling case can be made, however, for the advantages of partnerships among unlike institutions. The University of Illinois Library, for example, benefited considerably from its collaboration with several small, specialized libraries.[5] The small libraries frequently held copies of materials for loan that were checked out at the university library. The smaller libraries also owned niche collections not acquired by the larger library. Similarly, the rural Illinois project mentioned earlier proved the benefits of an alliance between school and public libraries.[6]

It is not surprising, of course, that geography plays a large role in selecting partners. Because CCD depends upon easy bibliographic access and fast delivery, libraries located physically near one another have traditionally become sharing partners, particularly for inter-library loan. Although new bibliographic linking capabilities and web-based document delivery software have reduced the significance of physical location, the benefits of local or regional CCD partners are still apparent. First, counterparts can easily meet in person. In addition, working with colleagues in a familiar cultural setting may nurture sustainable projects. Finally, despite physical proximity and this cultural familiarity, local areas offer diverse interests and resources that enable partnerships to make the most of complementary strengths.

One of the most dramatic advantages of geography is financial: collaboration among academic institutions within a political jurisdiction has proven effective for generating CCD funding. The Ohio-LINK, NAAL (Network of Alabama Academic Libraries), and MNSCU (Minnesota State Colleges and Universities System) programs are but a few examples of the many libraries receiving state funding to support their collaboration.[7] The Minnesota legislature actually mandated formation of the MNSCU, reinforcing the fact that when collaboration begins at the level of library funding agents, the potential for success increases dramatically. Such was the case when university provosts formed the Committee on Institutional Cooperation in 1958 among the members of the Big Ten Athletic Conference and the University of Chicago.[8] In South Africa, a Higher Education Act passed by Parliament in 1997 established the political basis for the formation of GAELIC (Gauteng and Environs Library Consortium). A network of sixteen academic and technical libraries representing both historically advantaged and disadvantaged libraries, GAELIC received funding from the Mellon Foundation for a common online system and resource sharing.[9] Although CCD is typically just one component among consortium initiatives, the organizational structure of the network and funding for collections are powerful incentives for using statewide partnerships to increase or begin CCD. It is not necessary for all members of a statewide consortium to participate in a particular CCD project. A few libraries in the network can pursue a pilot project with the potential for expansion.

Think creatively and broadly when considering potential CCD partners. The Books-Not-Bought In Ohio project described in chapter 3 pairs OhioLINK and book vendor YBP. This unusual team led to the design of a voluntary statewide approval plan with the goal of increasing the diversity of collections in the state.[10] An ambitious example is found in Wayne County, North Carolina. Wayne County is home to a community college library with strengths in literature and technical materials, a church-based college with a selective depository of government documents and a strong collection in the history of religion, a public library that collects genealogical materials, twenty-six public schools, and an Air Force base that offers public access to its excellent military collection as well as walk-in use of online databases.[11] Librarians at these institutions decided to address a common need among the diverse libraries. The result? A strengthening of their collective holdings in business reference tools.

CCD thrives or fails on the basis of the relationships among partners. As with any personal or professional relationship, a CCD partnership must have regular communication, a common vision, and a commitment to long-term investment in the affiliation. Thus, selection of appropriate partners is important. None will be perfect. Local participants will change; forgiveness will be required; partners will take turns providing encouragement and incentives. A good partner must be willing to invest more than a fair share, with the expectation that over time, all members will receive benefits from the collaboration. In the evolving digital collection development environment, collaborative frameworks can provide mutual support among subject counterparts, generate new ideas, and increase tolerance for risk. As is apparent in the many projects percolating around the world, a CCD partnership can be based on commonalities in subject, mission, funding agency, region, or vendor as well as combinations of these elements. The guidelines in figure 6-2 summarize considerations for selecting a consortium or individual libraries for collaboration. Once you have found desirable and willing partners, you are ready to begin the dynamic process of planning a future together.

FIGURE 6-2   *Guidelines for Selecting CCD Partners*

- Identify partner libraries that can help you achieve goals for your clientele.

- Build on established relationships with other libraries and librarians.

- Consider partnerships with libraries of different size and mission.

- For convenience, consider libraries in the same region.

- Identify partner libraries that complement your library's strengths, weaknesses, or both.

IDENTIFYING A MISSION AND GOALS

Well-crafted *mission statements* describe the purpose of a collaborative venture, clarify why participants have become involved, and communicate to local constituents and funding agents. *Goals* are statements of what the group hopes to achieve, and they guide *objectives,* measurable actions to be performed within a given time frame. A written mission statement and explicit goals are essential. A governance structure for the group helps to determine the process for taking action and resolving conflicts. The governance structure can evolve gradually as the group begins working on specific projects.

Some groups start their work with a definite mission in mind, such as developing a coordinated selection process, placing joint subscriptions to electronic databases, or, as in the case of the Brittle project, acquiring preservation photocopies at a reduced price.[12] In contrast, the Information Alliance partnership among the institutions represented by the authors of this book developed its mission after library directors brought department heads together for informal brainstorming sessions that led to the formation of the group.

Early in a CCD partnership, whether or not a mission is already defined, convene the counterparts who will be responsible for leading and implementing initiatives. Involve leaders at each institution in designing an organizational structure that will transcend its founders to serve future generations of participants. Information Alliance directors drafted a formal agreement (see figure 6-3) that was approved by the participants and signed by representatives of each university at the provost level. A CCD program was just one of the projects sponsored by the Alliance, which marks its tenth anniversary in 2004.[13] The Information Alliance mission statement is shown in figure 6-4.

Another strategy used by groups in the formative stages of a partnership is to engage the services of a *consultant.* In 1985, four public library districts in Colorado formed a consortium called APAL (Arapahoe Public Access to Libraries) and hired a contractor to develop a CCD plan.[14] Using ALA's *Guidelines for Collection Development,* librarians worked with the contractor on collection and use analysis. Participants collected data and calculated a budget for cooperative purchases, determining each library's level of responsibility for funding. By-products of the study included the purchase of unique new titles, local weeding, and service improvements. The contractor and the study helped APAL set policy and implement a CCD plan.

| FIGURE 6-3 | *Information Alliance Formal Agreement* |

The Libraries of the University of Kentucky, the University of Tennessee, Knoxville and Vanderbilt University are committed to a continuing partnership for resource sharing. An alliance between these organizations will strengthen library user access to regional resources and link information experts formally and informally. Three research libraries within a relatively close geographic area, the University of Kentucky, the University of Tennessee, Knoxville, and Vanderbilt University, can enhance their individual collections and services through an ongoing program of collaboration.

Through the Alliance we will address a variety of initiatives:

- List and Share Specialized Subject Expertise

- Develop Coordinated Collections

- Improve Physical Access to Materials

- Emphasize Bibliographic Access to Partner's Collection

- Pursue Experimental Services

We advocate information access as the key to the pursuit of excellence in all research and development endeavors for our organizations. This agreement represents a formal commitment to collaboration that is central to our individual library goals and objectives. Our library communities will receive enriched services and resources through the University of Kentucky— University of Tennessee, Knoxville, Information Alliance signed this second day of November 1994.

Eugene R. Williams
Vice President for Information Systems
The University of Kentucky

Marian S. Moffett
Associate to the Vice Chancellor for Academic Affairs
The University of Tennessee, Knoxville

Paul A. Willis
Director of Libraries
The University of Kentucky

Paula T. Kaufman
Dean, University Libraries
The University of Tennessee, Knoxville

Paul Gherman
University Librarian
Vanderbilt University
(December 23, 1999 signatory)

FIGURE 6-4	*Information Alliance Mission Statement*

The Information Alliance is a partnership founded on the principles of collaboration, cooperation, and resource sharing. Its purpose is to enhance information access and services for the member institutions. Information Alliance members facilitate bibliographic and physical access to holdings, share library collections (including digital information resources), share library staff expertise, develop new services, and seek funds to support collaborative projects. The Information Alliance helps members achieve individual and library goals through collaboration.

Partners can use *collection assessment* as an exploratory process to become acquainted with one another and their collections. The Conspectus, in spite of its flaws, offers a formal methodology for recording current collection practices. Numerous CCD initiatives have begun with systematic collection assessment using the Conspectus or its variants to gather information and establish benchmarks. Provided that the participants do not get mired in complexity and that they stay focused on their desire to identify a mission and goals, collection assessment can be an enlightening early step toward creating a partnership. Results of assessment enable participants to think systematically about what they have and what they might share, effectively leading the group to its mission.

Because *bibliographic access and delivery* are essential to the success of CCD, these functions should be addressed in the mission and goals, even if such services are already in place. As the purpose and directions for collaboration begin to take shape, partners are ready to tackle a specific project.

ACHIEVING RESULTS

Planning among counterparts will result in many possible projects with varied timetables for accomplishment. Focus on one or two projects with the potential for early results. Possibilities include:

starting a shared subscription to a database

purchasing complementary portions of an expensive specialized resource organizing subject counterpart meetings

completing a cataloging backlog in a specialized area to improve collection access

collaborating on collection review to prepare for weeding

If a project reported by another consortium relates to the needs of your users, consider replicating it or basing your plan on its successful features. A case study of a project to share translation journals among nine California academic libraries described the successes and difficulties experienced by the participants.[15] The authors' list of twelve steps to CCD success effectively outlines the communications process for developing a CCD framework:

1. Develop incentives. Matching funding is desirable.
2. Provide training on human as well as technical CCD issues.
3. Understand the purpose of, need for, and permanence of CCD.
4. Focus on the positive.
5. Focus on the customer.
6. Communicate clearly and often.
7. Make the written collaborative plan specific and complete.
8. Build a plan for change into the project contract.
9. Distribute work according to counterpart interests and emotions.
10. Appoint one bibliographic "guru" to monitor project maintenance.
11. Verify maintenance steps and changes to plans with written checklists.
12. Use electronic tools.

Figure 6-5 offers a dozen ideas for CCD projects that lend themselves to early results. Apply the preceding communication tips to the projects you take on, and chances are good that your partnership will soon have an accomplishment to celebrate.

PUBLICIZING SUCCESS

Publicizing CCD accomplishments heightens local appreciation for the benefits of collaboration while informing clientele and funding agents about the investment of local resources. Tell the national and

| FIGURE 6-5 | *What CCD Can Do for My Library Users: A Dozen Project Ideas* |

1. Sponsor a training session for counterparts on collection assessment techniques.

2. Purchase unique (to the consortium) materials in specialized areas.

3. Exchange information with subject counterparts regarding clientele demographics, use patterns, and collection statistics.

4. Increase awareness of collection strengths, specialties, and gaps through joint collection evaluation. Use data from or comparable to the North American Title Count.

5. Develop a template for an assessment progress report. (The MNSCU project required local plans for expending supplementary resources; a list of accomplishments, including statistics on funding received and the number and kind of resources purchased; examples and testimonials from library users; and concerns the local libraries wished to express.)[16]

6. Begin an acquisitions procedure of checking holdings at partner libraries and consulting selectors before ordering individual items that cost more than $500.

7. Create a collaborative wish list of needed electronic resources and establish group priorities.

8. Build on existing collection strengths in designated areas. (Examples of collecting areas: environmental studies for Northern Minnesota; contemporary poetry; women's studies; rural public administration; international cinema; community health education; telecommunications; fluid power; computerized video; music scores)[17]

9. Develop a shared archive of local publications online, such as PANDORA is doing in Australia.[18]

10. Create a shared off-site storage facility. Several groups have embarked upon such projects, including Washington Research Library Consortium, Southwest Regional Depository in Ohio, and the Five Colleges, Inc. (Amherst, Hampshire College, Mount Holyoke, Smith, University of Massachusetts).[19]

11. Share the services of a bibliographer, as done at the University of Arizona and Arizona State University.

12. Catalog a specialized backlog, such as the Arabic materials completed by the Information Alliance.

international community about your achievements to inspire others and to stimulate creativity in the scope of CCD possibilities. Because home institutions want local money to be spent on local needs, publicize the fact that another library is spending money to support your clientele. Marketing CCD success is so important that we devote chapter 9 to a discussion of promotion and publicity strategies.

ASSESSING PROGRESS

Partners in CCD want to know if their investments are valuable to local users. Goals, such as increasing the collection content in a specific area or developing a shared archive, must include a proposed method for assessing progress. Although CCD measures are subjective and can be interpreted both positively and negatively, a group of librarians sponsored by the Center for Research Libraries (CRL) is attempting to quantify CCD accomplishments using a modified balanced scorecard approach.[20] The balanced scorecard technique combines information from the perspectives of customers, internal data, financial success, and organizational learning and growth. The working group is incorporating the first three factors into performance measures that include numerical data (numbers of users, items purchased, collection size, and so on), use data, and customer satisfaction. By comparing relationships among these factors—for example, unit cost of materials per student by institution compared with the CCD group—it may be possible to quantify some aspects of CCD.

CCD partners should combine quantitative and qualitative measures because no single technique presents a full picture of progress. A count of the number of titles purchased cooperatively and their circulation records shows if anyone is using the new items. Title counts in specific subject areas can be taken before and after collaboration begins, with comparisons at both the local and system levels. Describing accomplishments toward a large goal, such as steps completed toward evaluating materials to be placed in a shared archive, helps participants gauge progress. Other evaluation options include tracking interlibrary loan (ILL) activity for a group of purchased materials or a collection; measuring comparative strength of local collections against standard checklists; counting database use; tracking use of serial titles; and conducting user surveys to explore the effectiveness of communication efforts and the perceived strength of individual and systemwide collections. Assessment requires staff resources to collect and interpret data, but the payoff is the opportunity to adjust CCD program priorities and promote results on the basis of tangible evidence. See chapter 10 for more about CCD assessment.

CREATING A SUSTAINABLE CCD STRUCTURE

Given the considerable investment in selecting CCD partners and determining appropriate projects, collaborators should be highly motivated to make their alliance a long-term affair. An effective governance structure and a commitment to nurturing a collaborative mind-set among local library staff will help to sustain CCD over time. The group needs a formal organizational structure to

1. set a direction for action
2. establish basic procedures
3. control the network by principles and not by persons
4. protect the participants by outlining expectations for financial obligations and the manner in which assets will be divided if the network dissolves
5. establish an operating entity that can be recognized by others
6. establish a standard by which library network effectiveness should be measured[21]

The organizational structure should encourage autonomy for the members and a high degree of flexibility. Examples of governance structures can be found on library network web pages, including those listed in the CRL survey. However, the process for crafting the structure is probably more significant than the document itself.

Let the organization evolve slowly to facilitate the goals outlined by the group. Over time, the group can make the structure more formal for easy comprehension and communication to new participants. A helpful resource for crafting the first organizational structure is the *Guide to Cooperative Collection Development*.[22] Early in designing a governance structure, record shared principles that illustrate the group's philosophy. Describe the scope of the program and eligibility for membership or participation. Identify contributions expected of the members. Describe a governing structure, particularly the process for making decisions. A budget, timeline, and evaluation process are standard and valuable management tools to stimulate the momentum that follows an energizing planning session. Although the *Guide* recommends developing procedures for withdrawing from the program and terminating the agreement, this step may be necessary only when members contribute large amounts of capital. Implementation includes a process for regular communication and meetings to conduct planning, consultation, and evaluation. Progress reports provide content for CCD publicity.

MAKING THE MOST OF HUMAN RESOURCES

A positive local climate helps to sustain CCD, and involving those who will implement objectives helps to develop their understanding and trust. Identify leaders and hold regular partner meetings that include orientation and training. Who should lead the emerging organization? Look for people in the organization who are interested in collaboration. For Information Alliance CCD initiatives, the leaders are the heads of collection development at the partner libraries.

Staff resources are essential, yet the lack of staff support and commitment are traditional CCD barriers. Clerical and bibliographic activities, such as gathering data and listing titles for consideration in a serials archive, require staff support. Staff members are also responsible for the technological infrastructure that supports many CCD projects. Computing staff provide shared catalogs and extract bibliographic and use data from local catalogs. Interlibrary loan staff make a tremendous contribution to local and partner libraries through their lending and document delivery operations. Librarians and other professional staff make web pages resonate with the benefits of shared resources for library users. All these human resources affect CCD success and sustainability. (See chapter 11 for more on sustaining CCD internally.) The significance of the human dimension should be acknowledged in the principles guiding the CCD program.

ESTABLISHING AN IMPLEMENTATION PROCESS

A formal structure to accomplish the CCD mission and goals will be welcomed by those responsible for implementation. As mission and goals emerge in the developing framework, give priority to actions with benefits for local users and envision ways to measure desired outcomes. The group should clearly understand the purpose for the program. Once general directions are outlined, participants need a process for implementation. Spelling out project structure and goals at the outset allows greater flexibility during implementation and preserves more local autonomy.

Incorporate the following factors into the implementation process to help participants recognize the value of the project for their local clientele:[23]

> Include clearly described steps for getting started.
>
> Identify contact people and their responsibilities.
>
> Schedule orientation and training for CCD tasks.
>
> Document and revise procedures as they are developed.
>
> Demonstrate organizational commitment to the project by allocating resources to it and acknowledging its value.
>
> Outline a process for helping staff with questions about processes.
>
> Evaluate the effectiveness of processes and make changes as needed.

Planning for such factors supports the development of a sustainable organization and provides links to assessment options.

Leaders should identify the individuals who will work on the project and describe their responsibilities. Opportunities for CCD participants to provide ideas and commentary about the program assure that full benefit is received from the wealth of perspectives held by the contributors. Develop orientation and training sessions to help new participants understand their role in the CCD project. Describe a plan for promotion and publicity that includes creation of printed materials and a web presence, as well as ways to inform the local community about the program. Design the structure to transcend its creators.

Obtaining Ongoing Support

Funding is critical for sustaining a CCD organization. Financial contributions to the partnership represent short-term allocation of resources for long-term gain. Because collaboration is heavily self-supported, CCD proponents must be especially creative in finding the funds to support projects. Paying for CCD incrementally works best for most participants. Use grant funding as seed money, ideally for three years so that the program becomes a traditional library function. Ultimately, funding must be provided over a period of years, so that CCD is supported through the library's budget process.[24]

CCD partners should provide fiscal support with the understanding that the framework will promote equity among the members' financial contributions. Cost savings should not be an expectation. The value of CCD derives from enhanced services and enriched resources.[25] Participants will likely reallocate funding to CCD projects as an investment toward more effective use of existing resources. They will increase support as results demonstrate benefits that justify the risk. Library networks have devised strategies to mitigate financial risk. SOLINET licenses, for example, contain a clause that permits libraries to discontinue participation in a group subscription if there are serious reductions in local funding. Other agreements specify that if a library withdraws from a consortium, its collection must remain accessible to the members. See chapter 8 for more detailed discussion about CCD economic issues.

CONCLUSION

To develop a CCD framework, start small and simple. As an initial step, explore the advantages of collaborating with a similar institution. Find a way to make the partnership an imperative from the parent organizations. Involve academic faculty and public library board members (trustees) in a CCD project. Target innovative subject areas, perhaps something multidisciplinary, to capture the imaginations of the participants. Devote particular energy to publicizing the partnership and its accomplishments. Be mindful of traditional barriers to CCD, so that new partnerships resolve issues before they become difficulties. For example, if a lack of exact counterparts at partner institutions is a barrier, make assignments more broadly or by function rather than by subject, with attention to personal communication styles. Approaches that preserve local autonomy and downplay competition will also diminish barriers. Give member organizations a formal opportunity to influence the network. Incorporate organizational checks and balances that promote CCD results. A sustainable framework for collaboration will enable the CCD partnership to move beyond simple, short-term projects into "deep CCD"—enduring endeavors such as shared collection management support, shared subject expertise, preservation, weeding, cancellation, and shared storage.

NOTES

1. K. Leon Montgomery and C. Edwin Dowlin, "The Governance of Library Networks: Purposes and Expectations," in *The Structure and Governance of Library Networks: Proceedings of the 1978 Conference in Pittsburgh, Pennsylvania, Co-Sponsored by National Commission on Libraries and Information Science and University of Pittsburgh*, ed. Allen Kent and Thomas J. Galvin, 181 (New York: Marcel Dekker, 1979).

2. Shasteen, "Cooperative Collection Management," 97–99.

3. Dominguez and Swindler, "Cooperative Collection Development," 470–96.

4. Haar, "Report of Working Group."

5. Hugh Atkinson, "Resource Sharing," in *Collection Management in Public Libraries: Proceedings of a Preconference to the 1984 ALA Annual Conference June 21–22, 1984, Dallas, Texas*, ed. Judith Serebnick, 44 (Chicago: American Library Association, 1986).

6. Shasteen, "Cooperative Collection Management," 99.

7. Haar, "Report of Working Group"; Richards, "One Size."

8. CIC http://www.cic.uiuc.edu/ (accessed November 7, 2003).

9. Edwards, "GAELIC."

10. Gammon and Zeoli, "Practical Cooperative Collecting."

11. Kester and Jones, "Birth and Growth," 116–20.

12. John Haar, "Cooperative Collection Development Survey Responses," Center for Research Libraries, "Creating New Strategies for Cooperative Collection Development," Follow-Up Working Groups from the AWCC 1999 Conference, http://www.crl.edu/awcc2002/ccdsurveyresults.htm (accessed October 16, 2003).

13. Information Alliance, *Formal Agreement*, http://www.lib.utk.edu/%7Ealliance/const.html (accessed July 30, 2003); Information Alliance, *Constitution*, http://www.lib.utk.edu/%7Ealliance/const.html (accessed July 30, 2003).

14. Edward P. Miller and Jodi Perlman Cohen, "Collection Development in a Multi-system Cooperative: An Acquisition Policy and Plan," *Library Acquisitions: Practice and Theory* 10, no. 4 (1986): 329–33.

15. Christy Hightower and George Soete, "The Consortium as Learning Organization: Twelve Steps to Success in Collaborative Collections Projects," *Journal of Academic Librarianship* 21, no. 2 (March 1995): 87–91.

16. Richards, "One Size," 108–12.

17. Ibid.

18. Haar, "Survey Responses."

19. Bridegam, "Collaborative Approach."

20. Steve Bosch et al., "Report from the Center for Research Libraries/Greater Western Library Alliance Working Group for Quantitative Evaluation of Cooperative Collection Development Projects," paper presented at the New Dynamics and Economics of Cooperative Collection Development Conference hosted by the Center for Research Libraries at the Aberdeen Woods Conference Center, Atlanta, GA, November 2002, http://www.crl.edu/awcc2002/Quant.%20Evaluation%20WG%20Report.pdf (accessed November 7, 2003).

21. Charles H. Stevens, "Governance of Library Networks," *Library Trends* 26, no. 2 (Fall 1977): 221–22.

22. Harloe, *Guide.*

23. Simpson, "Library Consortia," 87–88.

24. Carl W. Deal, "A Model Criterion for a Statewide Plan/Process/System," in *Coordinating Cooperative Collection Development: A National Perspective,* ed. Wilson Luquire, 218 (New York: Haworth, 1986).

25. Sheila T. Dowd, "Library Cooperation: Methods, Models, to Aid Information Access," *Journal of Library Administration* 12, no. 3 (1990): 79.

7

GOVERNANCE
CCD Documentation and Legal Agreements

By its very nature, collaborative collection development implies reciprocal commitments to a common goal. Whether that goal is modest or ambitious, the obligation to partners remains at the core of the relationship. Because individual and group decisions are based on the expectations underlying these consensual associations, the commitments made within the framework of ongoing CCD projects should be codified in written agreements. CCD agreements specify the arrangements binding the parties in common action and outline the parameters within which they work to achieve shared goals. Depending on the type and nature of the CCD activity, the written documentation governing the project can take a number of forms—from simple statements of common goals to enforceable contracts describing responsibilities and defining penalties for breach of contract terms. The nature and complexity of the proposed CCD activity and, above all, the inherent risk to participating institutions determine the level of formality and degree of legality of the documents that govern the cooperative effort.[1]

Not all CCD activity is governed by written agreements. Passive CCD accounts for a good portion of cooperative activities at many libraries. This type of "shadow CCD" is largely undocumented and remains unregulated except for informal and impromptu consultation by librarians. One step removed from passive forms of CCD are those projects implemented only by informal oral and nonbinding agreements of local colleagues. Many such CCD projects operate successfully simply with the consent of colleagues and their practical acknowledgment of a common goal. However, as the complexity of CCD projects increases, so too does the need for detailed written documentation to guide the execution of the projects.

As with other aspects of CCD, documentation and legal issues must be addressed in the planning phase. Formulating a clear concept of the CCD project ensures that participants identify issues to be regulated by a written statement or legal contract and draft appropriate documentation before implementing the project. Let the who, what, when, how, where, and why of the project guide you in identifying which elements to include in your CCD documentation. Who will collect what? At what intensity? What are the financial commitments? Will there be a fiscal agent to handle the financial transactions of the CCD participants? Who is responsible for training and how is it to be funded? How does the project affect staff time at local institutions, and how can CCD duties be equitably distributed among participants?

Complex CCD agreements have far-reaching legal ramifications. Drafting and implementing such agreements may require the services of legal experts. Contracts that carry penalties or entail potential financial liability are prime candidates for review by legal advisers versed in contract law. As a matter of practice, agreements and contracts should be submitted to governing agencies for review and approval. This chapter examines representative examples of current CCD agreements, project descriptions, and governance documents. We identify their essential components and collate those elements into a checklist for constructing CCD agreements.

INFORMAL AGREEMENTS

Many CCD projects are covered solely by informal written agreements that stipulate basic expectations of participants and forgo the threat of penalty or punitive action for noncompliance. Such agreements legitimize CCD activities and regulate support activities, such as cooperative cataloging and other technical service activities. A 1972 survey of academic library consortia suggested that informal agreements outlining basic commitments were a preferred, or at least a widely practiced, form of documentation.[2] The guidelines governing collaborative activities were generally articulated in informal written agreements that specified conditions for participation and defined circumstances for withdrawal from the cooperative, usually without penalty. The survey entry for the Committee of Librarians of the Washington Theological Consortium, founded in 1960, is representative. According to the Conditions of Participation, the committee operated by "informal agreement (no penalty for withdrawal); indefinite term of existence."[3] Only slightly more complex are the guidelines under which members of the Five Associated University Libraries (FAUL), founded in 1967 and later replaced by Nylink, operate: "Written agreement; indefinite term of existence; formal set of rules outlining conditions of participation (no penalty for withdrawal)."[4]

The results of a recent survey designed to map current collaborative projects and conducted on behalf of the Center for Research Libraries reveal that informal agreements are still the preferred governance vehicle for 35 percent of the respondents.[5] The rationale for using informal agreements is easy to understand. General, descriptive agreements are appropriate for those collaborative activities in which the participating institutions preserve a high degree of autonomy and independence, even though they closely coordinate selected collection development or collection support activities. Relying on a partner institution to collect more extensively in an area not represented in your library does not substantially jeopardize the ability of your library to meet the needs of local users. The low level of risk obviates the need for legal contracts because operations at the respective libraries run in parallel and are not inseparably intertwined. The appeal of informal agreements is their ease of implementation in contrast to more legalistic structures. Also, they have the advantage of flexibility and ease of implementation and often do not require the legal review necessary for more formal expressions of commitment to collaboration.

FORMAL AGREEMENTS

In the CRL survey just noted, 54 percent of the respondents indicated that their CCD projects operated on the basis of formal working agreements. These documents bear different designations—Memorandum of Understanding, Memorandum of Agreement, Charter, Constitution, Bylaws. Regardless of the term used, these instruments articulate the governance of the projects, delineate the relationship of the members of the project, and define their interaction within the scope and framework of the project. In this section, we will examine current examples of documents associated with CCD projects to gain a more detailed knowledge of the topics they address, the language they use, and the issues they raise. From these, we will construct a checklist of what to include as you craft a document to guide and govern your CCD project or activity.

Memorandum of Understanding or Agreement

The concise, one-page Memorandum of Understanding (MOU) that unites the Five Colleges of Ohio (Denison University, Kenyon College, Ohio Wesleyan University, Oberlin College, and the College of Wooster) in the CONStor project illustrates key elements of an agreement targeting a specific, well-defined CCD project—the long-term storage of lesser used but still valuable materials.[6] Divided into three sections, the brief document (see figure 7-1) gives the background of the project, addresses the commitments made by each of the participating institutions within the context of the project, and then defines the core regulations governing use of the CONStor facility itself.

As a Memorandum of Understanding, this document remains free of legalistic jargon, using instead straightforward language and simple phrasing. In fact, the force of the document resides in the statement "we agree" preceding each list of expectations and commitments. Although the assertion "we agree" perhaps expresses more a philosophical position than a contractual commitment, the obligations associated with participation are no less real. Despite the simplicity of the document, the terms are substantial and entail financial consequences. Guarantees of perpetual access, surrender of autonomous decision making about stored material to an appointed committee, and the acceptance of ongoing insurance costs for items no longer in direct ownership bind the members individually and reciprocally. The essential components defining the agents and objects of the collaboration are all present. The force of the agreement derives from its approval by the Library Committee, which is the facility's managing body, and the chief financial officers of the respective institutions, as attested by their signatures.

Depending on the nature of the project, a Memorandum of Understanding (MOU) can be more complicated and more detailed than the preceding example, as evidenced by the seven-page MOU

| FIGURE 7-1 | *Five Colleges of Ohio Memorandum of Understanding* |

Five Colleges of Ohio Memorandum of Understanding regarding Sharing of Library Materials

I. Background: Upon establishment of CONStor, the joint storage facility of the Five Colleges of Ohio Consortium, Inc., the library directors requested the creation of this Memorandum of Understanding in order to define ownership of and access to shared materials. The goal of this memorandum is to ensure that shared items, whether in CONStor or in the individual campus libraries, remain perpetually available to all members of the Five Colleges community. Decisions about CONStor usage and policies are made by the Library Committee (the library directors) of the Five Colleges with approval from the Five Colleges Board of Directors. OhioLINK and the international interlibrary loan community are secondary users of CONStor.

II. Concerning the College of Wooster, Kenyon College, Denison University, Oberlin College, and Ohio Wesleyan University campus collections, we agree that:

a. The five libraries will guarantee perpetual access to all circulating library materials, including those in CONStor, as long as the materials remain physically useable.

b. None of the five libraries will discard the last copy of any book or other type of library material, regardless of its location, without the agreement of all other member libraries. If a library does not agree, it will be given the item to add to its collection.

III. Concerning CONStor, we agree that:

a. The CONStor storage facility is a place for long-term storage of valuable but little-used library materials. It is not to be used as a way station for materials that should be discarded. Only materials in circulating condition may be placed in CONStor.

b. To maximize storage space and efficiency of operation, no duplicates will be permitted in CONStor.

c. Once a member library has deposited an item in CONStor, the other libraries may discard their copies of that item, if they choose, with the secure knowledge that the CONStor copy will always be available.

d. Materials sent to CONStor will remain the property of the original owners. The insurance for such items will be maintained by the owning libraries. If a library needs to return a stored item to its campus collection permanently, it will guarantee the other consortium libraries perpetual access to the item through OhioLINK channels, as long as it is in the circulating collection.

Approved 1/7/02 by Library Committee; 1/10/02 by Chief Financial Officers establishing the Wyoming Federal Depository Library Consortium (WYFDLC).[7] This document identifies participants, defines the purpose, and spells out responsibilities of individual members and the group as a whole. Unlike the CONStor MOU, the WYFDLC MOU contains a section called General Provisions that defines in more detail legal concepts that address very specialized issues, such as amendments, applicable law, severability (meaning that each part of the agreement applies independently of other segments), and sovereign immunity. Figure 7-2 is an excerpt, showing the terminology and exact wording of this section of the MOU. The signatures of official representatives (library directors, college presidents, state librarian) of the participating members confirm intent to abide by the terms and conditions of the MOU.

A Memorandum of Agreement (MOA) governs CALAFIA, the California Cooperative Latin American Collection Development Group, representing the libraries at Stanford University, the University of California System, and the University of Southern California.[8] The short document, which divides collecting responsibility for information resources from the northern Mexican states, is both consensual and operational in nature, reflecting the flexibility and adaptability of MOAs and MOUs. Again, the nonlegalistic language of the MOA and its specific focus make it attractive and acceptable to practitioners, the selectors who participate in drafting and implementing it. The CALAFIA MOA has two parts: Provisions and a Collection Profile. The nine-point Provisions section lists the Mexican border states assigned to each participating institution and enumerates expectations pertaining to cooperatively collected materials: modest commitment

FIGURE 7-2   *Excerpt from a Memorandum of Understanding*

Wyoming Federal Depository Library Consortium

MEMORANDUM OF UNDERSTANDING

AMONGST THE MEMBER LIBRARIES OF THE WYOMING DEPOSITORY LIBRARY CONSORTIUM CONCERNING THE ROLES AND RESPONSIBILITIES OF ALL LIBRARIES INVOLVED

16. **General Provisions.**

   A. **Amendments.** Any party may request changes in this MOU. Any changes, modifications, revisions or amendments to this MOU which are mutually agreed upon by and between the parties to this MOU shall be incorporated by written instrument, executed and signed by all parties to this MOU.

B. **Applicable Law.** The construction, interpretation and enforcement of this MOU shall be governed by the laws of the State of Wyoming. The courts of the State of Wyoming shall have jurisdiction over any action arising out of this MOU and over the parties, and the venue shall be the First Judicial District, Laramie County, Wyoming.

C. **Entirety of Agreement.** This MOU, consisting of seven (7) pages, represents the entire and integrated agreement between the parties and supersedes all prior negations, representations and agreements, whether written or oral.

D. **Prior Approval.** This MOU shall not be binding upon any party unless this MOU has been reduced to writing before performance begins as described under the terms of this MOU, and unless this MOU is approved as to form by the Attorney General or his representative.

E. **Severability.** Should any portion of this MOU be judicially determined to be illegal or unenforceable, the remainder of the MOU shall continue in full force and effect, and any party may renegotiate the terms affected by the severance.

F. **Sovereign Immunity.** The State of Wyoming and individual consortium members do not waive their sovereign immunity by entering into this MOU and each fully retains all immunities and defenses provided by law with respect to any action based on or occurring as a result of this MOU.

G. **Third Party Beneficiary Rights.** The parties do not intend to create in any other individual or entity the status of third party beneficiary, and this MOU shall not be construed so as to create such status. The rights, duties and obligations contained in this MOU shall operate only between the parties to this MOU, and shall inure solely to the benefit of the parties to this MOU. The provisions of this MOU are intended only to assist the parties in determining and performing their obligations under this MOU. The parties to this MOU intend and expressly agree that only parties signatory to this MOU shall have any legal or equitable right to seek to enforce this MOU, to seek any remedy arising out of a party's performance or failure to perform any term or condition of this MOU, or to bring an action for the breach of this MOU.

WYFDLC governance documents available at http://www-wsl.state.wy.us/sis/wyfdlc/feddeplbmou.html (accessed November 15, 2003).

of funds for targeted purchase of recent materials; responsibility for prompt technical processing; resource sharing through ILL; liberty to duplicate resources locally as needed; preservation of serial subscriptions; and annual review of the agreement. The Collection Profile section details the levels, types, and formats of publications collected, in twenty-one subject areas. Despite the brevity and simplicity of this document, the signatures of the collection development or technical services representatives of the participating institutions put in force a powerful vehicle for improving access to an important body of information about the northern states of Mexico.

Constitutions and Charters

As the preceding examples suggest, MOAs and MOUs are widely used for defining and initiating specific CCD projects. Another category of documents governing CCD activities includes constitutions and charters. These instruments focus on creating the framework for collaboration and provide the parameters within which specific projects are subsequently developed. They call entities and agencies into being and empower them to define tasks and projects within their scope.

The Information Alliance was created by a formal agreement.[9] Its activities are guided by a constitution consisting of five articles: Name, Purpose, Membership, Governance, and Meetings.[10] The wording of the Governance section is representative of this type of document whose essential purpose is to set in motion planning and implementation activities that will result in specific projects. As shown in figure 7-3, the document emphasizes "principles of collaboration, cooperation, and resource sharing," challenges alliance members to "enhance information access and services" by various means, and articulates the commitment to "[help] members achieve individual and library goals through collaboration." Within the framework of this constitution, training workshops have been held, CCD projects implemented (including annual meetings of selector counterparts), and the foundation laid for adapting to changes in the information environment.

The Portland Area Library System (PORTALS), a statewide consortium consisting of fourteen institutions, was created in July 1994 by the signing of a formal charter.[11] The founding document includes a mission statement, addresses organization and governance of the collaborative, and establishes requirements for membership. Intended to support the academic and research communities in a metropolitan area lacking an ARL-level library, PORTALS includes CCD as a major initiative. The expressions of commitment to CCD are found inter-

FIGURE 7-3 *Constitution of the Information Alliance*

Constitution

Article I: Name

The name of this organization shall be The Information Alliance.

Article II: Purpose

The Information Alliance is a partnership founded on the principles of collaboration, cooperation, and resource sharing. Its purpose is to enhance information access and services for the member institutions. Information Alliance members facilitate bibliographic and physical access to holdings, share library collections (including digital information resources), share library staff expertise, develop new services, and seek funds to support collaborative projects. The Information Alliance helps members achieve individual and library goals through collaboration.

Article III: Membership

The University of Kentucky and the University of Tennessee, Knoxville are founding members of The Information Alliance. Other libraries with common interests in collaboration may be invited to join the organization.

Article IV: Governance

The Library Directors of the member libraries have overall responsibility for Information Alliance initiatives and budgetary decision-making. An Executive Committee is appointed by the Library Directors for staggered two-year terms. The Executive Committee leads planning activities, communicates with the Library Directors and librarians working on Alliance projects, develops meeting agendas, makes local arrangements for meetings, and reports on Alliance activities. Ad-hoc groups appointed by the Library Directors and counterparts make decisions about specific projects.

Information Alliance projects address issues common to the member libraries. Activities range from formally described projects with a specific focus and charge, to informal consultation among counterparts. Projects that require budgetary support are proposed to the Executive Committee at any time during the year. The Executive Committee recommends funding or revision, and seeks budgetary support from the Library Directors. Project reports are given at Information Alliance meetings, and via electronic means.

Article V: Meetings

Meetings of The Information Alliance are held twice each year. Librarians from the member institutions participate in the meetings with their counterparts. Meeting agendas include information-sharing about developments in each library; reports about Information Alliance Projects; and discussion of issues affecting the members. Issues requiring decisions may be discussed at the semi-annual meetings.

Available at http://www.lib.utk.edu/~alliance/const.html (accessed November 20, 2003).

spersed in the bylaws governing the cooperative endeavor.[12] Figure 7-4 offers an excerpt pertaining to CCD intentions. The emphasis on the overarching importance of improving access to unique research materials, a major impetus for much of CCD, is reflected in the bylaws. Article 1.2.c.1 establishes an annual acquisitions budget figure as the first requirement for institutions seeking membership in PORTALS. But as Article 1.2.c.2 makes clear, more important than financial status is ownership of unique and valuable scholarly resources. Article 1.2.c.2 grants membership to those applicants who can expand access to otherwise unavailable research materials, even though they may not meet the financial requirement established in Article 1.2.c.1. Other statements also underscore the contribution that CCD is expected to make to the success of PORTALS. For example, participating institutions must be willing to share local resources with other libraries in the consortium (Article 1.2.e.3) and take part in the PORTALS-sponsored CCD program (Article 1.2.e.5). Although specific projects are not listed, the PORTALS charter and bylaws have created the climate in which CCD can flourish. Indeed, these documents make it abundantly clear that CCD is expected to improve access to important research and scholarly information resources.

COMPLEX CCD: STATE AND REGIONAL LEVELS

Given their frequency of use, MOAs, charters, and constitutions are convenient instruments for implementing CCD at the interinstitutional level. But when CCD is a component of the activities of statewide or regional cooperative efforts, relevant guidelines are often embedded within the bylaws or other governance documents applying to the consortium or network.

Bylaws and General Governance Documents

The membership and governance policy of the Keystone Library Network (KLN) of the Pennsylvania State System of Higher Education offers a typical example of guidelines as part of other governance documents. The policy offers a long list of member benefits, including cooperative collection development, a union catalog for access to consortial holdings, participation in aggregate electronic database licensing, and reciprocal access and borrowing privileges—all activities that lend themselves to specific CCD projects.[13] Because CCD is not the

FIGURE 7-4   *Excerpt from a Charter*

Bylaws of the Portland Area Library System (PORTALS)

PREAMBLE and MISSION

The Portland Area Library System (PORTALS) adopts these bylaws on 11/18/99 as amended on 5/17/01. PORTALS is a library consortium committed to meeting the research and educational needs of people in the greater Portland area through cooperative and creative access to information resources and services.

1.2 Membership Eligibility. To be eligible for membership, an institution must:

a. be a not-for-profit institution;

b. if it is a university or college, be fully accredited or, if it is a library, have a mission that supports scholarly activity;

c. provide evidence that the library has a significant collection and will continue to develop that collection:
   1. have an annual acquisition budget in excess of $200,000 (the amount will be adjusted yearly for inflation).
   2. alternately, an institution may demonstrate, to the satisfaction of the Council of Librarians, that it has, and will continue to maintain and develop, a valuable and distinctive collection of scholarly library and information resources that significantly enhances what is available through PORTALS.

d. provide the current necessary technology, to include:
   1. access to the Internet;
   2. an online catalog;
   3. machine readable records for its collection in an accessible database (or a commitment to meet this requirement); and
   4. access to a PORTALS-compatible document delivery system.

e. be willing to make the following institutional commitments:
   1. maintain library and information services;
   2. share costs of maintaining PORTALS;
   3. share collection resources with other members;
   4. comply with PORTALS standards for services;
   5. participate in PORTALS collection development program;
   6. maintain a current disaster preparedness plan and participate in mutual recovery aid when needed;
   7. participate in decision-making;
   8. participate in a periodic assessment and renewal of membership.

PORTALS governance documentation available at http://www.portals.org/bylaws.html (accessed November 15, 2003).

main purpose of the document, references to CCD are interspersed among many other regulations pertaining to membership. Taken as a whole, however, the document creates a framework in which to implement specific projects and establishes mechanisms to do that.

In a similar vein are the bylaws that govern the Illinois Cooperative Collection Management Program (ICCMP), a consortium creating a statewide collection of academic resources.[14] The program reiterates and amplifies the Statement of Principles, which places a premium on furthering cooperative ventures among partner libraries.[15] The ICCMP, like the KLN in the preceding example, does not delineate any specific CCD project, but instead signals the importance of CCD to the mission of the consortium. It accomplishes this by establishing CCD as two of the three pillars of ICCMP's guiding principles. The ICCMP bylaws comprise ten articles that address how the CCD purposes of the program are to be achieved. As the excerpt in figure 7-5 shows, Article 1 (Purpose) underscores the importance of CCD, explaining that to achieve the desired outcome, cooperative collection management and resource sharing must be considered guiding principles for the effort, along with ongoing professional development.

FIGURE 7-5	*Excerpt from Bylaws*

BYLAWS
ILLINOIS COOPERATIVE COLLECTION MANAGEMENT PROGRAM

December 2002

Article 1

Purpose

The Illinois Cooperative Collection Management Program (ICCMP) is committed to a shared statewide academic collection. The Consortium works to meet the diverse needs of faculty, students, and other library users in Illinois by encouraging cooperative library activity in order to make the best use of limited resources.

In order to achieve this vision, the ICCMP is organized around three guiding principles:

1. Cooperative collection management;
2. Resource sharing; and,
3. Continuing professional education.

Governance documents of the Illinois Cooperative Collection Management Program (ICCMP) available at http://www.niulib.niu.edu/ccm/bylaws.html (accessed November 15, 2003).

As these two examples suggest, many CCD governing documents simply establish a framework, first by underscoring CCD's importance in meeting collaborative goals, and then by calling into existence the organizational and governance structures that can initiate and implement specific projects. Statements of principle, charters, constitutions, bylaws, or similar governing documents establish the foundation for CCD, paving the way for detailed and focused CCD initiatives to be expressed through memoranda of agreement or understanding.

Legislative Mandate and 501(c)(3) Not-for-Profit Status

As noted in chapter 3, CCD can be the result of legislative mandate. In 1998, for example, the Minnesota legislature directed member institutions of the Minnesota State Colleges and Universities (MNSCU) system to coordinate acquisition of information resources and reduce duplication of esoteric materials within the system.[16] The legislative impetus for cooperation continues to bear fruit through the Minnesota Public Higher Education Compact. Minnesota House members praise efforts at library collaboration as libraries coordinate purchases and avoid duplication.[17] Likewise, many statewide cooperative endeavors are the result of legislative interest as articulated through governmental bodies, such as councils of higher education or boards of regents. The Kentucky Virtual Library owes its existence to advocacy by such legislative agencies, and OhioLINK was created and succeeds thanks to the support of the Ohio Board of Regents and legislature.

When the complexity of consortium goals increases, and especially when the interests of the consortium cross state lines, participants must consider more legalistic administrative vehicles for collaboration. Since the 1970s, interstate compacts and incorporation as a 501(c)(3) not-for-profit entity have grown in popularity.[18] Classification as a 501(c)(3) not-for-profit entity entails a lengthy application process, and the envisioned organization must meet the requirements spelled out for charities and nonprofits in the Internal Revenue Code. Today many statewide and regional consortia operate as not-for-profit corporations. Advantages include establishment of a group identity distinct from individual institutional identity, limitation of liability to the individual institution, and risk reduction via the representative agency. There is also the potential for greater longevity and more complexity in the projects undertaken because they have a foundation beyond the library. Because incorporation entails the establishment of an administrative body, oversight and promotion, without which many projects falter, are automatically in place.

As with contracts, 501(c)(3) incorporation may best suit the provision of specific services, not necessarily the coordination of parallel activities at numerous institutions located in different states. Still, many regional library cooperatives enable CCD among their members simply by bringing these members together under a common banner, thereby encouraging them to transcend passive consumption of negotiated and delivered products and services to become active initiators and implementers of CCD projects within the consortial framework.

An example of a 501(c)(3) organization for which CCD is an important component is the Center for Research Libraries (CRL). Although the governance documents of CRL do not expressly propose specific CCD activities, they do create administrative agencies that can formulate projects.[19] Dues and service charges fund purchase plans administered on behalf and with the input of members. CRL has likewise been a leader in promoting CCD through periodic conferences, workshops, and standing working groups or task forces that pursue a variety of CCD-oriented research and study.

The Greater Cincinnati Library Consortium (GCLC) also operates within the authority of 501(c)(3) status, providing administrative and coordinating services to its members: forty-four academic, public, school, and special libraries in the GCLC service area of northern Kentucky, Ohio, and southern Indiana. As an organization with far-ranging service interests, GCLC pursues a number of initiatives, including CCD. The Collection Management and Development Committee assists GCLC members in managing local collections in the context of the larger consortial collection by identifying local collection strengths and maintaining a database of member collection patterns and intensities.[20]

As these brief examples suggest, complex agencies operating on legislative mandate or 501(c)(3) status do not design and implement focused CCD projects. Their governance structures facilitate CCD through the creation of committees, working groups, and task forces that can pursue CCD at the project level.

COMPONENTS OF CCD AGREEMENTS: A CHECKLIST

In the preceding pages we reviewed a variety of sample documents used to implement and govern CCD, ranging from simple agreements to complicated legal instruments to 501(c)(3) status. The checklist in this section presents elements to consider in drafting a CCD agreement. The CCD project and the level of risk it entails will influence the choice and details of the components in your CCD agreement.[21]

Background

As orientation, consider providing a brief background to the project. This information can be designated Introduction, Preamble, Background, History, or any similar term that suggests its purpose, namely, to provide concise details about the genesis of the project and to set the stage for the remainder of the document.

Goals

A concise statement of the goals of the project communicates the essence of the endeavor to an external audience. The ability to capture the import of a project in a mission statement or other expression of purpose is a test of how clearly you have envisioned and focused the project.

Principles

A section on principles focuses on the philosophical contours underlying a project. Principles are articulated broadly and reflect the guiding insights that direct the planning of operational aspects of a project. Principles of executability and sustainability, comprehensibility and communicability, responsibility and accountability, and flexibility and adaptability, if not expressly articulated, should underlie the broad assumptions comprising this section of the CCD document.

Scope

Defining the scope of a CCD project makes the transition from the philosophical and abstract to the practical and executable. This section enables CCD managers to define and delineate the project's profile. They draw boundaries around and set limits and restrictions on the open-ended promises expressed or implied in goals or principles statements. Using this element to enumerate the benefits of the project transforms the abstract into the concrete.

Membership

The membership section can range from a simple list of participants, as is the case in MOAs, to a formal set of requirements, as is the case in the bylaws of large-scale consortial endeavors in which financial commitment and risk are greater. Depending on the complexity of the project, the membership section may need to define application procedures, establish categories or levels of membership (for example, charter, full, associate, affiliate), precisely define the responsibilities and commitments of members, and set minimum performance factors or fees for maintaining membership in good standing. Procedures for periodic review of memberships should also be established. To ensure the continued vitality of the collaborative effort, these procedures should outline the discipline, remediation, rehabilitation, or expulsion of noncompliant members.

Governance

Like the membership section, the governance section can be as short or lengthy as needed to capture the operational management of the project. A focused CCD project involving a few selectors working to avoid duplication in esoteric areas of their respective collections can probably function independently of a formal governance body. Beyond this, however, managing bodies need to be established and their source of authority and code of conduct outlined in bylaws or other such directives. The various governing bodies required for the management process should be established, including the mechanisms for determining representation and length of term of members on these bodies. If membership is by appointment, identify the appointing authority and detail eligibility requirements for appointment. If membership is by election, describe the voting process, the rights and responsibilities of the voting membership, and eligibility requirements for candidates. A committee of CD managers, a library council, a board of directors, subcommittees, user groups, and task forces are typical governing bodies for CCD projects and consortial enterprises.

In addition to describing and defining the corporate body tasked with managing a project or endeavor, the governance section must address the issue of how appropriate guidelines and regulations are formulated and formalized. Again, the extent of the undertaking will influence whether a brief set of guidelines will suffice or whether an elaborate and comprehensive set of bylaws, articles, sections, and subsections will be necessary to ensure smooth day-to-day operations and the transition from one phase of the project to the next. Methods for altering guidelines or amending bylaws should be included in the governance section.

Time Frame

CCD agreements, from the simplest to the most complex, and consortial arrangements of every type should contain a section specifying the time frame of the project. For projects of limited duration, a completion date and termination procedures are essential elements to clarify. For ongoing, opened-ended activities, such as statewide or regional consortia, or for long-term CCD among large academic institutions, specification of standard review intervals provides for scheduled oversight and assessment of the project. Establishing a timeline with intermediate check-in points for longer-term but limited projects should also be considered.

Budget and Finance

Every CCD project regardless of level and scope entails some financial commitment. CCD's impact on budgets should be addressed in terms appropriate to the extent of the project. It may be difficult to precisely calculate the costs and benefits of distributed responsibility for building a nonduplicating collection in a specific subject area. Still, the potential impact should be acknowledged rather than tacitly accepted or ignored. Complex environments may necessitate documents that are more detailed. If the project requires a budget of its own, this section would outline how that budget is established and how funding is apportioned. Membership fees must be clearly stated, and an explanation of how they were initially determined and will be calculated in the future should be part of an amplified financial declaration. The agreement should also note required monetary commitments to fund a project or stipulate the achievement of a specified level of financial performance as prerequisite to participation. Especially important for not-for-profit consortia or those activities commissioned by legislative mandate are standard and consistent accounting practices that allow for the proper distribution of funds within the guidelines of state and Internal Revenue Service (IRS) regulations. The budgetary section of the CCD agreement or governing bylaws can also address the fiscal support required for training, staffing, and the purchase of infrastructure and technological materials.

Assessment

All agreements and governance documents should provide for periodic review of a CCD project or the overall performance of a consortial activity. Although it is not necessary to detail the actual methods or instruments to be employed in evaluation, especially for complicated projects, participants should agree about basic approaches. Assessment results can be incorporated into the reports and updates required from the governing body.

Marketing and Communication

Governing agreements can contribute to the potential success of the projects they envision by including provisions for promoting and publicizing the activity. Mechanisms for pursuing these endeavors are built into the regulations guiding assessment activities. That is, when periodic reports are submitted to the governing body, adapt these updates for public consumption. Let the agreement specify that the accomplishments of the past year will be shared with the larger communities of interest, that plans for the coming year will be publicized and feedback invited from a wide audience, and that problems and obstacles will be shared, with an invitation for input by interested and affected members of the larger public.

Renewal/Withdrawal

CCD agreements should address means for continuing the project and for renewing or withdrawing membership. Establishing a periodic membership renewal date also offers a logical juncture for considering and implementing modifications of and amendments to the agreement. If active renewal is considered unnecessary, the agreement can state that renewal is presumed absent notification to the contrary. In the event that a member is no longer able to meet the requirements of participation or wants to opt out of the project, this section should specify procedures for disengagement. The agreement should specify a time frame for notification of intent to withdraw, detail any penalties for doing so, and establish guidelines about the disposition of the withdrawing member's material interests in the project. Creating guidelines for disengagement removes some of the risks associated with CCD by informing participants in advance of what happens to their contributions to the project should they no longer continue in the joint venture.

Termination

Finally, each CCD agreement should contain guidelines for termination of the project. For interinstitutional arrangements, the process may be as simple as discontinuing the active project. Coordinated development of nonoverlapping portions of separate collections may not have resulted in communally held resources, and staff members may have simply worked independently even while participating in the CCD initiative. In these instances, the intertwining of physical and materials resources is minimal or nonexistent, and termination of the project requires no additional attention. For more complex projects with more interdependence in which assets have been jointly acquired, termination requires more effort. Issues to be regulated include the distribution or disposition of financial assets and communal property. IRS regulations governing the financial activities of a 501(c)(3) entity are stringent, and the consortium must pay attention to devising methods in the initial agreement that can satisfy the requirements of federal legislation. Indeed, CCD agreements must anticipate issues of equity and fairness in the event of termination and make provisions at the beginning that consider the best interests of all parties associated with the project.

Perhaps no CCD agreement or consortial governing document incorporates all the elements discussed here. They are, however, core components that should be considered in the planning phase. Their inclusion or omission as discrete building blocks of an agreement can be a matter of choice, one based on the nature of the CCD project itself and dictated by the needs of the communities and interested parties involved in the design and implementation of the collaboration.

CONCLUSION

The importance of documenting CCD efforts cannot be overestimated. Informal acknowledgment may suffice for short-term or limited projects of mutual convenience. However, CCD achieves its full potential when practiced consistently and systematically over time and when contributions by each party are clearly defined. In these cases, the impact of CCD will have a lasting effect on the participating institutions. To ensure that all participants know and meet expectations, formal agreements should be crafted using input from those who will implement the plan. Authorized agents of participating institutions should endorse all agreements. Consultation with appropriate legal and financial agencies of participants' local institutions is highly advised for contractual commitments. The CCD agreement, duly signed by appropriate administrative and fiscal agencies, provides a sound and legal foundation for implementing specific activities.

The main components of a formal CCD agreement include:

a description of the participants and their purpose for collaboration

guidelines about project governance

a statement of financial and other resources needed to implement and support the project

a method for periodic review and assessment of the CCD activity

stipulations governing withdrawal from or termination of the project.

A well-crafted agreement with well-defined expectations is an essential step in ensuring that CCD projects, from the simple to the complex, succeed in improving and expanding access to a wider range of information resources for patrons.

NOTES

1. For a discussion of risk and risk management in the context of CCD, see Bernard Reilly, "Risk Management Aspects of Cooperative Collection Development Projects: A Paper and Presentation at Aberdeen Woods," presented at the New Dynamics and Economics of Cooperative Collection Development Conference hosted by the Center for Research Libraries at the Aberdeen Woods Conference Center, Atlanta, GA, November 8–10, 2002, http://www.crl.edu/awcc2002/Reilly%20paper.pdf (accessed November 15, 2003).

2. Diana D. Delanoy and Carlos A. Cuadra, *Directory of Academic Library Consortia* (Santa Monica, CA: System Development Corporation, 1972).

3. Ibid., 43.

4. Ibid., 66.

5. See Haar, "Report of Working Group."

6. CONStor documentation available at http://www.wooster.edu/library/OH5/CCCD/CCCD_MOU.html (accessed November 15, 2003); for background

information on CONStor and the Five Colleges of Ohio Consortium, see Margo Warner Curl, "Cooperative Collection Development in Consortium of College Libraries: The CONSORT Experience," and "Collection Assessment of the CONSORT Collections," *Against the Grain* 14, no. 6 (December 2002–January 2003): 52–53 and 53–57, respectively.

7. WYFDLC governance documents are available at http://www-wsl.state.wy .us/sis/wyfdlc/feddeplbmou.html (accessed November 15, 2003).

8. Information on CALAFIA is available at http://www-sul.stanford.edu/ depts/hasrg/latinam/calafia/northmex.html (accessed November 15, 2003).

9. The Information Alliance agreement is available at http://www.lib.utk .edu/~alliance/archive/agreemt.html (accessed November 15, 2003).

10. The Information Alliance constitution is available at http://www.lib.utk .edu/~alliance/const.html (accessed November 20, 2003).

11. Background information on the PORTALS project is provided in an online article entitled "A Virtual Research Library for Portland: The Progress of PORTALS," by Douglas Bennett, Executive Director, available at http://library .willamette.edu/publications/movtyp/spring1994/portals (accessed November 15, 2003).

12. PORTALS governance documentation is available at http://www.portals .org/bylaws.html (accessed November 15, 2003).

13. Keystone Library Network documentation is available at http://www .keystoneu.net/kln/subpages/governance.html (accessed November 15, 2003).

14. Governance documents of the Illinois Cooperative Collection Management Program (ICCMP) are available at http://www.niulib.niu.edu/ccm/bylaws .html (accessed November 15, 2003).

15. ICCMP documentation is available at http://www.niulib.niu.edu/ccm/ statepri.html (accessed November 15, 2003).

16. Richards, "One Size," 93–112.

17. Updates and reports on MNSCU activities are available at http://www .mnscu.eduLegislaltive/LegislativeUpdates/FY97/February_14.html; http:// www.mnscu.edu/NewsReleases/Fy98/January15.html (accessed November 15, 2003).

18. Harry S. Martin, "Coordination by Compact: A Legal Basis for Interstate Library Cooperation," *Library Trends* 24, no. 2 (October 1975): 191–213.

19. Documentation for the Center for Research Libraries is available at http://www.crl.edu/content.asp?l1=1&l2=9 (accessed November 15, 2003).

20. Greater Cincinnati Library Consortium documentation is available at http://www.gclc-lib.org/committees/collection.html (accessed November 15, 2003).

21. See also Harloe, *Guide,* 8–10.

CHAPTER
8

INVESTING IN SUCCESS
Economics of CCD

An enterprise based on human goodwill, such as collaborative collection development, eludes quantitative measures. Still, CCD represents financial benefits as well as tangible and intangible costs. Fiscal management is important to the success of CCD. Even though the economics of CCD verge on the subjective, leaders should consider costs and benefits throughout the decision-making process. What do participants hope to gain? What kinds of resources should libraries invest in a partnership? What level of investment is needed to make a difference? Is the benefit worth the cost? How can libraries be compensated for their contributions to a CCD consortium? This chapter explores the answers to these questions and related issues. It identifies CCD costs that have measurable financial impact, both as expenditures and as benefits.

CCD initiatives begin with the library director, who considers the economic aspects of developing a CCD framework as presented in chapter 6. A goal-based approach to CCD economics aims to reduce barriers, including those problems discussed in chapter 2. Determining desired outcomes helps to identify the investments needed to support start-up and ongoing costs.

Although a library should invest enough resources in CCD to achieve positive results, a large capital outlay is not required. If discretionary funds can be found to support a project on a trial basis, library staff can gain experience with cost requirements before making a specific allocation from the annual library budget. By incorporating CCD into the goals of existing staff and by using existing or supplemental operating money, a library does not have to include collaboration in the base budget until the library determines, over time, that the cost is worth the effort. CCD investments will most likely produce positive results if a specific product or outcome is intended. Occasionally, an unexpected CCD opportunity enables the library to achieve a goal if staff time or funding can be found. CCD investments require flexibility in resource allocation and willingness to take risks when occasion and goals suddenly converge.

QUESTIONS ABOUT CCD AND ECONOMICS

Our market culture stresses the importance of value. Unfortunately, costing and techniques to support economic management are among the weakest areas of library management.[1] One way to approach the economics of CCD is to identify cost centers in which specific outcomes provide a basis for considering the return on CCD investments. This strategy builds economic considerations into the library's planning and implementation process. Allocations for personnel, operations, and collections devoted to CCD will help the organization plan for results that are considered valuable by users, funding agents, and library staff.

What Do Participants Hope to Gain?

An overarching goal of CCD is to enhance and strengthen the combined collections of the partners for the benefit of local clientele. CCD demonstrates to funding agents a commitment to make the most of local resources through partnerships with organizations that enhance local strengths. Desired outcomes may include acquisition of more unique resources, preservation of existing collections, expansion of digital collections, increased available shelf space through coordinated archiving, and shared subject expertise. As noted in earlier chapters, planning creates the basis for a mutual understanding of CCD scope and goals.

The following example illustrates ways to incorporate projected costs and benefits into specific goals: Collaborative partners want to increase unique resources held among them. Steps to achieve this goal might include bringing counterparts together, developing policy and scope documents, targeting subject areas for purchase of resources, and allocating funds for specialized purchases. Each of these steps contains a cost for personnel, operating resources, and collection funding. Anticipating costs as well as benefits when setting goals provides a basis for evaluating progress or the value of CCD accomplishments. Purposeful projection of costs helps match expectations with results. To provide more unique resources in the shared collection, a library would invest in staff time, operating funds to support travel, and collection resources to purchase works in its assigned subject areas.

Participants expect resource allocations to support CCD plans and goals. Although CCD does not save money, it enables individual libraries to direct resources toward shared goals. For a library beginning a CCD program, an understanding among participants that library resources will be committed to support collaborative activities prevents anxiety about funding from derailing the focus on goals. Realistic expectations of organizational support will concentrate staff members' energy toward meeting the goals of the project and prevent them from digressing on cost concerns.

CCD enables libraries to manage local resources within the context of a larger entity—the partnership or consortium—to increase value for the cost. A librarian responsible for a $2,000 allocation in a library engaged in CCD will make selections using criteria different from those used by a librarian selecting independently. Although a portion of the $2,000 may purchase high-use materials that duplicate holdings in the partner library, another part will be spent on specialized, unique resources that complement the holdings of the entire group. When CCD leaders make resource commitments to CCD, the investment results in productive returns as librarians consider the information needs of both local clientele and partner libraries in making materials selections.

What Resources Should Libraries Invest in a Partnership?

Planning is a natural context for identifying costs and benefits of CCD. First, define the outcomes desired. Then, consider the support required for attaining those goals and whether resources will be new or reallocated. Costs common to nearly any CCD activity, regardless of scope, include staff time, travel, training, funding for materials purchases, shelf space, computer space, membership fees, telecommunications, and delivery service. Just as the library budget includes personnel, operations and facilities, collections, and intangible costs, CCD programs require these standard budget categories.

Personnel Costs

Staff members participating in CCD may range from the library director to clerical support personnel. The person or people responsible for collection development will have a significant role. Depending upon the scope of CCD projects and the size of the library, other personnel may include librarians who select information resources, support staff from numerous functional units, and student assistants. Personnel outside the library, such as legal counsel or technical support, may be needed. Each CCD library contributes creativity, motivation, data gathering, assessment, subject expertise, training, and accounting services. CCD leaders articulate project goals and communicate the results of collaborative activities to funding agents. Support staff members perform such CCD tasks as catalog searching and notation, spreadsheet compilation, and holdings comparisons that can be used for decisions about withdrawal or location in a shared archive. Staff can also assist with condition assessment, shifting, withdrawal, and shared conservation.

When planning for CCD personnel costs, consider the availability of existing staff to work on goals of the partnership. If additional funding can be designated for CCD, consider using it to "purchase" the time of an experienced librarian already on the staff who will be designated as CCD leader. Where possible, incorporate CCD tasks into existing staff responsibilities. Salaried employees may have considerable autonomy in structuring their work, so it is important that CCD goals be integrated into individual library staff responsibilities and expectations. Engage the creativity, commitment, and buy-in of library staff members by permitting them to take risks, to experiment, to fail, and to try alternate approaches. Such administrative support infuses the working environment with the high morale needed to sustain CCD projects. Each library already makes personnel investments. Drawing on these existing resources to achieve CCD goals makes good economic sense.

Over time, it will be possible to evaluate, even if subjectively, whether the CCD outcome has been worth the expenditure on personnel. Compare outcomes with the use of staff time to achieve them. Decide if staff should record hours spent on CCD to generate useful cost data. Consider other goals that staff members might have accomplished if they were not devoting time to CCD. Does the loss of library autonomy in the CCD project have a positive or negative effect on other library costs? For example, if the subject specialist at another library is selecting materials for your library to purchase, are you satisfied with the results? Consider the extent to which staff time invested in CCD activities has affected the perceptions of library clientele and funding agents about the benefits of collaboration.

Operations and Facilities Costs

CCD projects require operations budget support. Operations costs cover space for work and shelving, equipment, supplies, computing services, telecommunications, and travel. Postage and courier service expenditures also support CCD. By using the existing operations budget to accomplish collaborative project goals, a library buys staff and partner goodwill at minimal additional cost specifically devoted to CCD projects. Operations expenses can be shared, too. Libraries can take turns supporting staff travel, sharing the costs of external trainers, or contributing to joint storage facilities. If one library has already invested in a function, such as a conservation laboratory, partner libraries might pay for specific services. Such "outsourcing" will likely cost less than the expense of operating such a facility locally.

Collections Costs

A third major library budget category is collection resources. Because CCD does not substitute for a reduced materials budget, project goals will probably require some fund reallocation, so that money traditionally spent on one information resource can be used to pay for materials with high priority for the partners. Subject areas in which partners' high priorities converge could be particularly cost-effective. Availability of new funding earmarked expressly for CCD can be a powerful incentive for risk taking and creativity in collaboration. Two partners may already subscribe to an electronic resource. Adding a third partner could lower their cost. This represents a quantifiable benefit for the two original subscribers, albeit a new cost for the third partner. Still, the new subscriber gets a reduced price. Matching or other new funds (possibly designated from gift monies) could be awarded to support new purchases and promote success when librarians identify specialized areas in which to focus collection resources.

Spent collection funds represent a cost, while strengthened collections and the motivation of librarians to identify cooperative areas and coordinate purchasing are benefits. If use data on electronic journals purchased through a consortium are analyzed to identify potential cancellations and new subscriptions, patrons benefit from a resource more targeted to their needs. Cost per use is a tangible measure of benefit, while data about use provide a tool for making well-informed decisions about future subscriptions. Consortial subscriptions to journal aggregators provide a combination of increased access to journal titles, reduced cost per use over individual subscriptions, and valuable management information. Such subscriptions are usually expensive, however, and require librarians to reallocate funds or solicit new money from funding agents.

Intangible Costs

Beyond the predictable budget lines for personnel, operations expenses, and acquisitions, less-tangible costs should also be considered in the economics of CCD. For example, trust is one of the most essential elements of CCD. Lack of trust can be an economic as well as a psychological barrier. What price do we put on trust? There is a cost associated with being a trustworthy partner. If we agree to share the cost of a purchase, our autonomy has been reduced, because money now committed to a shared purchase is not available for something else. Because we trust another library to retain resources for our users, we may discard materials that will be impossible to replace in the future. Yet, as noted in chapter 2, CCD is an exercise in reciprocity, so we invest in collaborative organizations to sustain and encourage trust among CCD partners.

What is the cost of *not* acquiring something? Some of the points in chapter 2 about benefits and barriers contain powerful economic justifications for investing in CCD, a practice that encourages financial discipline and careful planning. The prohibitive costs of buying everything needed by the local clientele, paying for staff time to add items to the collection and apply preservation treatments, and purchasing more storage space are offset by the cost of interlibrary loan. Every function has its costs. Libraries expect to spend resources to achieve user satisfaction. Although a specific dollar amount cannot describe the cost of missing an opportunity to meet user needs, it is possible to imagine worthwhile collaborative investments that would be unattainable for a single library.

Sustaining the CCD framework represents another intangible cost. Over time, integrating CCD into organizational values and expectations requires moving beyond project-based activities, although the long-term process will differ for each library according to local needs and goals. Many activities that support the CCD framework are routine library functions easily incorporated into daily activities. Separated from other library functions, however, cooperation traditionally has been isolated in interlibrary loan (although libraries have long purchased cooperative cataloging). The cost of permeating library job descriptions and goals with CCD values may be impossible to measure, but the benefits of organizational commitment to CCD will be apparent in the library's ability to take advantage of new collaborative opportunities.

What Level of Investment Is Needed to Make a Difference?

CCD *cost centers* are the areas in which a library allocates resources to launch and sustain a CCD program. Recognizing CCD cost centers helps to budget and to determine the relative value of accomplishments. Many tasks related to CCD goals are probably already routine library functions. The local library and its partners can enjoy the benefits of collaboration by slightly expanding the scope of existing collection development and management tasks. Figure 8-1 divides several CCD activities among standard budget categories.

Recognizing CCD Costs

The following examples describe tasks frequently performed in CCD programs. Because cost and evaluation go hand-in-hand, each description offers a means for determining value. Use the illustrations to identify both start-up and continuing CCD costs to a library. Planning for the evaluation component at the outset helps to track costs and benefits.

COOPERATIVE BOOK PURCHASING

Libraries divide subject responsibilities in specialized areas; titles already held at partner libraries are considered lower priority purchases. Initial costs involve coordinating counterpart meetings to discuss potential areas for collaboration. Specific costs include the time of leaders at all participating libraries and travel to counterpart meet-

FIGURE 8-1	CCD Cost Center Activities

Personnel

- Develop policy
- Select and acquire unique resources
- Make decisions
- Conduct training
- Motivate staff
- Provide subject specialist services
- Conduct license and price negotiations
- Select titles to archive
- Select local titles to digitize
- Reduce work in given areas

Operations and Facilities

- Provide computer space
- Supply telecommunications access
- Make available library shelf space for shared archive
- Furnish delivery service courier

Collections

- Purchase unique resources
- Digitize local collections
- Pay for share of electronic resources
- Preserve materials
- Withdraw duplicate resources

ings. The time of counterparts to brief one another about their collections and clientele is also an investment. Ongoing costs include the time of counterparts to conduct collection assessment, to make decisions about dividing future selection responsibilities, and to make actual selections. Other ongoing costs include materials delivery among libraries as well as support staff time for checking respective library holdings and compiling management data. Increased funds for materials could accelerate purchasing. Evaluation includes overlap studies, a count of specialized materials purchased, and customer satisfaction studies of collection use.

SHARED STORAGE

Libraries divide responsibilities for retaining archives. Initial costs include librarian and support staff time to identify materials for consideration. Staff time, computer workstations, and telecommunications are essential for preparing spreadsheets with data to support decision making. Librarians make difficult decisions to determine which library will commit to retaining each title on behalf of the other libraries. The library that retains a title is considered the library of record. Staff at the library of record annotate the local catalog so that the title is not inadvertently discarded. Shipping services are used to exchange volumes to fill gaps. Each library maintains a storage facility in addition to open stacks. Interlibrary loan delivery is used for borrowing volumes. Evaluation considers the number of materials included in the archive, the number of items withdrawn, and the number of materials borrowed. Archived materials at a partner library save the local library from future investment in preservation and storage.

COORDINATED PRESERVATION

Libraries identify areas in which they will be responsible for preservation, thus enlarging the number of preserved items in the consortium. Such materials need be preserved only once within the network, generating savings for the partner libraries. Preservation librarians identify materials for preservation through collection condition surveys and consultation with selectors. They determine methods of preservation treatment. Other partner librarians create appropriate lending policies. Repair and conservation laboratories, including supplies, at participating libraries support appropriate treatments. Record keeping includes annotations of work done through the consortium. Evaluation considers subject areas of focus and numbers of materials preserved at each library in these areas.

JOINT CANCELLATION AND WEEDING

Libraries agree to cancel, not to cancel, to withdraw, or to consult with one another so that they are not discarding the same items. Collection development leaders share canceled or lower-priority serials lists as well as lists of encyclopedias and superseded reference works. Support staff and student assistants record bibliographic and location data on spreadsheets. Spreadsheets are shared electronically. Librarians make cancellation and weeding decisions in consultation with counterparts. Evaluation considers the number of titles canceled and/or withdrawn compared with the librarian time required. Money freed from cancellation of subscriptions can be reallocated to purchase new resources.

SHARED PURCHASES OF SPECIFIC TITLES

Libraries coordinate the purchase of specialized, expensive materials to maximize the number of unique titles held among them. By pooling their resources, the partners increase the funds available to purchase expensive materials. Counterparts discuss needs for costly, specialized materials. Travel may be required for in-depth discussion about options. Several meetings may be necessary to determine long-term goals for subject specialization. Librarians need time to consult clientele about options. Evaluation considers the number and significance of unique titles purchased.

The five preceding examples reflect commonalities that trigger recognition of the costs to start and maintain projects. Start-up is highly staff intensive. Staff time is an expensive and precious commodity, essential to the successful launch and implementation of a CCD project. Persistent time commitment from CCD leaders provides motivation, incorporation of CCD into staff goals, evaluation of progress, and communication about the projects within and beyond the library. Use of operations resources may increase slightly, but for the most part, CCD activities capitalize on existing allocations; no new equipment or additional telecommunications funding is required. Although additional collection resources increase incentives for participating in the project, they are not essential in any of the five examples. In most projects, something can be quantified for publicity about the CCD program. However, items counted do not provide the only basis for determining cost-effectiveness. The ultimate cost is staff time, which must be subjectively balanced against perception of value. Successful promotion of the activity within the library and publicity to clientele can enhance this perception, making it possible to fairly measure the benefits of CCD in meeting both immediate and long-term goals.

If CCD is a relatively new activity at the library, give particular attention to the cost of funding innovation. Exploring new areas requires taking risks and recognizing the potential for failure. Planning should encourage risk-taking along with expectations for results. Require a timetable and evaluation component for projects. The development process should include opportunities to consider continuation of the project and needed changes. In early stages of CCD, recognize that new initiatives require experimentation and that staff may experience several false starts before finding the course offering benefits to justify the investment.

CASE STUDY: CCD COST EXCEEDS BENEFIT

The Knox County Library and the University of Tennessee (UT) Libraries in Knoxville discovered an unexpected opportunity for CCD through an informal discussion between collection development counterparts about strategies for selecting current fiction. UT desired to collect current fiction with lasting research value. County librarians selected titles from McNaughton rental materials for retention in the local collection. Knox County Library secured permission from the McNaughton Company for a university librarian to select and purchase books at the same cost per volume paid by the public library. Cost centers embedded in this opportunity included the cost per volume balanced against the cost of the university librarian's time to go to the county library once every few months, make selections, and check the UT catalog for duplicates. Although over a hundred titles were selected during the first year, the practice was eventually discontinued because the cost of the librarian's time was too high for the number of books selected—the catalog check revealed that most titles were duplicates. However, the two libraries subsequently held a public ceremony establishing formal cooperative ties and now collaborate on several other projects.

Using CCD Cost Centers to Track Costs and Benefits

What CCD investments have the best chance for success? Figure 8-2 offers measures and outcomes for CCD activities as well as the kinds of resources required. Goals of the local library should suggest the type and extent of resources that will be allocated to CCD projects. Thus, if increased database access is a high local priority, a library may volunteer staff time to negotiate price and license terms with a vendor on behalf of the partners. Success will be apparent in the number of databases acquired and the cost savings realized in the shared purchase. Likewise, if staff members are indifferent to cooperation, leaders may choose to make the greatest investments in training and in counterpart introductions to garner support for CCD. Measures include the number of training sessions and assessment of changing staff enthusiasm for CCD, perhaps through an evaluation survey or anecdotal observation of increased staff initiative toward cooperative tasks.

Tangible outcomes of CCD programs are:

- policy development
- addition of unique resources
- work reduction in given areas
- increased print storage space
- help with decision making
- training

FIGURE 8-2	*Calculating Return on CCD Investments*

Cost Center	Measure	Outcome	Investment Required
Personnel			
Develop policy	Policies accepted by all partners	Smooth-functioning processes, without additional use of staff time	Staff time
Select and acquire unique resources	Number of unique titles added	Cooperative purchase of books	Staff time
Make decisions	Process includes sharing ideas, consultation with colleagues, specific outcomes	Clear communication about goals, accomplishments	Staff time
Conduct training	Number of specific sessions conducted	Staff prepared for specific tasks or generally more motivated	Staff time, travel
Motivate staff	Assess staff enthusiasm for CCD	Staff energized to devote quality effort to CCD	Staff time, travel
Provide subject specialist services	Report of tasks initiated; collection strength	Consultation for library users and collection development staff	Staff time, travel
Conduct license and price negotiations	Number of licenses and deals considered and completed; cost savings	Shared purchases of specific titles	Staff time
Select titles to archive	List and count titles selected; space saved	Fewer volumes retained locally	Staff time
Select local titles to digitize	List and count titles selected	Shared purchases of specific titles	Staff time; server space
Reduce work in given areas	Cite specific tasks conducted by partners	Time available to spend on other tasks	Staff time

FIGURE 8-2 (*continued*)

Cost Center	Measure	Outcome	Investment Required
Operations and Facilities			
Provide computer space	Amount of space for shared files, such as serials archive, journals overlap lists, etc.	Data management for shared collection items	Purchase or dedicate server space
Supply telecommunications access	Description of access; hours access is available	24-7 access to catalogs and shared data files	Staff time; network upgrades; software
Make available library shelf space for shared archive	Number of linear feet of shelving; description of physical facility used	Shared storage	Designated shelving; staff time
Furnish delivery service courier	Number of items delivered and cost per item	Efficient turnaround for users	Staff time; supplies; courier fees
Collections			
Purchase unique resources	Number of items added in given subject category and cost	Ability to rely on another collection for resources	Allocation of funding
Digitize local collections	List of collections identified; cost savings estimate for avoiding duplication	Online access to local resources	Staff time; server space
Pay for share of electronic resources	Actual amounts spent and saved	Online access to commercial products	Staff time; cost share
Preserve materials	Documentation of categories or titles shared	Coordinated preservation	Staff time; preservation supplies
Withdraw duplicate resources	Number of items withdrawn	Joint cancellation and weeding	Staff time; shipping costs

- motivation
- university digital collections of faculty research (institutional repositories)
- shared subject specialist services
- increased access to databases
- titles added to storage archives
- selection of local collections to digitize
- assistance with license and price negotiations to secure reduced subscription prices

Each of these outcomes represents a cost and, it is hoped, a benefit.

To the extent that CCD can be integrated into routine library functions, the chances increase for library staff to embrace its values and goals. Because staff time is clearly the most needed resource to support CCD, we recommend spending as little as possible on operations infrastructure and investing as much as possible in personnel. Delegate to one staff member the responsibility for leading projects; this will identify a point person and demonstrate the commitment of the library to the CCD program. Such an assignment may be as minimal as 5 percent of a librarian's time. If the responsible person already has staff support, some CCD clerical work can be handled within the unit. Depending upon the nature of the CCD program, it is likely that technical services and business staff may also contribute to tasks in the course of their routine assignments. Although new funding to support CCD in personnel, acquisitions, or operating budget lines can accelerate the program, it is possible to achieve success with existing resources, provided that there is some flexibility in decision making about expenditures. Where possible, incorporate CCD tasks into existing functions for maximum cost efficiency.

CASE STUDY: INFORMATION ALLIANCE CCD IN ANTHROPOLOGY

Consider the economics of the following activity among Information Alliance librarians responsible for collecting materials in anthropology. Note the cost centers that are embedded in activities as the CCD relationship advances, and consider how the outcome provides a measure of success.

Librarians in charge of collection development organized counterpart meetings to allow the anthropology specialists to get acquainted (cost center: Personnel/Motivate staff).

Bibliographers and subject librarians shared information about their respective users and collections (cost center: Personnel/Provide subject specialist services).

The conversation revealed that two of the three libraries held a subscription to a portion of the Human Relations Area File (HRAF) and that all three wanted to subscribe to a second HRAF database, given available funds.

One of the three subject specialists agreed to ask the vendor for pricing and learned that the existing subscription cost for two members would be reduced if the third subscribed (cost center: Personnel/Conduct license and price negotiations).

The vendor offered the second database at reduced cost to all three.

The subject specialists successfully appealed to their collection development heads for funding (cost center: Collections/Pay for share of electronic resources), and one of the three subject specialists placed the order on behalf of the Information Alliance.

Costs to implement this project included the price of the database, the time of the collection development and subject librarians, and the time of technical services and business office personnel who handled the billing. Beneficiaries of the collaboration were HRAF users. The example reflects both quantifiable and subjective economic issues. The total cost of the subscription to each of the three libraries was less because of the group order. The investment of librarian time provided more information resources for users, while it strengthened relationships among counterparts with comparable subject assignments. Once the librarians had identified a desired resource and allocated funding, the remainder of the work required to place the order and add the item to local database menus was incorporated into routine library functions. Without the impetus of consortial action, it is unlikely that the individual libraries would have given high priority to the HRAF subscription.

Is the Benefit Worth the Cost?

Few, if any, empirical methods have been proven to measure CCD cost. However, combining quantitative and qualitative measures offers some basis for assessing the value of CCD outcomes. For example, the relative success of collaborative archiving might be judged by calculating shelf space saved, comparing past and present use of titles in the archive, and observing interlibrary loan turnaround time for delivery of requested materials. Each project requires a customized set of indicators to be determined in the planning process.

Use data is one way to illustrate benefits. Other indirect measures include user satisfaction surveys, speed of information delivery, statistics on titles selected or withdrawn, and costs of products and services. CCD stakeholders include present and future library users, spreading both costs and benefits across generations. Today's clientele enjoy access to new databases provided through consortial purchases. Researchers of the future will benefit from coordinated selection that develops comprehensive collections in specialized areas.

Recognizing the need for more quantitative measures to evaluate CCD effectiveness, a Working Group for Quantitative Evaluation of Cooperative Collection Development Projects sponsored by the Center for Research Libraries presented a progress report at the second Aberdeen Woods Conference on Cooperative Collection Development in November 2002.[2] Using a modified balanced scorecard approach, the group identified categories of quantitative measures, such as local data (for example, student enrollment, use of electronic resources versus number of electronic resources, user satisfaction), number of staff, and number of items purchased. The Working Group is seeking collaborators to test performance measures. They plan to develop "tool boxes," or templates, for measuring performance in various types of CCD projects. (Chapter 10 contains more details about the balanced scorecard approach.) Although the cost of administering structured quantitative performance measures today likely exceeds the benefits realized from CCD, this group is breaking ground in a difficult area. The work shows promise for developing standard measures to calculate CCD costs and benefits. Until the promise is fulfilled, those engaged in CCD activities will use more descriptive assessments to determine the cost and value of achievements.

How Can Libraries Be Compensated for Their Contributions to the Consortium?

When partners jointly purchase a resource or database subscription at a reduced cost, payback is immediate and apparent. If partners share a position, each receives services according to the contract. However, much compensation from a CCD partnership is intangible. Among the benefits that are difficult to quantify are policy development, work reduction in given areas, expanded collection resources, help with decision making, staff training, motivation derived from the synergy of collaborating with counterparts, and the institutional goodwill generated from publicity about CCD accomplishments.

INVESTING IN A PARTNERSHIP

What kinds of resources should be invested in a partnership? Membership dues, while easily quantified, are perhaps among the smallest of contributions to a partnership. Most significant is staff time, which forms a pool of expertise to conceive and implement collaborative projects to solve local challenges. Partners also share space for meetings or for housing collections, funding for travel, and the expenses of specific projects, such as a delivery service. In some partnerships, the members or their funding agents contribute to a fund for purchasing information resources.

Numerous models exist for sharing costs among all partners. Membership dues frequently support the organizational infrastructure. Members purchase services or products that the consortium offers at a cost lower than the individual library price. In addition, members contribute the expertise of their librarians for consortia boards and task forces. Among the benefits of consortia membership are pooled buying power, help with license negotiation, intellectual contributions to solving difficult problems, and leadership toward major projects, all of which augment local expenditures in these areas. Another model, one that works well for smaller groups, involves a formal charter or governing structure to express overarching goals, while members share costs of specific projects. An example of this model is the Information Alliance among the university libraries of Kentucky, Tennessee, and Vanderbilt in which a Memorandum of Understanding and bylaws outline a general perspective that the collections of all three universities will be considered as one. Each library has designated its head of collection development as the responsible leader for CCD initiatives. The heads allocate discretionary funds for collection purchases recommended by subject librarians and bibliographers. Library directors take turns sponsoring annual counterpart meetings that include costs of travel, meeting space, and meals. Information Alliance CCD projects rely on the existing infrastructures of their respective libraries to support the selection, collection management information, materials transfer, and catalog updates essential to fulfilling CCD goals.

Evidence that each of the partners is contributing in these areas sustains collaboration. Taking turns at tasks as mundane as taking minutes or initiating conference calls demonstrates the participants' commitment to supporting the partnership. Neither a detailed cost account of the contributions of each nor a quid pro quo mind-set is necessary or practical. Anticipated costs and benefits should be incorporated into determination of objectives, which will subsequently be used as a basis for evaluating outcomes. CCD economics involves not only the costs (and benefits) to individual libraries, but also the resources of the partnership.

CONCLUSION

Librarians who show that they understand and care about the relationships between costs and productive outputs have credibility with funding agents.[3] Participants in CCD programs want assurance that they are making worthwhile investments in activities with the potential for improving the ability of the local library to provide services and resources. Although the economics of CCD involve a high degree of subjectivity, this chapter outlines cost centers that affect CCD financial planning and assessment. Success of collaborative ventures depends on the confidence of funding agents and participants who believe that investments are returning good value. National attention continues to be focused on defining benchmarks and quantifying relationships among data that will offer empirical measures of CCD economics in the future.

CCD costs and benefits are cumulative. Staff time devoted to developing infrastructure, data gathering, and making purchase or withdrawal decisions can take years to be fully appreciated from an economic perspective. Fortunately, CCD also produces short-term outcomes that demonstrate immediate and quantifiable benefits. Increasingly, we share human resources in an information environment in which the library is viewed as both access provider and archive. Expanding collection strength to increase access is a primary goal supported through CCD initiatives. Although formal metrics do not presently support a CCD balance sheet, economic issues permeate all aspects of the endeavor, from selecting the right partners to assessing outcomes. Perhaps the most important lessons of CCD economics can be summarized in this advice: Spend as much as the library can afford on CCD. Expect to contribute more to partnerships than you gain initially. Capitalize on CCD investments by publicizing successful outcomes.

NOTES

1. Steven A. Roberts, *Financial and Cost Management for Libraries and Information Services,* 2nd ed. (West Sussex, UK: Bowker-Saur, 1998), 4.

2. Bosch, "Working Group for Quantitative Evaluation."

3. Martin M. Cummings, "Cost Analysis: Methods and Realities," *Library Administration and Management* 3, no. 4 (Fall 1989): 183.

CHAPTER
9

OUTREACH
Promoting and Publicizing CCD

Despite the widespread appeal of collaborative collection development, at least as a theoretical concept, getting CCD projects started takes substantial effort. Strong leadership, a positive collection development atmosphere, and logistical solutions to bibliographic access and prompt delivery are key elements in making CCD work. Increasingly, library administrators and collection development managers also recognize the need to systematically market CCD as well as its products and services. *Marketing* is a general term for communicating with internal and external customers. Figure 9-1 provides a graphic representation of the interrelated areas encompassed by this all-purpose term. Public libraries long ago recognized the need to market their products, programs, and services as the competition for resources and customers (library users) intensified. Within the past two decades, public, academic, and special librarians alike have increasingly recognized the need to become adept at public relations. They have learned how to work with local media to advertise their programs. Also, librarians have focused time and financial resources on developing and maintaining mutually beneficial relationships with their users by promoting and publi-

Collaborative Collection Development

FIGURE 9-1   *The Interrelationship of Marketing Activities*

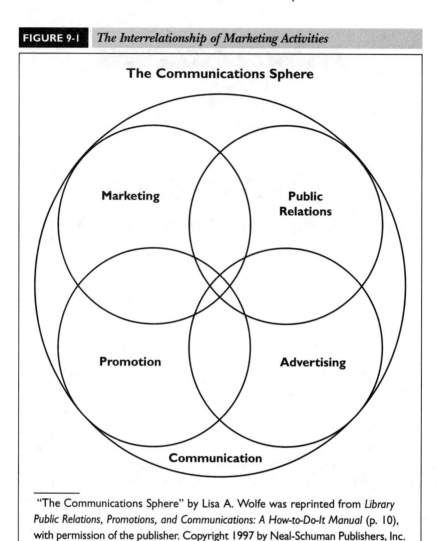

The Communications Sphere

Marketing

Public Relations

Promotion

Advertising

Communication

"The Communications Sphere" by Lisa A. Wolfe was reprinted from *Library Public Relations, Promotions, and Communications: A How-to-Do-It Manual* (p. 10), with permission of the publisher. Copyright 1997 by Neal-Schuman Publishers, Inc.

---

cizing the unique services available through the library. We suggest that a systematic, consistent marketing plan specifically for CCD is not only helpful, but essential if participating libraries and their clients are to derive maximum benefit from collaborative efforts.

A comprehensive marketing plan consists of several interconnected components. Activities common to most marketing plans include analysis and selection of target audiences, design and testing of products, evaluation of services by survey and focus group feedback, and review and redesign.[1] Early on, the core of marketing was circumscribed by the so-called Four Ps: product, place, price, and promotion.[2] Over time, other aspects have been added, such as packaging.[3] The traditional Four Ps have recently been expanded to the more comprehensive Seven Ps to address services-as-products by including people, process, and physical evidence as essential aspects of the marketing mix.[4] Alternatively, the Four Cs (customer, convenience, cost, communication) were introduced as more appropriate to the marketing of services.[5] These key words are shorthand for the complicated and extensive processes underlying how products are developed, how they are valued, where they are offered, and how they are introduced. They also convey how the interaction between producer and consumer is structured, how the exchange encounter between provider and customer is organized, and how the tangible elements of an otherwise invisible service are deployed to give evidence of the quality level of that service. Several of these elements have already been addressed in this guide because the planning that goes into creating a framework for CCD contains some parts of the marketing mix. During the framework phase, for example, the product, namely the particular CCD project being proposed, is designed, priced, and placed.[6]

In this chapter, we focus on the promotion component of the marketing mix. This is not to suggest that marketing can be reduced to promotion alone.[7] Indeed, all the elements reciprocally influence one another. However, this chapter concentrates on those practical steps for communicating with internal and external customers. For the sake of discussion, we divide promotion into its two complementary aspects: promotion and publicity. We use the term *promotion* to refer to activities that address the needs and concerns of internal customers, namely, the library staff and related agencies who participate directly or indirectly in proposing, supporting, and implementing CCD. In this sense, promotion implies an ongoing dialogue between those who establish CCD projects as part of the framework phase and their counterparts (for example, local library staff or consortial partners) who evaluate and implement the products and services of CCD. Together, these constituencies define CCD and influence its shape. The goal of promotion is to persuade those involved that a proposed project is an appropriate and efficient means of meeting a need identified by the community of participating libraries.

Whereas promotion is persuasive in nature, seeking to gain support for a project among potential participants, publicity is informative, serving to acquaint an audience not involved in the project with its scope and impact. *Publicity* encompasses the strategies needed to make a particular CCD project known to an external audience—whether that audience is situated inside or outside the library as organization. Publicizing CCD seeks to inform external customers (end-users) of the existence of a particular project so that these individuals can use the results of the collaborative effort. External customers also include individuals within the library community who are not involved in the creation and implementation of a CCD project, but who, like library patrons, will take advantage of its benefits. As components of an overall marketing strategy, promotion and publicity are crucial to the success of CCD and CCD projects.

PROMOTING CCD

The time to begin promoting a CCD project among library staff, collaborative partners, and library-relevant agencies is early in the planning phase of the project itself. In fact, a promotional plan should be a constituent part of the overall design and implementation of the project. Promotion needs to begin early because it is this effort that helps to identify experts and stakeholders whose support will increase the potential for success of the project. This plan does not have to be perfect from the beginning, but it should be flexible and adaptable to changing circumstances as the planning process evolves. Moreover, creating a promotional plan requires no esoteric knowledge or arcane skills. Instead, commonsense approaches and practical strategies that encourage dialogue will serve the no-nonsense, results-oriented attitudes of most librarians.[8] Key determinations in designing a promotional plan include:

> who is in charge of developing and implementing the plan
> what product is being promoted
> to whom the project is being promoted
> how and where details about the project are communicated
> how to periodically review and retool the plan

Designate the Promotional Plan Coordinator

Just as a CCD program or project should have a dedicated manager, someone must take charge of designing and coordinating the accompanying promotional plan. Identifying this individual is the first step in creating a promotional plan.[9] Better yet, consider using a team approach with diverse expertise and assignments. Who promotes a CCD project within a particular library or collaborative group may depend on the nature of the project and the type of activities that constitute the project. The promotional plan coordinator must first work at an abstract level to articulate the project vision and mission well before proceeding to elaborate the details of the plan. Only within the framework of this guiding vision can the discrete elements of a promotional plan be assembled.

The promotional plan coordinator will assume responsibility for reviewing the needs of the organization, analyzing the dynamics of the marketplace, setting objectives for the plan, deciding which strategies to use in promoting the project, and articulating the details of activating the plan.[10] In addition to performing the preliminary analysis of the environment for promoting the CCD project, the coordinator assembles core information about the goals of the project, serves as a contact person for the project, creates a consistent profile for the project, and, most importantly, involves the staff, whose participation and support are crucial.

The choice of a coordinator will have an impact on the scope of the promotional plan and the resources that are available for promotion. The director of the library will employ one approach to seek support for CCD, while a selector in a subject discipline will opt for another. Regardless of the level at which the plan coordinator serves, that individual will assume responsibility for a series of strategic steps in promoting the specific CCD project or program. Taken together, the steps that follow constitute the nuts and bolts of the promotional plan the coordinator will implement. Let's assume that you are responsible for marketing in your organization. You are also your library's representative to the consortium providing the context for the CCD project. You have been given the task of promoting CCD projects and programs to your coworkers and consortial colleagues. The following steps should serve as a useful guide for implementing a promotional plan.

Identify the Product

The product is central to the marketing process.[11] The framework phase identifies a specific CCD project, ranging from expedited interlibrary loan to coordinated collection development in a particular subject area. As marketing manager, you must promote this project—

that is, this "product"—to the internal customer, namely, those within the local or partner library whose support is needed to actually make the project work. A logical starting point here is to describe the project in a manner that identifies it as a natural extension of the institutional mission. To persuade internal customers to buy into the project, demonstrate that the product offers benefits, provides solutions to problems, or delivers improvements over existing products.[12] Your promotional plan must persuade the internal customers, namely administration, staff, and consortial partners, of the value of the project. Only then have you laid the groundwork on which later steps of the promotional plan will be built.

And take note: You must identify the project not only at the objective, but also at the subjective, or perhaps more accurately, the affective level. This means that for the nominal product, a corresponding psychological and emotional construct of that product must also be factored in. In fact, identifying and promoting the product's psychological construct may be more important to getting buy-in from internal customers than depending solely on the hard data associated with the product. A project to coordinate monograph acquisition in a subject area among participating institutions can be captured in quantitative terms: dollars saved in less duplication, increased number of unique titles available regionally, shared expertise in building a more comprehensive collection, and so forth. This is the objective CCD product. But what about the affective factors that figure into this project? What are the emotional costs to those who will be asked to implement this plan? More work, more meetings, less control over the local collection. To address some of the obstacles, use the psychological construct of the product to connect it to one or more of the CCD principles discussed in chapter 3. Coordinated CCD, for example, assumes and advances the essential unity of all libraries as a single institution. The emotional appeal of this concept may counterbalance concerns about additional duties or a more complicated workflow. An alternative may be to promote cooperation itself as the affective product. At any rate, identifying the product requires acknowledging and addressing the multidimensional nature of products in the promotional plan.

Identify Target Audiences

In preparation for drafting the content of marketing materials, those promoting CCD projects must identify and define the target audiences for the advertising they will create and deploy to build support for CCD projects. In marketing terms, this step is known as *market segmentation*.[13] Essentially, market segmentation means finding common elements and building cohesive relationships among the larger universe of consumers the promotional material addresses. Within the library context, you can segment the market in many different ways: public services and technical services; administration and staff; librarians and paraprofessionals; proponents of electronic products and supporters of print products, to name just a few possibilities. As promotional plan manager, you must analyze the environment by asking who needs to know what about the project and why. Defining the constituencies that need information allows the promotional plan manager to tailor messages to specific groups.

Use market segmentation techniques to pinpoint the needs and concerns of specific customer groups. Anticipate and address the issues a particular constituency might raise. Assess the library itself and prepare for dealing with organizational barriers. Most importantly, use the information gained from market segmentation analyses to tailor messages to the needs of the specific group whose support you seek.[14] Even though you think and work in terms of a constituency, remember that these groups are composed of individuals. Seek a convergence of individual and group needs, and exploit that mutually reinforcing relationship whenever possible.

Tailor the Promotional Message

After you have identified the who, what, and how of a CCD project, the next step is to create texts that describe the project to those internal customers who need to support it or who may be called on to implement it. Package details about the project in such a way that you can take the message to those who need to hear it, whether it be a member of the administration who must be convinced of the legitimacy of the project, an advisory council or committee tasked with reviewing institutional strategic initiatives, or skeptical colleagues who suspect that any new project will mean an added workload and infringe on their ability to accomplish primary tasks and professional goals.

Marketing managers know that a CCD project description can be pivotal to its acceptance. The rhetoric of persuasion requires sensitivity to choice of words and phrasing, the tone and flavor of the document. Exercise keen judgment, sensitivity, adaptability, and flexible thinking—traits and skills you will need to develop early on if you have been asked to promote CCD projects. Consider that, in many respects, preparing a report or proposal recommending the implementation of a CCD project parallels the stages of generating a grant application. In effect, seeking support for a CCD project mirrors the submission of a funding request of any other type. For that reason, the language—its content, tone, and level—must be carefully considered.

Tailor a CCD proposal to the audience that must comprehend and act on it. Adapt generic CCD proposals to the local circumstances. Otherwise, promotional texts lose their appeal, and getting buy-in becomes more difficult. After all, promotion is about building consensus. A message describing a CCD activity to be implemented by a particular target audience should address likely concerns of that group.[15] An administrator, for example, may be interested in the financial details of the proposal, while a bibliographer will want to know how the project brings new and deeper content to a particular subject area. Such targeted messages have their own format and structure and may require some time and energy to craft, but they are worth the effort. All constituencies affected by the CCD project should understand the project through a promotional descriptive text configured for their needs. Indeed, although the message promoting CCD needs to be widely disseminated, the more specific it can appear to a particular audience, the greater its chances of gaining support for the project and for the eventual success of the project itself.

Communicate the Message

Once you have crafted the texts promoting a CCD project, tailored their content and structure to the intended audience, and established their format, you must find channels for communicating the message. Create a persuasive narrative that lays out the proposed project and details its advantages in terms specific to the local institution. Determine who needs to carry the message; match the text to the intended audience and the occasion; and try to anticipate how that audience will receive the message. When these elements come together as a successful whole, the narrative will demonstrate the value of the project to your constituency and offer convincing evidence that the project is in the institution's or the group's best interests. Unless the message can communicate something positive and worthwhile to be gained from the effort—specific resources, prestige, acclaim, or any other of innumerable payoffs for collaboration—the chances of the plan being adopted are remote. Carefully articulate the rewards of participation, so that the project will be well received.

Identify Promotional Venues

After you have created the narrative describing a CCD project, you are ready to go public. Find outlets for presenting your project description to participants and other stakeholders. Audiences who need to hear the pitch include both direct and indirect stakeholders—those who implement the project as well as those who will feel the impact of the project's implementation. Do not define stakeholders or beneficiaries too narrowly. Seek advice about improving or adapting the project to make the narrative more convincing. The goal is to create an ongoing dialogue that keeps the project in the spotlight.

Informal Networking

At the most elementary level, use personal networking to promote the CCD message. Social and professional occasions present ideal opportunities to advance the CCD cause within the home institution. A conversation over lunch with a coworker from another department can lead to a synergistic exchange of insights. You can increase the understanding of CCD and thereby generate local support for the proposed project. Networking with colleagues also offers an ideal way to gauge potential enthusiasm for cooperation and to garner broad-based support. Networking breaks down emotional barriers and addresses individuals' need to be consulted before having to voice positions in a formal arena. Conversational networking will go far toward paving the way for a CCD project within the library setting. Informal discussions and exchanges of ideas at meetings on campus can also set the stage for CCD outside the confines of the library system.

Formal Outlets

At some point, it will be necessary to get the topic on the agenda when various library groups, such as selectors, technical services staff, administrators, or similar constituencies, meet. For example, informational presentations at technical services department meetings will alert those individuals to the project and allow them to assess how it might impact them.

Broadening the scope, consider conferences, workshops, and similar professional gatherings at the state, regional, national, and even international levels. These sites represent ideal venues for presenting information about existing and proposed CCD activities. In addition to the social contacts that can be used to promote a project, for example, with potential partners and counterparts, the formal programs often offer outlets for presenting more official papers and reports. The board of directors of a public library, the senate at a university or college, a departmental faculty meeting, or a special interest committee likewise are often receptive to presentations and welcome advance information about new initiatives still in the planning stages.

Manage the Promotional Plan

Once you have established your promotional plan and have assembled the resources to get it under way, you will need to spend time and energy managing that plan as an ongoing operation.

Create Expectations

Promoting CCD creates expectations. As with other products, create a perception of a need and then show how the CCD project can satisfy that need. CCD supporters must communicate the sense of excitement that first gripped them as they evoke expectations in others about what CCD can accomplish. An expectation anticipates an event. Collaboration requires participants to focus forward on a deferred, yet realizable goal. It helps, of course, if there are intermediate steps along the way, shorter-range objectives leading to accomplishments that reinvigorate the effort. Creating expectations means crafting these near-term opportunities for success into the CCD plan. When will the first books of a shared purchasing plan begin to arrive in the library? And how will their arrival be heralded? How can the establishment of a shared expedited courier service be used to encourage users to look forward to taking advantage of resources at a partner institution? Such routine CCD components can and should be exploited regularly to foster enthusiasm for the services offered through CCD. They offer opportunities for the project managers to give the effort that periodic shot in the arm.

Schedule Feedback

Promoting the project on an ongoing basis can be as simple as sharing implementation details, creating a timeline if appropriate, and providing background on the genesis of the project. Regular updates and progress reports focus attention on the project and remind those on the periphery of the project of what it is supposed to accomplish.[16] By preventing the project from fading into the background, from becoming routine, you purposefully invite continuing quality improvement of the project, with input from those who directly influence its profile. As one writer puts it, "the library staff is the best communications tool available to you. What a circulation clerk says over her or his back fence will have much greater impact than any flyer or slick brochure."[17] Finding out what that circulation clerk or any of her or his colleagues has to say is a part of the feedback loop that consists of providing and soliciting information and ideas.

Maintain Momentum

The success of a complex and complicated CCD project is built on the successes and sacrifices of the many individuals who have contributed to the project. Promoting CCD includes promoting those individuals who have participated in establishing the project. As a general concept, CCD does not happen of its own accord, but is made to happen by those who see it as a tool for improving the materials and services available to users. Specific CCD projects require institutional resources as well as real time and energy from staff. Keep enthusiasm and commitment from flagging through ongoing recognition. Take time to offer thanks and give recognition to those who keep the project on track. Doing this regularly and randomly can maintain a level of expectation and positive suspense that reflects attention on the project itself each time someone is recognized. Individuals who were initially skeptical or who did not choose to participate may be won over by the celebration of success and those responsible for that success.

Manage Expectations

Although CCD holds great promise, promising more than it can deliver will only lead to disappointment and may contribute to the failure of the project. And although creating expectations in conjunction with promoting CCD is a legitimate, even necessary, task, keep in mind that CCD has its appropriate uses, but is not a cure-all for collection development concerns. Promoting CCD does not require creating fantastic scenarios of infinite and unrealistic possibilities. Most information professionals are immediately skeptical of overblown claims, but appreciate the true benefits that modest and sustainable efforts can achieve. When promoting CCD, remind your audience that CCD is one strategy for building collections and improving services, but not the only strategy.

PUBLICIZING CCD

As the preceding section has suggested, promoting a CCD project to the internal audience is the first, essential step to getting information about a CCD activity or program out to those who can influence its profile and contribute to its contours. Once a CCD program has been designed and successfully implemented, the next step is to publicize it to external audiences. In our discussion, the key difference between promotion and publicity is that promotion focuses on the process of creating the CCD product, while publicity deals with the availability of that product for use by consumers. Publicity increases the chances that the project will achieve its full potential and will be continued as a cornerstone of the services available through the partner libraries. A marketing plan for publicizing CCD will share many of the same elements that the promotional plan includes. Publicity is directed at external customers and end-users who need to be guided in using and appreciating the benefits of the CCD project. Design publicity campaigns to inform and educate as well as to reinforce the contributions of CCD as a collection-building tool.

In many respects, the components of a publicity campaign mirror those of a promotional plan. As with the promotional plan, you need to identify the product, identify the audiences for that product by analyzing market segmentation, create effective advertising texts, and determine the most effective venues and formats for disseminating the information to end-users. Formalized communication methods and tools have been developed for publicity efforts. Figure 9-2 offers examples. Formats for channels of communication are limited only by the imagination of marketing personnel. Fortunately, learning to create these formats is relatively straightforward. A number of useful practical manuals provide examples and walk you through the mechanics of writing publicity texts.[18]

Staging Publicity

Think of a publicity campaign as a series of ever-widening, concentric circles moving out from the center. Initial publicity efforts target the

FIGURE 9-2	*Publicity: Tools of the Trade*

- Press releases
- Press conferences
- Public service announcements (PSAs)
- Radio and TV features
- Newspaper and magazine articles
- News bulletins
- Advertisements
- Newsletters
- Brochures
- Pamphlets
- Flyers
- Posters
- Postcards
- Monthly/Annual reports
- Library guides
- Personal visits
- Telephone surveys
- Direct mailings
- E-mail announcements

- Exhibits
- Displays
- Kiosks
- Library's website/home page
- Online exhibits
- Badges/Identification tags
- Bulletin boards
- Storyboards
- Bookmarks/with logos
- New books display/Book reviews
- New books lists
- Presentations
- Computer slide shows
- Focus groups
- Events/Receptions
- Special programs
- Training seminars/Workshops
- Promotional gifts (pencils, bookmarks, notepads, etc.)

most immediate audience. Subsequent communications target audiences at wider rings. The circle of attention expands systematically until all audiences have received information about the CCD project.

Start Local

The best place to begin a publicity campaign to advertise a CCD project is at your own library. Naturally, since the project is CCD based, coordinate the campaign with counterparts at partner libraries, unveiling parallel efforts simultaneously. Because not all staff members may have been involved in the planning and implementation of a CCD project, they are the first "external" audience that publicity efforts should target. This has practical implications because library staff members deal directly with the public and regularly receive feedback. The local audience must be as informed as possible in order to assist with later inquiries from outside the library. As a test audience, they can help fine-tune publicity materials before you go public with those messages.

To publicize CCD projects to the home crowd, use formats and venues that regularly reach them. Meeting summaries, news digests, or internal "press releases" that are distributed, circulated, or routed within the organization offer channels for communicating news to staff. Others in the organization will call on those involved in the project once initial announcements are disseminated. Public service announcements can provide concise details while touting the appeal of the project. Standard library publications, such as staff newsletters, news bulletins, or similar official channels for announcements, offer convenient venues for short news notes or periodic updates. Power-Point presentations and feature pieces at staff meetings, library events, and similar outlets expand the scope of familiarity with the project. When CCD projects are featured in officially sanctioned publications, such as library newsletters, brochures, or flyers, their acceptability increases in the perceptions of staff. Publicity thus legitimizes as it informs about CCD activities.

As a transitional area between internal and external customers, the library's website offers an excellent channel for publicizing CCD projects. A column or section devoted to a specific CCD project in the library electronic newsletter is a useful publicity tool that can be exploited to advantage. Links to CCD project initiatives from the library's home page offer "on-demand" publicity. Major or extensive CCD projects deserve their own websites. Figure 9-3 shows how the Information Alliance (consisting of the University of Kentucky, the University of Tennessee, and Vanderbilt University) maintains a public presence on the Internet. Also, resources stemming from CCD projects in specific disciplines can be branded on subject pages that collate resources related to a particular area of study and research. Even local notes in the MARC record publicize CCD activities. The Information Alliance's Serials Archive, for example, seeks to distribute responsibility for maintaining backfiles of selected print journals. In terms of publicity, the note that is added to the 856 field of the

FIGURE 9-3 *Home Page of the Information Alliance (University of Kentucky, University of Tennessee, and Vanderbilt University)*

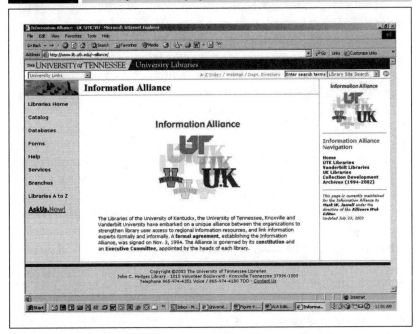

MARC record to identify the library of record for a particular title functions as a persistent advertisement for the existence of the collaborative endeavor. As a version of branding, this note serves as a registry for action and an acknowledgment of the efforts that went into pursuing a cooperative goal.

Expand Horizons

In addition to publicizing CCD projects to audiences within your library, expand your horizons to campus, community, and consortium customers. Audiences include faculty, students, staff, Friends groups, special borrowers, drop-in users, special interest groups, and others. Identify specific channels for getting the word out to them, and match the information format to the audience and the communication opportunity. On a college campus, the student newspaper can be a good venue for informing students about collaborative projects and inviting them to take full advantage of CCD products and services. Many colleges and universities have other publications that target faculty and staff. They exist, in print and online, to celebrate campus initiatives. Figure 9-4 reproduces an article from the *Vanderbilt Register* describing the collaborative collection development activities of the Information Alliance.

Public and school libraries often use flyers and direct mailings sent to patrons' homes to get the information on CCD projects where it needs to go. Newsletters of Friends groups and community newsletters are ideal for reaching the local audience. A brief e-mail alert can inform patrons on an electronic broadcast list about new developments and programs at the library. Also, a well-scripted short text printed on a bookmark inserted at check-out or upon receipt from a partner library may be an effective tool in certain contexts. Posters and exhibits make information about CCD projects available to drop-in users on-site. If appropriate, consider special kick-off events to publicize projects that are just getting under way. Other outlets unique to individual institutions undoubtedly exist as well. Imagination is often the only limitation to ensuring that CCD projects and programs get the attention they need and deserve.

Go Regional and Beyond

The size and scope of a CCD project determine the breadth and reach of publicity efforts. A statewide CCD activity, such as the creation of a virtual library, should be publicized at the statewide level or risk being ignored and underused by segments of the population for which it was established. Although CCD seldom has the glitz and glamour of sensational stories, attracting the attention of print and media journalists to a CCD project as a newsworthy subject may not be as difficult as you think.[19] Learn how the various media work. Build strong positive relationships with local media representatives.[20] Many newspapers and radio and TV stations feature articles on local initiatives. A CCD project with the potential to improve local citizens' access to information resources certainly fits this category. Communicate the public interest aspects of CCD projects in language free of the jargon and acronyms that characterize much library publication. As coordinator of publicity, take the initiative to funnel these stories to the appropriate media contacts.

In addition to exploiting media such as newspapers, local radio, and TV, CCD participants can publicize their efforts through more narrowly focused professional venues at the local, state, regional,

FIGURE 9-4   Vanderbilt Register Article on the Information Alliance's CCD Initiative

Vanderbilt Register Article on the Information Alliance's CCD Initiative

2 *VANDERBILT REGISTER*   *APRIL 6-12, 1998*

IRIS partnership brings more library resources to VU, UT and UK researchers

by Ann Marie Deer Owens

A new collaboration of the three largest research university libraries in Tennessee and Kentucky will make more than six million volumes available to students and faculty via the Internet.

IRIS (Information Resources for Interinstitutional Sharing) — a joint initiative of Vanderbilt University, the University of Tennessee, Knoxville, and the University of Kentucky — was announced April 3 during the dedication of the William T. Young Library at the University of Kentucky.

The initiative establishes a World Wide Web-based system for seeking, identifying and ordering books for interlibrary loan that speeds the delivery of these volumes to students, faculty and staff at the three universities.

IRIS will foster broad cooperation in collection development and access by the three institutions, according to Paul Gherman, Vanderbilt University librarian. "Now faculty and students can search simultaneously the catalogs of all three libraries and receive requested material through expedited interlibrary loan. By the fall, users will be able to directly request books via their local library system from all three libraries without needing to contact their interlibrary loan office," Gherman said.

Paula Kaufman, dean of libraries at the University of Tennessee, Knoxville, said each library's collection brings unique strengths that make the IRIS collection an important resource for scholars. "For example, the University of Tennessee Library possesses outstanding hold-

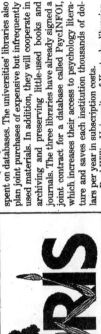

ings in English and American literature, materials science and civil engineering," Kaufman said.

"The University of Kentucky Library collects broadly in Southern history, architecture and agriculture, while the Vanderbilt University Library has extensive resources in Latin American studies, education and religion."

IRIS and cooperative license agreements between the universities will help improve the cost efficiency of money spent on databases. The universities' libraries also plan joint purchases of expensive but infrequently used materials. In addition, they will cooperate in archiving and preserving little-used books and journals. The three libraries have already signed a joint contract for a database called PsycINFO1, which increases their access to psychology literature and saves each institution thousands of dollars per year in subscription costs.

Paul Willis, University of Kentucky librarian, said Project IRIS will significantly enrich UK's access to books at the University of Tennessee and Vanderbilt University at the same time that the William T. Young Library offers improved resources.

"No one library can hope to meet the information needs of its students and faculty today, and our joining with our two strongest neighbors assures us of a rich information resource into the future," Willis said.

IRIS is accessible through each library's Web page. The address for the Vanderbilt Library home page is www.library.vanderbilt.edu/

national, and international levels. Professional journals, conferences, and discussion groups provide a sounding board for the community of information professionals. Articles in professional journals, poster sessions at conferences, and discussion groups all offer opportunities to publicize CCD activities. These channels of communication also make it possible to solicit feedback and suggestions. This evaluation phase forms the groundwork for product revision and further development. Then the marketing cycle begins anew.

CONCLUSION

To be an effective instrument for improving collections and library services, CCD projects must be promoted and publicized vigorously. Successful CCD efforts do not come into existence in and of themselves, but only through the dedicated efforts of those who see the potential benefit of such cooperation. Individuals who are interested in marketing CCD must organize their efforts. A systematic approach to promoting and publicizing consists of designating a marketing coordinator, identifying products and target audiences, and creating an action plan for packaging, presenting, and communicating the messages that focus on CCD programs, projects, and services.

CCD must be promoted to the internal audience. The support of this constituency is vital to developing and implementing CCD projects. CCD products and services must also be actively publicized. Publicity introduces CCD projects to wider audiences and garners the support of groups external to the project itself. Publicity keeps the project viable over the long term, even in tenuous budget circumstances. It focuses on the benefits and documents the contribution that CCD makes to the libraries and their clienteles. Promoting and publicizing CCD projects, parallel tracks with similar methods and complementary goals, should accompany all cooperative activities from their inception, through the planning phases, to their implementation, and beyond.

NOTES

1. Cosette Kies, *Marketing and Public Relations for Libraries* (Metuchen, NJ: Scarecrow, 1987), 73–85.

2. Eileen Elliott de Sáez, *Marketing Concepts for Libraries and Information Services* (London: Library Association Publishing, 1993), 38–54; Keith Hart, *Putting Marketing Ideas into Action* (London: Library Association Publishing, 1999), 10–14.

3. Kies, *Marketing and Public Relations*, 78.

4. Jennifer Rowley, *Information Marketing* (Aldershot: Ashgate, 2001), 6–8.

5. De Sáez, *Marketing Concepts*, 39; Linda Ashcroft, "The Marketing and Management of Electronic Journals in Academic Libraries: A Need for Change," in Rejean Savard, ed., *Education and Research for Marketing and Quality Management in Libraries*, 178 (Munich: K. G. Saur, 2002).

6. Darlene E. Weingand, *Marketing/Planning Library and Information Services*, 2nd ed. (Englewood, CO: Libraries Unlimited, 1999), 9 ff.

7. Ibid., 1.

8. De Sáez, *Marketing Concepts*, 1; Katharina J. Blackstead and Eric C. Shoaf, "Synergy in Library Public Relations, Marketing, and Development Activities," in Rashelle S. Karp, ed., *Powerful Public Relations: A How-to Guide for Libraries*, 5 (Chicago: American Library Association, 2002).

9. Lisa A. Wolfe, *Library Public Relations, Promotions, and Communications: A How-to-Do-It Manual* (New York: Neal-Schuman, 1997), 3; Weingand, *Marketing/Planning*, 141-42; Blackstead and Shoaf, "Synergy," 2.

10. Blackstead and Shoaf, "Synergy," 1–3.

11. Rowley, *Information Marketing*, 13; Weingand, *Marketing/Planning*, 81 ff.

12. Sally Gardner Reed, *Making the Case for Your Library: A How-to-Do-It Manual* (New York: Neal-Schuman, 2001), 13–14; Blackstead and Shoaf, "Synergy," 6.

13. Hart, *Putting Marketing Ideas*, 24–33.

14. Ibid., 30.

15. Ibid., 34.

16. Kies, *Marketing and Public Relations*, 51.

17. Wolfe, *Library Public Relations*, 36.

18. Anne F. Roberts and Susan Griswold Blandy, *Public Relations for Librarians* (Englewood, CO: Libraries Unlimited, 1989), 7, 16; Wolfe, *Library Public Relations*, 75–164; Reed, *Making the Case*, 25 ff; Rashelle S. Karp, ed., *Powerful Public Relations: A How-to Guide for Libraries* (Chicago: American Library Association, 2002), 8 ff.

19. Greg Kowalski, David Crumm, and Herb Gunn, "How to Get Your Library's Story in the Local Newspaper," *Unabashed Librarian*, no. 125 (2002): 29–31.

20. Roberts and Blandy, *Public Relations for Librarians*, 31–32; Wolfe, *Library Public Relations*, 78.

CHAPTER

10

CCD'S IMPACT
Assessment and Evaluation

$\mathbf{A}$lthough cooperation may seem intuitively valuable and collaborative collection development, in theory, obviously beneficial, illustrating the positive cost-benefit ratio of specific CCD projects with concrete numbers has proven difficult and elusive. The literature on collection assessment is extensive.[1] Still, there is no generally accepted method for quantifying and evaluating CCD activities. However, collection-centered or user-centered instruments deployed to measure the quantity and quality of a single library's collection can be adapted to the CCD context.[2] As with the assessment of individual collections, a number of instruments focusing on discrete collection components can be combined to address the various segments of a CCD project. Although a comprehensive evaluation of CCD remains an unrealized dream, the evaluation of CCD activities is becoming ever more important, with a growing number of CCD efforts increasing emphasis on costs of services and interest in outcomes-based performance. This chapter describes key approaches to assessing CCD activities.

Evaluation of a collaborative project should be a core part of the CCD planning process. Consider assessment methods in the beginning phase of CCD discussions so that evaluation instruments will be appropriate to the type of CCD project under review. Make assessment and evaluation part of the comprehensive CCD package. Clarify what these processes should accomplish. Delineate the areas of focus and establish the ground rules under which assessment is to be undertaken. For many CCD projects, evaluation instruments must be considered in advance because the project often requires a collection assessment at the beginning of the project for benchmarking purposes. CCD projects show an amazing variety of types; the instruments selected or developed to evaluate them will also vary.

ESTABLISHING THE ASSESSMENT STRATEGY

The primary imperative is to tailor assessment strategies to the individual project or specific type of project. Factors that affect the selection of assessment approach include the scope and extent of the CCD project, its formality and complexity, and the level of accountability and reporting required of project's managers. Assessment must address a myriad of questions: Will updates to external agencies be required? How often will evaluation be performed and by whom? How will CCD financial commitments be tracked? By what standards will fiscal responsibility be demonstrated? As participants design the evaluation instrument, they should agree on definitions of what constitutes progress or, in the event of a completed project, what determines success to ensure that planning and implementation match input to expected outcomes. Now more than ever, the library, as a service unit, must be concerned with dimensions of user satisfaction. CCD project managers must make significant efforts to determine how CCD activities affect user attitudes and assumptions. Although some of these factors have proven to be virtually unquantifiable, they must be addressed when CCD activities are considered. Use the categories, questions, and tag words in figure 10-1 to organize for CCD assessment.

INFORMAL ASSESSMENT AND EVALUATION METHODS

Not all CCD projects require elaborate and complicated assessment instruments. In fact, some CCD activity may elude direct assessment. This is often the case with "shadow CCD," that form of CCD in which

| FIGURE 10-1 | *Organizing for CCD Assessment and Evaluation* |

Purpose: What purpose does the assessment serve?
- Initial benchmarking
- Interim progress
- Phase/stage analysis
- Final audit

Focus: What component or aspect does the evaluation address?
- Collection
- User
- Hybrid, combination, compromise
- Holistic

Scope: What will the assessment cover? To what extent?
- General
- Targeted
  - Subject area focus
  - Specific cost center
- Comprehensive

Formality: Does the evaluation need to be formal or informal?
- Rigid
- Flexible
- Adaptable

Agency: Who initiates or performs an evaluation?
- Commissioning agent
- Performing agent
  - Advocate
    - Internal
    - External
  - Independent reviewer
    - Internal
    - External
  - Appointed, assigned, retained

Time Frame: When should an evaluation be undertaken? How often?
- Periodic intervals
- Anchored time points
- Initial and final

Format: What is the most appropriate report structure for the assessment?
- Digests
- Narrative/executive summaries
- Statistical charts, diagrams

Reporting: At what levels and in what venues are assessment results to be reported?
- Internal
- External
- Areas/units affected
- Professional publications

Articulation: How can the evaluation serve the needs of the individual institution and those of the consortium?
- External review agencies
- Consortial partners
- Accreditation teams
- Public audience

librarians make purchase decisions based on what they know of the collections at nearby libraries, but have made no explicit agreement with librarians at those institutions. Because this type of CCD occurs without any expressed agreement between individuals or institutions, the level of accountability is low and evaluation may be discretionary. In the absence of any formal arrangements and lacking any defined project, documenting the day-to-day practice and volunteering periodic updates may serve as the checks-and-balances framework most appropriate to this brand of CCD.

CCD projects in which an explicit understanding or an informal oral agreement between selectors and institutions exists require periodic review. Many short-term or limited CCD projects fall into this category. For these less formal, less extensive projects, casual assessment strategies will work. These methods are less stringent and may even rely on anecdotal evidence, but they are no less effective if the chosen approach addresses the stated objectives of the CCD activity. In some instances, the project suggests the evaluation approach to use. For example, if CCD is being used to complete a single project, such as the acquisition of a multipart microfilm collection through shared purchases coordinated among a number of libraries, the appropriate method for evaluating the project is defined by the goals of the project. Progress is measured by the number of segments purchased over time and shared on an ongoing basis among the participating libraries. Success is achieved and the project completed when the consortium has acquired all segments. In another scenario, bibliographers at neighboring institutions may informally agree to divide collecting responsibility in certain areas and to avoid duplication of esoteric materials. As long as this remains an informal project operating under general guidelines, periodic check-in with counterparts and updates to supervisors by selectors may suffice as assessment methods.

Casual methods avoid the potential high costs and extensive staff time and expertise that more formal assessments require. Generally, in these ad hoc situations, each library continues to collect core materials and may simply forgo purchase of the materials covered by the informal agreement. Risk to each institution is therefore limited. Projects based on a predefined shopping list shared among participants fall into this category. A checklist of titles from a bibliography, a list of publishers, or subject classification ranges divided among counterparts all represent CCD projects in which the description of the project implies a de facto form of assessment. When division of collecting responsibility becomes part of a written CCD agreement, or other responsibilities are distributed among consortial partners, more detailed techniques should be used to assess compliance. Formal projects call for formal assessment methodologies.

FORMAL ASSESSMENT AND EVALUATION METHODS

Extensive, long-term CCD projects governed by written agreements and involving a number of participating libraries in close coordination require vigorous and systematic evaluation strategies. Typically, such formal assessment methods are data driven and require outcomes to be quantified as accurately and comprehensively as possible. Often, not all aspects of a large project can be accommodated by a single formula or accomplished in a single pass. In this situation, individual components can be isolated and evaluated on their own terms. A narrative report will describe how the various components all fit together and will serve as an overall qualitative assessment.

Statistical Measures

Libraries have long used measures of quantity, such as title counts, circulation statistics, ILL transactions, and dollar savings, to evaluate their activities.[3] For CCD projects, title counts and associated statistical measures have frequently served as the point of departure and subsequent yardstick for comparison purposes. Holdings data are assumed to signal collection strengths, allowing partner institutions to distribute responsibilities for filling gaps identified by such quantitative methods. Interim goals can be established and progress measured at specified intervals by recounting. The Boston Library Consortium employed various quantitative measures to define the goals of its Asian Business and Economics CCD agreement. The initial agreement setting out the 1996–1998 project indicated that success was be measured by four factors: titles purchased; total cost/average cost per book; unique titles [within the Consortium]; and average circulations per title.[4] Each of these input measures represents facets of collection development that are tracked routinely.

North American Title Count (NATC)

Because collection counting is central to many assessment methods, libraries have made a number of efforts to standardize this process and create a historical record to provide measurements over time. The North American Title Count (NATC) is the premier example of such an effort at the national and international levels.[5] The methodology used by the participants in this statistical assessment conducted every four years ensures that the extensive time and resources libraries invest will result in a high degree of interoperability and comparability of data. The statistics collected and correlated over the years comprise a rich database for relative benchmarking of collections. Moreover, the accuracy of the data is steadily increasing as more and more participants switch from manual to machine title counting. NATC data make it possible for libraries that divide collecting responsibilities based on subject classification to track progress and monitor compliance with long-term CCD target goals. For example, a consortium member library that has assumed responsibility for collecting French Canadian literature (LC classification PS 9001-9599) on behalf of the consortium could demonstrate fulfillment of its commitment by assessments showing that the number of titles purchased in this range as a percentage of the local collection has increased over time.

Conspectus Approach

In 1980, the Research Libraries Group created the RLG Conspectus to facilitate collection development and management in response to tight budgetary conditions and, subsequently, to evaluate library collections from a cooperative point of view.[6] The Western Library Network (WLN) further refined the RLG original and produced worksheets and software used by many libraries from the mid-1980s onward to survey and describe their collections. Although use of the Conspectus may have peaked in the mid to late 1990s, it remains a useful tool for collection assessment and is readily adaptable to CCD purposes.

The Conspectus approach accomplished two important tasks. First, it defined fixed areas of focus for comparative purposes based on Library of Congress (LC) classification ranges (LC/Dewey conversion charts were created later). This is similar to the approach taken by the NATC, which also bases its count on classification ranges. As with the NATC, this strategy ensures that all libraries using the Conspectus are measuring the same object. But the Conspectus goes a step farther by addressing issues related to how the collection under assessment came to be, how it is behaving in the present, and how it might change over time. The Conspectus was able to add these dimensions of analysis by establishing standardized descriptors to indicate how a particular library was performing in a particular LC classification range, and it tied those descriptors to defined numerical ratings.

Five levels of collecting intensity (ranging from 1, signifying minimal collecting activity, to 5, representing comprehensive responsibility) define each of the three categories of collecting commitment (current collection, acquisition commitment, and collection goal). These standards make it possible to triangulate a library's precise collecting behavior (past, present, and future) for a given classification range. By introducing more structure into the collection description process, the Conspectus brought libraries a step closer to a common language for assessing past, present, and future collection development plans. Armed with the Conspectus worksheets, collection managers could describe their collecting behaviors and intentions with a granularity and specificity that enabled collaboration as never before.

On the basis of the Conspectus assessment, consortial partners can select specific and well-defined slices of subject areas for attention and specify precisely the collecting intensity level for the CCD project. One library of a consortium may agree to take responsibility for collecting French Canadian literature at a higher-intensity goal level (GL) on behalf of other members. Those members can maintain the status quo of their current acquisitions commitment (AC) or perhaps downgrade it in favor of increasing the acquisitions commitment in another area on behalf of the consortium. With agreed-to definitions and a clear understanding of commitments in place from the beginning, tracking progress over time becomes systematic, results repeatable, and the assessment process sustainable.

In 1983, working with the Research Libraries Group, the Association for Research Libraries (ARL) began the North American Collections Inventory Project (NCIP) using RLG Conspectus data. The project's long-term goal was to develop an online North American inventory of research collections that could assist scholars in locating materials needed to support their scholarship. As a corollary result, the inventory was expected to enhance coordinated maintenance of these vital resources. In the early 1990s, the Western Library Network (WLN) developed Conspectus-derived PC software, the Collection Assessment and Analysis Services, that enables libraries to create or to maintain a local collection assessment database.

Commercial and Vendor Tools

Although the offerings are not extensive, a number of commercial or vendor-based software options are available for collection evaluation and comparison. Perhaps best known among these tools is OCLC's Automated Collection Assessment and Analysis Services (ACAS).[7] ACAS studies can address the age and content of a collection; compare the target collection to recommended lists, such as those based on *Books for College Libraries* or *Choice Outstanding Academic Titles;* and focus on format, academic level, or language. Among the types of automated reports ACAS can provide, a quantitative analysis and comparison of the collections of a consortium's libraries can address the particular needs of CCD assessment. ACAS allows the flexibility of linking results to Conspectus categories and levels or to other collection aspects, such as publication date, content level, format, and language. The downside of the ACAS solution is its cost, which can be a serious impediment to CCD needs. In many CCD projects, an initial assessment serves as a baseline, and a number of subsequent evaluations at specified intervals are needed to demonstrate progress toward the goal of the CCD activity. The costs of repeated ACAS studies can be considerable, and their value must be weighed against the other cost factors associated with the project.

Bowker, publisher of the print and electronic *Ulrich's Periodicals Directory,* offers a product for serials analysis, the Ulrich's Serials Analysis System (USAS).[8] Unlike OCLC's ACAS, USAS is focused solely on serials, but it can perform a number of useful analyses. One option is to compare the target library's serials subscriptions to a core collection or to the comprehensive list of active titles included in the Ulrich's database. As a subscription product, USAS can be used as often as participating libraries deem necessary without incurring additional costs with each use. This feature makes shorter-term projects attractive because assessment feedback is available at any point during the project.

Vendor-supplied reports can also be used effectively to monitor and evaluate CCD agreements. The advantage is that they can offer immediate feedback as well as provide short- and long-term collection management analysis. An example is YBP's GobiTween feature of its Gobi2 interactive ordering system.[9] This software enhancement allows selectors to use real-time feedback on monograph purchasing at partner institutions to build their local collection. The Books-Not-Bought In Ohio (NBIO) project, jointly undertaken by YBP and Ohio-LINK, demonstrates how such vendor services enable clients to pursue CCD projects.[10] The NBIO project is not the basis for setting up yet another approval plan, but it is used to coordinate the acquisition of retrospective titles by informing OhioLINK libraries which books have not been purchased through the various approval plans already in effect. As a result, collection developers can target the nonacquired titles and build broader holdings with more unique titles within the comprehensive OhioLINK collection. Periodic collection assessments are showing the availability of a higher number of unique titles within Ohio than would have been probable without the NBIO service.

QUALITATIVE AND MULTIFACTOR LOCAL APPROACHES

Although statistics-based approaches to collection assessment tend to predominate, they provide only one view of a complicated mosaic. Qualitative methods, though they are often more expensive and labor intensive, complement information provided by title counts, ILL transaction numbers, and the like. The title count in a particular LC class may give a general indication of the relative importance of that subject area to the holding library, but that raw number says little about the quality of the holdings. To address issues of quality, libraries rely on such assessment methods as checking holdings against standard bibliographies, hiring consultants with specialized subject expertise, or surveying the researchers and scholars who are experts in the particular discipline. A number of collection checklists were created in conjunction with the development of the Conspectus. Other tests of collection strength were developed independently.

These qualitative assessment tools are readily adaptable to the CCD environment. For example, short tests of collection strength can be applied to a single library's collection or to that of a collaborative. Applying a short test to the Information Alliance's French collection quickly reveals that a unified, consortial collection is qualitatively better than the independent collections of Information Alliance libraries. This should not come as a great surprise. Access to a broader range of resources expands as the responsibility for creating value through acquisition of these items is distributed across institutions.[11]

Collaborative CCD projects, though they generally appear to focus on collection building, have an impact on support and ancillary services. Areas like ILL, cataloging, and reference may not always participate directly in collaborative activities, but they often bear the burden of collection development initiatives. Chapter 8, focusing on the economics of CCD, identifies cost centers associated with implementing particular types of projects. With growing attention on the costs of services, quantifying the impact on support services as part of CCD assessment calls for a variety of approaches that consider not only the cost of an acquired item, but also the costs of technical processing, staff assignments, patron wait times, and similar factors.

Determining the underlying costs of complex information transactions has a long tradition in the library. For years, cost and time studies have been used to compute financial factors in ancillary areas, and economics of information analyses address these concerns in a theoretical manner. For example, a CCD project of distributed acquisition generally presumes some form of resource sharing. This arrangement puts pressure on the interlibrary loan operations of the partner libraries as books, journals, and other transportable resources are in constant transit. An assessment of CCD must include an acknowledgment of the cost-benefit impact of this arrangement. In this scenario, a resource, once a "private" good held by the local library, becomes a "public" good shared among many libraries. Economic efficiency will be calculated based not just on the value of the commodity to the holding institution, but on the potential benefit to the collective.

On the one hand, economic efficiency increases as the unit cost of an item decreases by being shared across an expanded number of users—the user population of the holding institution versus the combined user populations of the CCD consortium. On the other hand, the users who may now wait longer for delivery of materials not owned locally pay a price, possibly offsetting the savings accrued through economic efficiency. In the end, CCD managers may be compelled to decide at what point the benefits to the consortium population outweigh the needs of individual users of a single participating institution—economic efficiencies to the consortium versus costs to individual users. Finding the balance between these benefits and costs represents a major task of CCD assessment. Complex formulas underlie these calculations and may be beyond the requirements of all but the most stringent assessment needs. However, such issues must be factored into the design of CCD evaluation instruments that seek to be inclusive, comprehensive, and feasible.[12]

BALANCED SCORECARD

Efforts continue to identify and develop holistic collection assessment instruments. Recently, librarians have explored methods from the business world for possible application in the library arena. The balanced scorecard now being used by some innovative companies seeks an optimum combination of financial and operational factors on which to base decisions.[13] In a nutshell, the balanced scorecard integrates financial information about a company with so-called operational features, such as customer satisfaction, internal workflows, and innovation and product/services improvement efforts, all of which ultimately impact the financial performance of the company. The goal is to achieve a timely and accurate snapshot of the company as a whole, balancing financial performance with other factors, such as research and development costs.

In the library setting, the balanced scorecard approach takes an integrative look at collection management, assessment, and evaluation. Whereas the NATC or the Conspectus approach offers many details about collection strengths and weaknesses, these statistical techniques do not directly address other issues, such as the ancillary or indirect costs associated with CCD—staff time, storage and retrieval, user satisfaction, library funding, and the like. The balanced scorecard aims to use the quantitative and qualitative data that libraries already routinely collect to provide an overall assessment of the library's performance. How this is to be accomplished is the subject so far of only a limited number of projects. One such developmental effort involves three of the largest academic research libraries in Germany.[14] This project takes into consideration the unique status of libraries, which, unlike commercial ventures, do not choose the products and services they market, the customers they want to attract, or the sectors in which they compete. Instead, libraries are intermediaries with a mission not to maximize profits, but to offer the best service possible. The balanced scorecard focuses on four areas and their interrelationships to achieve a multidimensional, integrated view of the products and services provided by the library. These four areas are financing, clientele, work procedures, and ability to innovate or adapt to changing environments.[15]

For each of the four areas, strategic goals and performance measures are established consistent with the overall mission of the library. For libraries, the two most important stakeholders are the parent/ host institution, which allocates funding for the library, and the clientele to be served. To be considered successful, a library must fine-tune internal workflows and seek innovative ways of making the best use of the funding provided by the host institution. Through evaluation and assessment, the library must demonstrate that users are getting the highest level of service for the investment.

The balanced scorecard makes use of the quantitative and qualitative data that libraries have long collected, but now seeks to establish a cause-effect relationship between them as previous methods have not attempted to do.[16] For example, to set strategic goals and performance indicators, libraries begin by asking leading questions for the four key areas: users, funding, internal procedures, and innovation. Of paramount importance, libraries ask how they can best fulfill user expectations, the primary goal of the library. They ask how they can use funding most efficiently to meet that goal. They review internal procedures and seek to determine how workflow can best be organized to meet user expectations. Finally, they address the issue of adaptability to a changing information environment and consider ways to secure additional funding, redesign workflows, or improve the performance of staff. To define each of these areas, concrete data are assembled and analyzed—a process that gives the balanced scorecard its high value as a data-driven instrument that can potentially measure both quantity and quality.

Adapting the Balanced Scorecard to CCD

How the balanced scorecard approach can be adapted to CCD has not been thoroughly studied. Consequently, no body of literature exists to guide its implementation. Applying the principles and analysis processes of the balanced scorecard to a specific CCD project remains to be undertaken, but it appears attractive and feasible. To explore this possibility, the Working Group for Quantitative Evaluation of Cooperative Collection Development, established by CRL in conjunction with its initiative on collaborative collection development, reported at the 2002 Aberdeen Woods Conference on the intent to create a toolkit, a collection of targeted measures to use for the evaluation of CCD activities.[17] The team is working on defining performance measures and data points for assessing user satisfaction, financial commitments, and number of information resources. By combining performance measures in these areas, the team expects to be able to define outcomes more operationally and meaningfully. Success or failure of a CCD project will be based on the interaction of a variety of data, not just on input or output statistics.

How might some of the key concepts of the balanced scorecard be adapted to a CCD project? Consider the proposal by members of the Information Alliance to begin sharing audiovisual (AV) materials among the three partner institutions via interlibrary loan. Using the balanced scorecard approach to design and then to assess this project would require that the four components described earlier be integral parts of the overall plan. The assessment instrument would establish performance measures and identify data points to track ILL transactions specific to the sharing of AV materials. How do CCD partner libraries distribute the funding from their host institution to support the audiovisual collection before and after the decision to share audiovisual resources via ILL? Budget allocations and expenditures for audiovisual materials as well as AV-specific ILL transactions are data items that would be collected to plan and assess this project. At the same time, participating libraries would need to examine and possibly revise existing policies and procedures that govern the handling of AV materials. Staff time, transport costs, and replacement costs for lost materials are data items that can quantify the review of internal procedures.

The value to users of an expanded, though distributed, audiovisual collection would also require assessment. Aspects of this value can be quantified by determining the total cost of the collection before and after the implementation of the project. The impact on users—access to a wider universe of materials versus the wait time for delivery of needed resources—must also be determined. Often, this component is addressed by user satisfaction surveys or focus groups.

Elements of costs and benefits to users could be approximated by measuring expanded access versus shortened or lengthened wait times for titles not owned locally.

The implementation of a new approach and attitude to the handling of audiovisual materials would represent innovative thinking in this area of the collection because AV materials traditionally have been exempt from interlibrary loan. Such innovation would demonstrate that the participating libraries had examined the information environment and had responded in an innovative manner based on a changed set of forces—budgetary, philosophical, and practical. In the final analysis, to demonstrate success of this project, the balanced scorecard assessment would need to document the extent of aggregate collection use increase, unit cost decrease, and higher overall satisfaction of users within the consortium. Although the development of balanced scorecard–based measurements may take time, this integrative approach will provide a more complete, more accurate assessment of CCD activities—and do so in terms that can be more easily communicated to the public.

CONCLUSION

Evaluation and assessment of CCD projects are essential components of collaborative activities. CCD partners can ensure that reciprocal commitments are being met and that the project is achieving its stated goals only by periodic assessment using mutually accepted evaluation techniques. The scope of the activity will influence the formality or informality of the assessment approach, which in turn will determine the specific tools used. Ideally, the particular technique chosen will result in a balanced assessment that addresses library-centered and user-centered concerns.

There is an inherent danger, however, in reducing evaluation and assessment to efforts to determine a price tag for CCD projects, placing too much emphasis on the unit costs of CCD. The basic difficulty in evaluating CCD primarily from the cost perspective is that we are compelled to use tools that can quantify costs, but that cannot easily measure value. Costs are quantifiable, but value is harder to pin down. Value possesses a qualitative dimension that can arguably only be appreciated and approximated. In the end, the costing operations that seem to be gaining favor recently can account for much, but not all. Once again, the CCD whole is greater than the sum of the parts.

Libraries can add up prices and compute costs per transaction or other unit. But value is ultimately established by the user. That value is not intrinsic to the CCD project, but derives from the interchange between user and information resource. For this reason, we suggest that CCD has its costs; its value, however, lies beyond the bottom line.

NOTES

1. See, for example, Michael R. Gabriel, *Collection Development and Collection Evaluation: A Sourcebook* (Metuchen, NJ: Scarecrow, 1995); G. E. Gorman and Ruth H. Miller, eds., *Collection Management for the 21st Century: A Handbook for Librarians* (Westport, CT: Greenwood, 1997).

2. Blaine H. Hall, *Collection Assessment Manual for College and University Libraries* (Phoenix, AZ: Oryx, 1985); Subcommittee on Guidelines for Collection Development, Collection Management and Development Committee, Resources Section, Resources and Technical Services Division, *Guide to the Evaluation of Library Collections* (Chicago: American Library Association, 1989).

3. Gabriel, *Collection Development*, 77–137.

4. Soete, *Collaborative Collections Management Programs*, 30.

5. *North American Title Count: Titles Classified by Library of Congress and National Library of Medicine Classifications,* prepared for the Association for Library Collections and Technical Services, a division of the American Library Association, by the Library Research Center, the Graduate School of Library and Information Science (Urbana-Champaign, IL: University of Illinois, 2002). CD-ROM. Excerpts at http://www.ala.org/Content/NavigationMenu/ALCTS/Publications6/Catalog/Collection_Management1/2001_North_American_Title_Count.htm (accessed November 5, 2003).

6. Olson and Allen, *Cooperative Collection Management.* Many of the chapters in this survey work contain useful background information and suggestions, specifically the article by Sally Loken entitled "The WLN Conspectus," 31–42.

7. Information on the Automated Collection Assessment and Analysis Services is available at http://www.oclc.org/acas/ (accessed October 15, 2003).

8. Information on the Ulrich's Serials Analysis System is available at http://www.ulrichsweb.com/ulrichsweb/analysis/ (accessed October 15, 2003).

9. Information on GOBI2 and GobiTween is available at http://www.ybp.com/ (accessed October 15, 2003).

10. Gammon and Zeoli, "Practical Cooperative Collecting."

11. Howard D. White, *Brief Tests of Collection Strength: A Methodology for All Types of Libraries* (Westport, CT.: Greenwood, 1995). See specifically chapter 6, "Gains in Strength through a Consortium," 89–105, and chapter 7, "The French Literature Test," 107–20, including the actual brief test, 169–71.

12. Bruce R. Kingma, *The Economics of Information: A Guide to Economic and Cost-Benefit Analysis for Information Professionals* (Englewood, CO: Libraries Unlimited, 1996). See specifically chapter 12, "Resource Sharing," 153–62.

13. Robert S. Kaplan and David P. Norton, "The Balanced Scorecard—Measures That Drive Performance," *Harvard Business Review* 70, no. 1 (January–February 1992): 71–79; Robert S. Kaplan and David P. Norton, *The Balanced Scorecard: Translating Strategy into Action* (Boston: Harvard Business School Press, 1996).

14. Roswitha Poll, "Performance, Processes and Cost: Managing Service Quality with the Balanced Scorecard," *Library Trends* 49, no. 4 (Spring 2001): 709–17; Peter Hernon and Robert E. Dugan, *An Action Plan for Outcomes Assessment in Your Library* (Chicago: American Library Association, 2002): 68–69.

15. Klaus Ceynowa and André Coners, *Die Balanced Scorecard für wissenschaftliche Bibliotheken* (Frankfurt am Main: Vittorio Klostermann, 2002). See pp. 5–57 for general overview and basic concepts.

16. See "Standards for Libraries in Higher Education," *C&RL News* (May 2003): 329–36 for discussion of areas that libraries measure as part of standards assessment.

17. Bosch et al., "Working Group for Quantitative Evaluation."

CULTIVATION
Sustaining CCD
in the Local Library

Partners accomplish CCD goals through local library operations. The internal process for implementing CCD tasks complements the framework for an effective CCD partnership discussed in chapter 6. In preceding chapters, we explored principles, benefits, barriers, and varieties of CCD practice, describing many options for collaborative programs that enhance partner collections. At the core of CCD are the local library practitioners who must evaluate local conditions and establish with partners a framework for an effective collaboration program. This concluding chapter addresses the role of the local library in creating a work environment that nurtures CCD, sustaining the investments in documentation and legal agreements, financial commitment, outreach, and assessment covered in chapters 7–10.

Integrating CCD into work patterns of the home organization assures an internal process for achieving CCD goals. The local culture and interpersonal dynamics among librarians and support staff will have a much more profound impact on sustaining collaborative collection development than will bibliographic or economic conditions.[1] Because CCD as a function is relatively new or not yet present in most library organizational cultures, tasks required to implement projects may seem unnatural to staff, or at least unwelcome in an already heavy workload. Thus, developing and cultivating a culture of collaboration, both within the library and among the community of library constituents, should receive special attention from leaders.

PROVIDING PRO-ACTIVE LEADERSHIP

Building and sustaining a collaborative culture begins with the library leader. Leaders of the partner libraries should guide the general direction of the consortium or network, an organization that may focus beyond CCD collaboration alone. The library director or CEO can be a powerful advocate to colleagues and constituents about the benefits of all types of collaboration, including CCD. CCD initiatives, in particular, need a leader. In a small organization, the CCD leader may be the library director, but in a larger library, the director will delegate responsibility for CCD to a colleague, such as the head of collection development, reference, or library outreach. In a smaller environment, the library director will be the champion of all collaboration and may enlist the board of directors or other opinion leaders to gain recognition and support for investing in partnerships. Planning similar to that discussed in chapter 6 applies to the home library: leaders should help local colleagues select projects of local value that are compatible with the general directions of the consortium and its CCD program.

Winning the acceptance of home library personnel requires sustained attention of the leader. Both subtle and direct approaches can achieve internal sanction. Involve local librarians and staff in the network at the outset, so that they and their counterparts can brainstorm about relative merits of various options and develop projects together. Mention the collaboration often to library staff members and to the library board of directors, campus administrators, or company CEO. Incorporate small routines for checking partner library catalogs into existing local practices for determining ownership to encourage a sense of joint ownership of the collections. Consider sharing with partner libraries the results of data compilation about the local collection. New developments in library organizational structure and issues of high local interest will affect collection practices and may be of interest to other members of the network. The CCD leader should continually demonstrate that collaboration is a high organizational priority. Ultimately, genuine commitment to CCD from the local librarians and staff will reflect the energy and enthusiasm of a leader invested in CCD.

DEMONSTRATING ORGANIZATIONAL COMMITMENT

Perhaps the most tangible way of demonstrating a high priority for CCD in the local organization is to allocate resources to CCD tasks. Chapter 8 covers ways to recognize costs and allocate resources to CCD. By calling attention to the use of collection funds or other resources to support CCD projects, the library leadership makes a statement about the value of CCD in the organization. Planning discussions about allocation of library resources present an opportunity to earmark specific funds for purchasing materials or dedicating staff time to CCD projects. In this way, CCD becomes a visible priority. Figure 11-1 offers several ideas for allocating organizational resources to CCD.

If the benefits of CCD can be recognized most clearly in the context of local limitations, another way to demonstrate support for CCD is to depend on a partner library to lead a project.[2] Perhaps a partner librarian will agree to serve as principal investigator for a grant proposal. In consultation with other members of the consortium, this librarian will write the proposal and, when it is funded, be

---

FIGURE 11-1 *Resource Allocations That Demonstrate CCD Support*

- *Identify CCD liaison positions.* These may be the director, collection development or reference librarians, or systems personnel. Their time commitment represents organizational support for CCD.

- *Accept responsibility for some aspect of the partnership.* For example, if centralized billing is required to purchase subscriptions, one library can provide the staff resources to accomplish this task.

- *Allocate a specific amount of collection money to fill gaps identified through collection studies.*

- *Purchase software that will create a union catalog of the consortium.*

- *Designate funds to pay membership fees.* These payments are distinct financial commitments to CCD.

responsible for budget management, liaison with the funding agent, and preparation of the final report. When a group of libraries decides to compare use statistics from a journal aggregator to reduce overlap, one librarian skilled in statistical analysis or spreadsheet creation may synthesize the collective data, contributing valuable expertise and time to the partnership. These examples illustrate local benefits of membership in a CCD enterprise that pools its human resources for the benefit of the entire group. Each library in the group is expected to contribute something, and resources on even the smallest scale are valuable. Such cooperation makes a vivid impact on internal organizational dynamics.

ORGANIZING THE LOCAL LIBRARY FOR COOPERATION

The prospects for accomplishing CCD goals are best when tasks that support CCD can be integrated with existing routines. Once the internal planning process has identified CCD initiatives, responsibility for performing the tasks necessary to achieve goals should be incorporated into staff job descriptions. Figure 11-2 lists several local tasks that support CCD.

The library's CCD leader should see that appropriate tasks are assimilated into staff responsibilities, personal goals, and timetables. If a CCD project requires counterparts to work collaboratively, personal goals might include getting acquainted, developing specific actions to be taken, and creating a timeline to complete a project. If one staff member usually handles bibliographic searching and verification for library acquisitions, CCD-related searching could be assigned to this person. A staff member who organizes collection management projects, such as retention review, may be well-suited to develop processes for a CCD project that draws on many of the same procedures used for internal collection management.

Figure 11-2 presents many types of collaborative activities in which staff might engage; it is likely, however, that a single institution would work on only a few of these at a time. In making commitments to pursue CCD projects, a challenge for each local institution is to incorporate new tasks into existing routines. The Information Alliance Serials Archive mentioned in previous chapters is an example. Librarians and staff are pursuing a goal to create a shared collection of journal backfiles. One library agrees to serve as library of record and

FIGURE 11-2	*CCD Tasks Managed Locally*

▉ Conduct bibliographic verification.

▉ Host CCD training.

▉ Compile and report user demographics.

▉ Compile and report collection use statistics.

▉ Compile and report electronic resource use statistics.

▉ Create processes for activities, such as monitoring purchases over $500 and notifying partners.

▉ Compile spreadsheets for shared access.

▉ Arrange travel and accommodations for meetings with partners.

▉ Devise project scope, implementation plans, communications processes, and evaluation methods for an individual project, such as creating a shared electronic archive of local publications.

▉ Develop policy.

▉ Catalog a shared backlog.

▉ Report space constraints or availability of space.

▉ Organize the work of a shared subject specialist or other CCD-related position.

▉ Create processes to make collaborative decisions for locating low-use materials in storage collections.

retain journal volumes so that the other libraries can discard their holdings if they wish. Tasks include compiling lists of journal titles that are candidates for the serials archive, verifying that physical holdings match those listed in the catalog, verifying holdings among the partner libraries, sharing spreadsheets with bibliographic information, developing local criteria for retention decisions, and consulting Information Alliance counterparts for library of record decisions.

Heads of collection development are the project leaders for the serials archive. They solicited help from colleagues in the local organization and assigned work to staff in their immediate work group. Librarians developed goals for the project as well as criteria for retention review. Because criteria for retention review apply to the entire local collection, the process of recommending content for the serials archive draws on existing procedures. Support staff identified journal titles for potential withdrawal from the local library. Student assistants and clerical staff collected journal holdings information from respective library catalogs and entered data onto spreadsheets that are accessible through library internal networks and shared among counterparts. Librarians and counterparts at the partner institutions use the information to decide which titles should receive library of record status so that other libraries may withdraw them. Among the candidates for withdrawal are titles included in the JSTOR collection to which all Information Alliance members subscribe. JSTOR is an archive of prominent scholarly journal backfiles available on a subscription basis. As of September 2003, the growing collection contained 322 journal titles.[3] Heads of collection development review project goals with subject librarians and bibliographers during each step of the process. As librarians make recommendations about retention and library of record commitments, the information is recorded on shared spreadsheets.

The time spent by the heads of collection development to implement and sustain the serials archive figures in their personal CCD goals. Librarians and support staff spend approximately 30 percent more time beyond routine retention review and clerical tasks to incorporate the serials archive into their workflow. Technical services staff enter local notes in the catalog for the library of record, so that titles will not inadvertently be discarded in the future. Because this work is not time-sensitive, and because decisions trickle through as counterparts have an opportunity to review lists together, catalog entry can be done as time permits. As the work progresses, the heads of collection development must continually assess progress and adapt goals to accommodate changing environments, all in the context of creating additional storage space through collaboration. Leaders manage the tasks required to create and sustain the Information Alliance Serials Archive by following existing procedures where possible and by adding personnel resources specifically dedicated to the CCD project.

REEVALUATING POLICIES TO PROMOTE THE PARTNERSHIP

Tasks may be substantially different when the goal is to develop policy. Drawing again on the experience of the Information Alliance, the following example involves subject area counterparts who wished to strengthen the Information Alliance shared collection of materials that support research in women's studies. Because considerable content for research and instruction is contained on videotapes not held by any of the partner libraries, the counterparts wanted to devise a program of collaborative acquisitions in which the shared collection would be accessible to all users. Although interlibrary loan policies have improved access for researchers through expedited delivery, audiovisual formats traditionally have been excluded from interlibrary loan. Thus, appropriate local librarians needed to examine policies that seemed to put the needs of local clientele and Information Alliance users in competition with one another.

Could a special agreement for Information Alliance users be developed among the interlibrary loan and audiovisual units in the partner libraries to offer benefits for all users of the libraries? Interlibrary loan leaders consulted local stakeholders about ways that existing policy could be adapted to permit sharing of audiovisual materials. The resulting policy recognizes the fragility of videotape as well as local use patterns in which users expect audiovisual materials to be available on a reserve basis—always on the shelf unless in use within the library. Extending access to the Information Alliance libraries presents increased risk to local collections. However, it also offers access to a much larger and deeper collection than could be offered by any of the individual libraries. The time spent by librarians and support staff to update this policy promises to be a one-time investment that will support future CCD initiatives. A revised policy for audiovisual loans among Information Alliance partners will provide a foundation for many other CCD projects as diverse as collecting musical scores or highly specialized area studies content in multiple formats. A restructured policy that reduces the loan period, relies on the expedited courier service for delivery, and assesses materials damage and user satisfaction will serve all Information Alliance clientele, local and distant. This example illustrates the necessity for and value of using staff time to create CCD-friendly policy at the local library level.

UPGRADING LOCAL CATALOGS
TO IMPROVE PRODUCTIVITY

The local library catalog and access to catalogs of consortium members are critical to sustaining CCD projects. Although periodicals holdings information is sometimes not accessible through the public catalog, local library staff rely on the accuracy, comprehensiveness, and speed of partner and local catalogs to conduct their CCD tasks. To the extent that library catalogs are compatible with one another and available to all the participants, less time is needed to track down holdings. Some libraries have, for decades, included the holdings of other libraries in a shared catalog. Local catalog upgrades, such as streamlined searching features, have tremendous benefit for CCD while they also meet the needs of local users. The investment of library systems and technical services staff time in online catalog development improves CCD productivity and promotes overall job satisfaction for anyone who conducts cross-catalog searching. This indirect organizational bonus for collaboration promotes timely completion of CCD tasks and serves as an incentive for new CCD ventures. By encouraging and funding upgrades to its library catalog, an organization strengthens its support for CCD.

ASSESSING PROGRESS

Rapid change within local institutions, as well as in the partnership, demands continuing assessment, including the review of tasks related to CCD. The library process for monitoring goals should incorporate appraisal of CCD-related activities, from confirmation of progress on projects to review of cost-benefit indicators. Assessment of progress and purpose should be conducted both locally and within the partnership on at least an annual basis. Keep assessment activities as simple as possible so they do not interfere with the completion of CCD tasks. Allow plenty of room for ambiguity, and give benefit of doubt to initial slow progress that may leap forward once procedures are developed and false starts abandoned. When considering the best way to conclude a project, consider the investment to date and, if necessary, adjust the goals or schedule to improve the cost-benefit relationship. Use timetables and target dates liberally once project implementation has begun. The initial phases may focus on simply bringing people together to brainstorm; once goals are set, however, monitor progress carefully and document results from the participants. If you are the CCD leader, be sure to leave yourself time and energy to coach, assess, and promote by delegating tasks to colleagues and support staff.

Because CCD can stimulate and promote progress in areas of local interest, initial assessment projects of specific collection areas may inspire staff to review the local collection and to become familiar with the resources of the entire consortium. The results of collection assessment can become the basis for a CCD plan. Chapter 10 discusses techniques for creating and using evaluation tools.

INVESTING IN TRAINING

Until CCD becomes more routine in library internal operations, allocating resources to training provides formal occasions for staff to codify practices and understand the context for CCD tasks. CCD training and promotion are complementary because a well-conceived training program solidifies staff commitment through understanding. As staff members develop new processes, training ensures that all who participate understand routines and their purpose. Whenever possible, explain the reason for doing a task. To eliminate confusion and redundant effort, verify frequently with the stakeholders that a process is being implemented correctly. As tasks unfold, think about strategies to sustain ongoing projects, and formulate a process for future communication about the tasks. Get it in writing. The developmental process includes planning for future productivity. Because tasks can be complex, time devoted to training will help to reinforce instructions and to avoid mistakes. Some aspects of training will apply only to local practice, although opportunities for counterparts to participate in training across the consortium offer the added benefit of increasing counterpart contact.

CCD training can be formal or informal, task-oriented or visionary, depending on the needs of the participants. The CCD leader should create opportunities to discuss general directions and progress of the program, involving colleagues and support staff in making choices about priorities and areas of emphasis. To share procedures, staff can document processes and train one another. Staff from one library may provide training to representatives from the partner libraries. When launching a major new direction, the network may elect to hire an outside trainer with expertise not available among the partners. Or, an outsider may present a potentially controversial issue from an impartial distance. Training for subject librarians and bibliographers can incorporate both general and specific CCD issues. A logical goal for new participants is to become acquainted with counterparts in the network. Besides covering procedural matters, training should affirm that CCD is a high priority for the organization, with the expectation that personal goals will include CCD tasks.

ILLUSTRATING BENEFITS THROUGH OUTREACH

A university vice president recently quipped that perception is reality. A positive spin on CCD progress enhances the perception of its value in the local organization and thus helps to sustain CCD benefits. Opportunities abound for publicizing CCD achievements. Chapter 9 describes a systematic approach to promoting CCD within the organization and publicizing results to the public. Considering the energy required to launch a CCD program, outreach can easily be neglected. However, time spent on demonstrating appreciation for staff accomplishments and illustrating benefits is a sparkling opportunity to illuminate CCD at the local level. Set some easy targets for timing and content. Figure 11-3 offers a few simple ways to celebrate CCD; combine these with the tools of the trade for publicity listed in figure 9-2. As the leader of CCD initiatives, or as the supervisor of a

---

FIGURE 11-3 *Outreach: Sustaining CCD through Celebration*

- If your library has an electronic bulletin board, post a message when you begin work on a CCD project. If the project has already started, post a progress report.

- Include a section about CCD initiatives in the library annual report.

- Announce specific benefits from CCD activities as they occur. For example, when you begin a new subscription at discounted rates offered to the consortium, write a brief press release for the local newspaper or newsletter.

- Celebrate staff accomplishment of CCD goals. Write a note to a supervisor observing the completion of a spreadsheet or a policy revision. Send a thank-you letter to the staff member who accomplished the task.

- Show your superior written documentation as it is created to support CCD. That person will be impressed and may have the opportunity to pass it along to her or his superior.

- Write short project updates for library and other organization literature.

- Write research reports for scholarly publication and presentation at conferences.

- Notify the person in charge of fund-raising at your institution about CCD projects. The collaborative angle might capture the imagination of a donor who may decide to support CCD.

leader, acknowledge the power of marketing. Devote energy to public relations. The effort will likely generate more goodwill and support than any other CCD task you tackle.

CONCLUSION

Nearly every library belongs to one or more networks. Library users are no longer constrained by the resources of their local collection. Local libraries are now windows on the world for their users, nodes in the global network.[4] Today's wired environment encourages CCD programs. Library leaders who incorporate CCD tasks into the functional structure of their organizations will be well positioned to increase the scope and depth of collections available to their library users.

This chapter explored ways to establish CCD in the local organization. To expand local support for CCD programs, mention them frequently. Include CCD in library and staff goals. Communicate your expectations for CCD progress through training and assessment. Depend on your partners to accomplish some CCD tasks, and publicize the benefits to the local community. Publicize your investments in the partnership. Celebrate CCD achievements. One of the greatest satisfactions a CCD leader can experience is to guide the organization toward embracing the values of cooperation. An organization that views collaboration positively has an excellent chance of reaping benefits for its users. Local organizations effectively performing CCD tasks may be the most important of all the components in developing a CCD program. Your goal is to sustain CCD commitment in a constantly changing environment.

NOTES

1. Ross Atkinson, "Crisis and Opportunity: Reevaluating Acquisitions Budgeting in an Age of Transition," in *Declining Acquisitions Budgets: Allocation, Collection Development, and Impact Communication,* ed. Sul Lee, 53 (New York: Haworth, 1993).

2. Darlene E. Weingand, *Administration of the Small Public Library* (Chicago: American Library Association, 2001), 173.

3. JSTOR http://www.jstor.org/ (accessed September 2003).

4. Weingand, *Administration,* 185.

Allen, Barbara McFadden. "Consortia and Collections: Achieving a Balance between Local Action and Collaborative Interest." *Journal of Library Administration* 28, no. 4 (1999): 85–90.

———. "Theoretical Value of Conspectus-based (Cooperative) Collection Management." *Collection Building* 13, no. 2/3 (1993–95): 7–12.

Allen, Barbara McFadden, and Arnold Hirshon. "Hanging Together to Avoid Hanging Separately: Opportunities for Academic Libraries and Consortia." *Information Technology and Libraries* 17, no. 1 (March 1998): 36–45.

Association for Library Collections and Technical Services. "2001 North American Title Count." http://www.ala.org/Content/NavigationMenu /ALCTS/Publications6/Catalog/Collection_Management1/ 2001_North_American_Title_Count.htm (accessed October 16, 2003).

Association of Research Libraries. "AAU/ARL Global Resources Network." http://www.arl.org/collect/grp/grp.html (accessed April 5, 2004).

———. "Issues in Scholarly Communication: Open Access." http://www .arl.org/scomm/open_access/index.html (accessed May 14, 2003).

Atkinson, Hugh C. "Atkinson on Networks." *American Libraries* 18, no. 6 (June 1987): 431–39.

———. "Resource Sharing." In *Collection Management in Public Libraries: Proceedings of a Preconference to the 1984 ALA Annual Conference, June 21–22, 1984, Dallas, Texas,* edited by Judith Serebnick, 38–48. Chicago: American Library Association, 1986.

Atkinson, Ross. "Access, Ownership, and the Future of Collection Development." In *Collection Management and Development: Issues in an Electronic Era. Proceedings of the Advanced Collection Management and Development*

Institute, Chicago, Illinois, March 26–28, 1993, edited by Peggy Johnson and Bonnie MacEwan, 92–109. Chicago: American Library Association, 1994.

———. "Crisis and Opportunity: Reevaluating Acquisitions Budgeting in an Age of Transition." In *Declining Acquisitions Budgets: Allocation, Collection Development, and Impact Communication,* edited by Sul Lee, 33–55. New York: Haworth, 1993.

———. "Old Forms, New Forms: The Challenge of Collection Development." *College and Research Libraries* 50, no. 5 (September 1989): 507–20.

———. "Preservation and Collection Development: Toward a Political Synthesis." *Journal of Academic Librarianship* 16, no. 2 (May 1990): 98–103.

———. "Rationality and Realpolitik: Prospects for Cooperative Collection Development in an Increasingly Networked Environment." In *Scholarship in the New Information Environment: Proceedings from an RLG Symposium Held May 1–3, 1995, at Harvard University,* edited by Carol Hughes, 25–31. Mountain View, CA: Research Libraries Group, 1996.

Baird, Lynn. "Idaho Union List of Serials: Old Dream, New Tool." *PNLA Quarterly* 53, no. 3 (Spring 1989): 18–19.

Baker, Shirley K. "The Future of Resource Sharing: Introduction." *Journal of Library Administration* 21, no. 1/2 (1995): 1–3.

Ballard, Tom. "Public Library Networking: Neat, Plausible, Wrong." *Library Journal* 107, no. 1 (April 1982): 679–83.

Battin, Patricia. "Research Libraries in the Network Environment: The Case of Cooperation." *Journal of Academic Librarianship* 6, no. 2 (June 1980): 68–73.

Billings, Harold. "Shared Collection Building: Constructing the 21st Century Relational Research Library." *Journal of Library Administration* 31, no. 2 (2000): 3–14.

Bosch, Steve, et al. "Report from the Center for Research Libraries/ Greater Western Library Alliance Working Group for Quantitative Evaluation of Cooperative Collection Development Projects." Paper presented at the New Dynamics and Economics of Cooperative Collection Development Conference Hosted by the Center for Research Libraries at the Aberdeen Woods Conference Center, Atlanta, GA, November 8–10, 2002. http://www.crl.edu/awcc2002/Quant.%20Evaluation%20WG%20Report.pdf (accessed October 16, 2003).

Bostick, Sharon L. "The History and Development of Academic Library Consortia in the United States: An Overview." *Journal of Academic Librarianship* 27, no. 1 (March 2001): 128–30.

Branin, Joseph J. "Cooperative Collection Development." In *Collection Management: A New Treatise*, edited by Charles B. Osburn and Ross Atkinson. Foundations in Library and Information Science, vol. 26, Part A, 81–110. Greenwich, CT: JAI, 1991.

———. "Shifting Boundaries: Managing Research Library Collections at the Beginning of the Twenty-first Century." *Collection Management* 23, no. 4 (1998): 1–17.

Branin, Joseph, Frances Groen, and Suzanne Thorin. "The Changing Nature of Collection Management in Research Libraries." *Library Resources and Technical Services* 44, no. 1 (January 2000): 23–32.

Bridegam, Willis E. "A Collaborative Approach to Collection Storage: The Five-College Library Depository." 2001. http://www.clir.org/pubs/reports/pub97/contents.html. (accessed October 16, 2003).

Bril, Patricia L. "Cooperative Collection Development: Progress from Apotheosis to Reality." In *Collection Management in Academic Libraries*, edited by Clare Jenkins and Mary Morley, 235–58. Brookfield, VT: Gower, 1999.

Brown, Doris Rahe. "Cooperative Collection Development: The Illinois Experience." In *Collection Management for the 1990s: Proceedings of the Midwest Collection Management and Development Institute, University of Illinois at Chicago, August 17–20, 1989*, edited by Joseph J. Branin, 145–46. Chicago: American Library Association, 1993.

Brownson, Charles W. "Modeling Library Materials Expenditure: Initial Experiments at Arizona State University." *Library Resources and Technical Services* 35 (January 1991): 87–103.

Buckland, Michael. *Redesigning Library Services: A Manifesto.* Chicago: American Library Association, 1992.

Budd, John M., and Bart M. Harloe. "Collection Development and Scholarly Communication in the 21st Century: From Collection Management to Content Management." In *Collection Management for the 21st Century: A Handbook for Librarians*, edited by G. E. Gorman and Ruth H. Miller, 3–25. Westport, CT and London: Greenwood, 1997.

Burgett, James, John Haar, and Linda Phillips. "The Persistence of Print in a Digital World: Three ARL Libraries Confront an Enduring Issue." In *Crossing the Divide: Proceedings of the Tenth National Conference of the Association of College and Research Libraries, March 15–18, 2001, Denver, Colorado,* edited by Hugh A. Thompson, 75–80. Chicago: Association of College and Research Libraries, 2001.

Bush, Carmel, William A. Garrison, George Machovec, and Helen I. Reed. "Prospector: A Multivendor, Multitype, and Multistate Western Union Catalog." *Information Technology and Libraries* 19, no. 2 (June 2000): 71–83.

Butler, Meredith A., Karen R. Hitchcock, Clifford Lynch, Timothy Ingoldsby, Colin Day, and Malcolm Getz. "Part X: The Economics of Information and the Need for Collaboration—Creating a Research Agenda." *Journal of Library Administration* 26 (1998): 271–96.

Byrd, Jacqueline. "A Cooperative Cataloging Proposal for Slavic and East European Languages and the Languages of the Former Soviet Union." *Cataloging and Classification Quarterly* 17, no. 1/2 (1993): 87–96.

Carpenter, Kathryn Hammell. "Competition, Collaboration, and Cost in the New Knowledge Environment." *Collection Management* 21, no. 2 (1996): 31–46.

Case, Mary, and Deborah Jakubs. "Building the Global Collection—World Class Collection Development: A Chronicle of the AAU/ARL Global Resources Program." *Journal of Library Administration* 28, no. 1 (1999): 63–80.

Center for Research Libraries. "Creating New Strategies for Cooperative Collection Development, November 12–14, 1999, Aberdeen Woods Conference Center, Atlanta, Georgia." http://www.crl.edu/awcc2002 /99confinfo.htm (accessed October 16, 2003).

———. "The New Dynamics and Economics of Cooperative Collection Development." A Triennial Conference Hosted by the Center for Research Libraries, Atlanta, GA, November 8–10, 2002. Papers available at http://www.crl.edu/content.asp?l1=2&l2=48&l3=94&l4=41 (accessed October 16, 2003). To be published in forthcoming issues of *Collection Management.*

Chapman, Elizabeth. "Buying Shares in Libraries: The Economics of Cooperative Collection Development." *IFLA Journal* 24, no. 2 (March 1998): 102–6.

Claus-Smith, Diane. "Starting Small, Dreaming Big: The OSLIS Project Brings Resources Statewide." *Multimedia Schools* 6, no. 5 (November–December 1999): 28–31.

Cochenour, Donnice, and Joel S. Rutstein. "A CARL Model for Cooperative Collection Development in a Regional Consortium." *Collection Building* 12, no. 1/2 (1993): 37–38.

Crowe, William J., and Nancy P. Sanders. "Collection Development in the Cooperative Environment." *Journal of Library Administration* 15, no. 3/4 (1991): 37–48.

Cummings, Martin M. "Cost Analysis: Methods and Realities." *Library Administration and Management* 3, no. 4 (Fall 1989): 181–83.

Curl, Margo Warner. "Collection Assessment of the CONSORT Collections." *Against the Grain* 14, no. 6 (December 2002–January 2003): 53–57.

———. "Cooperative Collection Development in Consortium of College Libraries: The CONSORT Experience." *Against the Grain* 14, no. 6 (December 2002–January 2003): 52–53.

Dannelly, Gay N. "Coordinating Cooperative Collection Development: A National Perspective—the LAPT Report." *Library Acquisitions: Practice and Theory* 9, no. 4 (1985): 307–15.

Deal, Carl W. "A Model Criterion for a Statewide Plan/Process/System." In *Coordinating Cooperative Collection Development: A National Perspective,* edited by Wilson Luquire, 215–32. New York: Haworth, 1986.

Delanoy, Diana D., and Carlos A. Cuadra. *Directory of Academic Library Consortia.* Santa Monica, CA: System Development Corporation, 1972.

De Sáez, Eileen Elliott. *Marketing Concepts for Libraries and Information Services.* London: Library Association Publishing, 1993.

Diedrichs, Carol Pitts. "Designing and Implementing a Consortial Approval Plan: The OhioLINK Experience." *Collection Management* 24 (2000): 18–20.

Distad, Merrill. "Cooperative Collection Development and Resource Sharing in Alberta." *PNLA Quarterly* 53, no. 3 (Spring 1989): 17–18.

Dominguez, Patricia Buck, and Luke Swindler. "Cooperative Collection Development at the Research Triangle University Libraries: A Model for the Nation." *College and Research Libraries* 54, no. 6 (November 1993): 470–96.

Dorst, Thomas J. "Cooperative Collection Management at the Crossroads: Is There a New Social Paradigm for Resources Sharing?" *Illinois Libraries* 76, no. 2 (Spring 1994): 97–100.

———. "Employing Collection Management as an Institutional Change Agent." In *Cooperative Collection Management: The Conspectus Approach,* edited by Georgine N. Olson and Barbara McFadden Allen, 91–96. New York: Neal-Schuman, 1994.

Dougherty, Richard M. "A Conceptual Framework for Organizing Resource Sharing and Shared Collection Development Programs." *Journal of Academic Librarianship* 14, no. 5 (November 1988): 287–91.

————. "Library Cooperation: A Case of Hanging Together or Hanging Separately." *Catholic Library World* 46, no. 8 (March 1975): 324–27.

————. "Resource Sharing among Research Libraries: How It Ought to Work." *Collection Management* 9, no. 2/3 (Summer/Fall 1987): 79–88.

Dowd, Sheila T. "Library Cooperation: Methods, Models, to Aid Information Access." *Journal of Library Administration* 12, no. 3 (1990): 63–81.

Dowler, Lawrence. "The Research University's Dilemma: Resource Sharing and Research in a Transinstitutional Environment." *Journal of Library Administration* 21, no. 1/2 (1995): 5–26.

Dunn, John A., Jr., and Murray S. Martin. "The Whole Cost of Libraries." *Library Trends* 42, no. 3 (Winter 1994): 564–78.

Dwyer, Jim. "Consortial Review and Purchase of Networked Resource: The California State University Experience." *The Bottom Line* 12, no. 1 (1999): 5–11.

Dykhuis, Randy W. "OhioLINK: Vision, Money, and Technology." *Computers in Libraries* 15, no. 2 (February 1995): 16–21.

Eaton, Nancy L. "Resource Sharing: The Public University Library's Imperative." *Journal of Library Administration* 21, no. 1/2 (1995): 27–39.

Edwards, Heather M. "South Africa's GAELIC: The Gauteng and Environs Library Consortium." *Information Technology and Libraries* 18, no. 3 (September 1999): 123–28.

Erbes, Bill. "If CCD Is Good, CCCD Is Better: The IVLS Approach." *Illinois Libraries* 71, no. 1 (January 1989): 18–20.

Evans, G. Edward (with the assistance of Margaret R. Zarnosky). "Cooperative Collection Development and Resource Sharing." In *Developing Library and Information Center Collections*. 4th ed., 454–87. Englewood, CO: Libraries Unlimited, 2000.

Farrell, David. "The NCIP Option for Coordinated Collection Management." *Library Resources and Technical Services* 30, no. 1 (March 1986): 47–56.

Farrell, David, and Jutta Reed-Scott. "The North American Collections Inventory Project: Implications for the Future of Coordinated Management of Research Collections." *Library Resources and Technical Services* 33, no. 1 (January 1989): 15–28.

Feller, Judith M. "Assessing 'Readiness for Resource Sharing' in an Academic Library." *Collection Building* 6, no. 1 (Spring 1984): 3–9.

Fiels, Keith Michael. "Coordinated Collection Development in a Multitype Environment: Promise and Challenge." *Collection Building* 7, no. 2 (Summer 1985): 26–31.

Fiels, Keith Michael, and Margie Epple, eds. *Multitype Library Coopera-tion: An Annotated Guide to Working Documents.* Chicago: American Li-brary Association, 1988.

Filstrup, Christian E., Jordan M. Scepanski, and Tony K. Stewart. "An Experiment in Cooperative Collection Development: South Asia Vernaculars among the Research Triangle Universities." *Collection Management* 24, no. 1/2 (2000): 93–104.

Fink, Norman A., and Richard Boivin. "MultiLIS Book Exchange Pro-cess: A 'Shuttle' Approach to Collection Development." *Library Hi Tech* 6, no. 2 (1988): 63–70.

Foote, Brenda J. "Process to Promise: The CCM Plan." In *Cooperative Collec-tion Management: The Conspectus Approach,* edited by Georgine N. Olson and Barbara McFadden Allen, 101–3. New York: Neal-Schuman, 1994.

Forcier, Peggy. "Building Collections Together: The Pacific Northwest Conspectus." *Library Journal* 113, no. 7 (15 April 1988): 43–45.

Franklin, Brinley. "The Cost of Quality—Its Application to Libraries." *Journal of Library Administration* 20, no. 2 (1994): 67–79.

Gabriel, Michael R. *Collection Development and Collection Evaluation: A Sourcebook.* Metuchen, NJ: Scarecrow, 1995.

Gammon, Julia A., and Michael Zeoli. "Practical Cooperative Collecting for Consortia: Books-Not-Bought in Ohio." Presented at the New Dynam-ics and Economics of Cooperative Collection Development Conference Hosted by the Center for Research Libraries at the Aberdeen Woods Conference Center, Atlanta, GA, November 8–10, 2002. http://www.crl .edu/awcc2002/GammonZeoliPaper.pdf (accessed October 16, 2003).

George, Lee Anne, and Julia Blixrud, comps. *Celebrating Seventy Years of the Association of Research Libraries, 1932–2002.* Washington, DC: Asso-ciation of Research Libraries, 2002.

Gerstein, Christine Wondolowski. "Liaison with Teaching Faculty: Effec-tive Strategies for Collaborative Collection Development." *Public and Access Services Quarterly* 1, no. 4 (1995): 85–90.

Getz, Malcolm. "Resource Sharing and Prices." *Journal of Library Admin-istration* 21 (1995): 77–108.

Gherman, Paul M. "Vision and Reality: The Research Libraries and Net-working." *Journal of Library Administration* 8, no. 3/4 (Fall–Winter 1987): 51–57.

Go, Fe Susan. "Is Cooperative Cataloging Realistic? Thoughts of a South-east Asian Bibliographer." *Cataloging and Classification Quarterly* 17, no. 1/2 (1993): 169–79.

Goodman, Naomi J., and Carole J. Hinchcliff. "From Crisis to Cooperation and Beyond: OhioLINK's First Ten Years." *Resource Sharing and Information Networks* 13, no. 1 (1997): 21–38.

Gorman, G. E., and Ruth H. Miller, eds. *Collection Management for the 21st Century: A Handbook for Librarians.* Westport, CT: Greenwood, 1997.

Grimes, David. "Assessing Assessment: A Researcher's Evaluation of 'Conspectus.'" *Catholic Library World* 60, no. 6 (May–June 1989): 259–75.

Grover, Mark L. "Cooperative Cataloging of Latin-American Books: The Unfulfilled Promise." *Library Resources and Technical Services* 35, no. 4 (October 1991): 406–15.

Gwinn, Nancy E., and Paul H. Mosher. "Coordinating Collection Development: The RLG Conspectus." *College and Research Libraries* 44, no. 3 (March 1983): 128–40.

Haar, John. "Cooperative Collection Development Survey Responses." Center for Research Libraries. "Creating New Strategies for Cooperative Collection Development." Follow-Up Working Groups from the AWCC 1999 Conference. http://www.crl.edu/awcc2002/ccdsurveyresults.htm (accessed October 16, 2003).

———. "Report of Working Group to Map Current Cooperative Collection Development Projects." Presented at the New Dynamics and Economics of Cooperative Collection Development Conference Hosted by the Center for Research Libraries at the Aberdeen Woods Conference Center, Atlanta, GA, November 8–10, 2002. http://www.crl.edu/awcc2002/Project%20Mapping%20WG%20Report.pdf (accessed October 16, 2003).

Hall, Blaine H. *Collection Assessment Manual for College and University Libraries.* Phoenix, AZ: Oryx, 1985.

Hamaker, Charles A. "Some Measures of Cost Effectiveness in Library Collections." *Journal of Library Administration* 16, no. 3 (1992): 57–69.

Hamilton, Beth A., and William B. Ernst Jr., eds. *Multitype Library Cooperation.* New York: Bowker, 1977.

Harloe, Bart. "Cooperative Collection Development and Partnerships—Panel of Representatives of Distinct Library Cooperatives Focused on Long-Standing and Traditional or New Forms of Cooperation." *Library Collections, Acquisitions, and Technical Services* 23, no. 4 (1999): 477–78.

———, ed. *Guide to Cooperative Collection Development.* Chicago: American Library Association, 1994.

Hayes, Sherman, and Don Brown. "The Library as a Business: Mapping the Pervasiveness of Financial Relationships in Today's Library." *Library Trends* 42, no. 3 (Winter 1994): 404–19.

Heady, Donna M. "Cooperation Works! Successful Models of Cooperative Collection Development: Report of a Program." *Library Acquisitions: Practice and Theory* 20, no. 2 (1996): 190–92.

Hernon, Peter, and Robert E. Dugan. *An Action Plan for Outcomes Assessment in Your Library.* Chicago: American Library Association, 2002.

Hewitt, Joe A., and John S. Shipman. "Cooperative Collection Development among Research Libraries in the Age of Networking: Report of a Survey of ARL Libraries." *Advances in Library Automation and Networking* 1 (1987): 189–232.

Hightower, Christy, and George Soete. "The Consortium as Learning Organization: Twelve Steps to Success in Collaborative Collections Projects." *Journal of Academic Librarianship* 21, no. 2 (March 1995): 87–91.

Holley, Robert P. "Cooperative Collection Development: Yesterday, Today, and Tomorrow." *Collection Management* 23, no. 4 (1998): 19–35.

Howrey, Morrison. "Partners in Illinet: A Study in Two Parts." *School Library Media Annual* 9 (1991): 155–63.

Ionesco, Medea. "Regional Cooperation for Research Collections." *Collection Building* 9, no. 2 (1989): 7–11.

Jakubs, Deborah L. "The AAU/ARL Global Resources Program: Both Macrocosm and Microcosm." *ARL: A Bimonthly Report on Research Library Issues and Actions from ARL, CNI, and SPARC,* no. 206 (October 1999): 1–7.

Johnson, Peggy. "Symposium on Cooperative Collection Development: A Report." *Library Acquisitions: Practice and Theory* 20, no. 2 (1996): 157–62.

Johnson, Peggy, and Bonnie MacEwan, eds. *Collection Management and Development: Issues in an Electronic Era. Proceedings of the Advanced Collection Management and Development Institute, Chicago, Illinois, March 26–28, 1993.* Chicago: American Library Association, 1994.

Kachel, Debra E. *Collection Assessment and Management for School Libraries: Preparing for Cooperative Collection Development.* Westport, CT: Greenwood, 1997.

Kaiser, John R. "Resource Sharing in Collection Development." In *Collection Development in Libraries: A Treatise,* edited by Robert D. Stueart and George B. Miller Jr., 139–57. Greenwich, CT: JAI, 1980.

Kaplan, Robert S., and David P. Norton. "The Balanced Scorecard—Measures That Drive Performance." *Harvard Business Review* 70, no. 1 (January–February 1992): 71–79.

————. *The Balanced Scorecard: Translating Strategy into Action*. Boston: Harvard Business School Press, 1996.

Karp, Rashelle S., ed. *Powerful Public Relations: A How-to Guide for Libraries*. Chicago: American Library Association, 2002.

Kent, Allen. "Library Resource Sharing Networks: How to Make a Choice." *Library Acquisitions: Practice and Theory* 2, no. 2 (1978): 69–76.

Kent, Allen, and Thomas J. Galvin, eds. *The Structure and Governance of Library Networks: Proceedings of the 1978 Conference in Pittsburgh, Pennsylvania, Co-sponsored by National Commission on Libraries and Information Science and University of Pittsburgh*. New York: Marcel Dekker, 1979.

Kester, Diane D., and Shirley T. Jones. "The Birth and Growth of Library Resource Sharing in Wayne County." *North Carolina Libraries* 53, no. 3 (Fall 1995): 97–123.

Kies, Cosette. *Marketing and Public Relations for Libraries*. Metuchen, NJ: Scarecrow, 1987.

Kingma, Bruce R. *The Economics of Information: A Guide to Economic and Cost-Benefit Analysis for Information Professionals*. Englewood, CO: Libraries Unlimited, 1996.

Kohl, David F. "Farewell to All That . . . Transforming Collection Development to Fit the Virtual Library Context: The OhioLINK Experience." In *Restructuring Academic Libraries*, edited by Charles A. Schwartz, 108–20. Chicago: American Library Association, 1997.

Kopp, James J. "Library Consortia and Information Technology: The Past, the Present, the Promise." *Information Technology and Libraries* 17, no. 1 (March 1998): 7–12.

Kowalski, Greg, David Crumm, and Herb Gunn. "How to Get Your Library's Story in the Local Newspaper." *Unabashed Librarian*, no. 125 (2002): 29–31.

Kraus, Joe W. "Prologue to Library Cooperation." *Library Trends* 24, no. 2 (October 1975): 169–81.

Kreimeyer, Vicki R. "Washington's Cooperative Collection Development Project." *PNLA Quarterly* 53, no. 3 (Spring 1989): 26–28.

Krueger, Karen. "A System Level Coordinated Cooperative Collection Development Model for Illinois." In *Coordinating Cooperative Collection Development: A National Perspective*, edited by Wilson Luquire, 49–63. New York: Haworth, 1986.

Kulleseid, Eleanor R. "Cooperative Collection Development in the School Library Revolution." *Bookmark* 50, no. 1 (Fall 1991): 21–23.

LaCroix, Michael J. "MINITEX and ILLINET: Two Library Networks." *Occasional Papers* (University of Illinois at Urbana-Champaign. Graduate School of Library and Information Science) 178 (May 1987): 1–42.

Lange, Janice. "The Conspectus: A Tool for Collection Assessment and Description." *Encyclopedia of Library and Information Science*, 65–78. New York: Marcel Dekker, 2000.

Leonard, Barbara G. "The Metamorphosis of the Information Resources Budget." *Library Trends* 42, no. 3 (Winter 1994): 490–98.

Lopresti, Robert. "Sharing the Law: A Cooperative Legal Materials Project." *Advances in Library Resource Sharing* 3 (1992): 17–27.

Lougee, Wendy Pradt. *Diffuse Libraries: Emergent Roles for the Research Library in the Digital Age.* Washington, DC: Council on Library and Information Resources, 2002.

Maass, Barbara. "The New Mythology: Co-operative Collection Development." *Canadian Library Journal* 46, no. 1 (February 1989): 23–29.

Machovec, George S. "Model Strategic Plan for a Multitype Library Consortium." *Online Libraries and Microcomputers* 14, no. 8/9 (September 1996): 1–4.

Mahoney, Brian D. "Electronic Resource Sharing in Community Colleges: A Snapshot of Florida, Wisconsin, Texas, and Louisiana." *Community and Junior College Libraries* 9, no. 2 (2000): 31–35.

Martin, Harry S. "Coordination by Compact: A Legal Basis for Interstate Library Cooperation." *Library Trends* 24, no. 2 (October 1975): 191–213.

McCallister, Myrna J., and Roderick F. Gregory. "The Western North Carolina Library Network: An Experiment in Resource Sharing." *Advances in Library Resource Sharing* 3 (1992): 106–23.

Medina, Sue O. "The Evolution of Cooperative Collection Development in Alabama Academic Libraries." *College and Research Libraries* 53, no. 1 (January 1992): 7–19.

Medina, Sue O., and William C. Highfill. "Effective Governance in a State Academic Network: The Experience of the Network of Alabama Academic Libraries." *Library Administration and Management* 6, no. 1 (Winter 1992): 15–20.

Miller, Edward P., and Jodi Perlman Cohen. "Collection Development in a Multi-system Cooperative: An Acquisition Policy and Plan." *Library Acquisitions: Practice and Theory* 10, no. 4 (1986): 329–33.

Millson-Martula, Christopher A. "The Greater Midwest Regional Medical Library Network and Coordinated Cooperative Collection Development: The RLG Conspectus and Beyond." *Illinois Libraries* 71 (January 1989): 31–39.

Montgomery, K. Leon, and C. Edwin Dowlin. "The Governance of Library Networks: Purposes and Expectations." In *The Structure and Governance of Library Networks: Proceedings of the 1978 Conference in Pittsburgh, Pennsylvania, Co-sponsored by National Commission on Libraries and Information Science and University of Pittsburgh,* edited by Allen Kent and Thomas J. Galvin, 179–209. New York: Marcel Dekker, 1979.

Mosher, Paul H. "Collaborative Collection Development in an Era of Financial Limitations." *Australian Academic and Research Libraries* 20 (March 1989): 5–15.

———. "Cooperative Collection Development Equals Collaborative Interdependence." *Collection Building* 9, no. 3/4 (1989): 29–32.

Mosher, Paul H., and Marcia Pankake. "A Guide to Coordinated and Cooperative Collection Development." *Library Resources and Technical Services* 27, no. 4 (October–December 1983): 417–31.

Naru, Linda A. "The Role of the Center for Research Libraries in the History and Future of Cooperative Collection Development." *Collection Management* 23 (1998): 49–50.

North American Title Count: Titles Classified by Library of Congress and National Library of Medicine Classifications. CD-ROM. Prepared for the Association for Library Collections and Technical Services, a division of the American Library Association, by the Library Research Center, Graduate School of Library and Information Science. Urbana-Champaign, IL: University of Illinois, 2002. Excerpts available at http://www.ala.org/Content/NavigationMenu/ALCTS/Publications6/Catalog/Collection_Management1/2001_North_American_Title_Count.htm (accessed November 5, 2003).

Nye, Julie Blume. "A New Vision for Resource Sharing: TRLN Document Delivery Project." *North Carolina Libraries* 53, no. 3 (Fall 1995): 100–104.

Oberg, Larry R. "Evaluating the Conspectus Approach for Smaller Library Collections." *College and Research Libraries* 49, no. 3 (May 1988): 187–96.

O'Connor, Steve, and Stephen Pugh. "Collaborative Purchasing: A Model for Financially Straitened Times." *Collection Management* 24, no. 1/2 (2000): 57–77.

Olson, Georgine N., and Barbara McFadden Allen, eds. *Cooperative Collection Management: The Conspectus Approach*. New York: Neal-Schuman, 1994.

Patrick, Ruth J. *Guidelines for Library Cooperation: Development of Academic Library Consortia*. Santa Monica, CA: System Development Corporation, 1972.

Payne, Lizanne. "The Washington Research Library Consortium: A Real Organization for a Virtual Library." *Information Technology and Libraries* 17, no. 1 (March 1998): 13–17.

Perrault, Anna H. "The Printed Book: Still in Need of CCD." *Collection Management* 24, no. 1/2 (2000): 119–36.

Peters, Paul Evan. "Cost Centers and Measures in the Networked Information Value Chain." *Journal of Library Administration* 26 (1998): 203–12.

Poll, Roswitha. "Performance, Processes and Cost: Managing Service Quality with the Balanced Scorecard." *Library Trends* 49, no. 4 (Spring 2001): 709–17.

Potter, William Gray. "Recent Trends in Statewide Academic Library Consortia." *Library Trends* 45, no. 3 (Winter 1997): 416–34.

Reed, Sally Gardner. *Making the Case for Your Library: A How-to-Do-It Manual*. New York: Neal-Schuman, 2001.

Reed-Scott, Jutta. *Manual for the North American Inventory of Research Library Collections*. Rev. ed. Washington, DC: Association of Research Libraries, 1988.

Richards, Diane. "Making One Size Fit All: Minnesota State Colleges and Universities Manage a Legislative Mandate for Cooperative Collection Development." *Library Collections, Acquisitions, and Technical Services* 25, no. 1 (Spring 2001): 93–112.

Roberts, Anne F., and Susan Griswold Blandy. *Public Relations for Librarians*. Englewood, CO: Libraries Unlimited, 1989.

Roberts, Elizabeth P. "Cooperative Collection Development of Science Serials." *Serials Librarian* 14, no. 1/2 (1988): 19–31.

Roberts, Stephen A. *Financial and Cost Management for Libraries and Information Services*. 2nd ed. West Sussex: Bowker-Saur, 1998.

Robinson, Barbara M., and Sherman Robinson. "Strategic Planning and Program Budgeting for Libraries." *Library Trends* 42, no. 3 (Winter 1994): 420–47.

Rowley, Jennifer. *Information Marketing*. Aldershot: Ashgate, 2001.

Rutstein, Joel S. "National and Local Resource Sharing: Issues in Cooperative Collection Development." *Collection Management* 7, no. 2 (Summer 1985): 1–16.

Savard, Rejean, ed. *Education and Research for Marketing and Quality Management in Libraries*. Munich: K. G. Saur, 2002.

Schaffner, Bradley L. "Specialized Cooperative Efforts in Collection Development: An Analysis of Three Slavic Programs." *Collection Management* 24, no. 3/4 (2000): 263–80.

Shelton, Cynthia, et al. "Best Practices in Cooperative Collection Development: A Report Prepared by the CRL Working Group on Best Practices." Presented at the New Dynamics and Economics of Cooperative Collection Development Conference Hosted by the Center for Research Libraries, Atlanta, GA, November 8–10, 2002. http://www.crl.edu/awcc2002/BESTPRACTICESRPTrev.pdf (accessed November 7, 2003).

Shoaf, Eric. "The Effects of Consortia Membership on Library Planning and Budgeting." *Library Administration and Management* 13, no. 4 (Fall 1999): 196–201.

Shreeves, Edward. "Is There a Future for Cooperative Collection Development in the Digital Age?" *Library Trends* 45, no. 3 (Winter 1997): 373–90.

Simpson, Donald B. "Library Consortia and Access to Information: Costs and Cost Justification." *Journal of Library Administration* 12, no. 3 (1990): 83–97.

Sinclair, Michael P. "A Typology of Library Cooperatives." *Special Libraries* 64 (April 1973): 181–86.

Sloan, Bernard G., and J. David Stewart. "ILLINET Online: Enhancing and Expanding Access to Library Resources in Illinois." *Library Hi Tech* 6, no. 3 (1988): 95–101.

Sloan, Bernie. "Testing Common Assumptions about Resource Sharing." *Information Technology and Libraries* 17, no. 1 (March 1998): 18–30.

Soete, George J., comp. *Collaborative Collections Management Programs in ARL Libraries*. SPEC Kit 235. Washington, DC: Association of Research Libraries, Office of Leadership and Management Services, 1998.

Sohn, Jeanne. "Cooperative Collection Development: A Brief Overview." *Collection Management* 8, no. 2 (Summer 1986): 1–9.

Stevens, Charles H. "Governance of Library Networks." *Library Trends* 26, no. 2 (Fall 1977): 219–40.

Subcommittee on Guidelines for Collection Development, Collection Management and Development Committee, Resources Section, Resources and Technical Services Division. *Guide to the Evaluation of Library Collections.* Chicago: American Library Association, 1989.

Thornton, Glenda A. "Impact of Electronic Resources on Collection Development, the Roles of Librarians, and Library Consortia." *Library Trends* 48, no. 4 (Spring 2000): 842–56.

Twiss, Thomas M. "A Validation of Brief Tests of Collection Strength." *Collection Management* 25, no. 3 (2001): 23–37.

Vikor, Desider L., George Gaumond, and Fred M. Heath. "Building Electronic Cooperation in the 1990s—the Maryland, Georgia, and Texas Experiences." *Journal of Academic Librarianship* 23, no. 6 (November 1997): 511–14.

Wagner, Ralph D. *A History of the Farmington Plan.* Lanham, MD: Scarecrow, 2002.

Wall, C. Edward, and Donald Riggs, eds. "State of the State Reports: Statewide Library Automation, Connectivity, and Resource Access Initiatives." *Library Hi Tech* 14, no. 2/3 (1996): 1–352.

Walters, Edward M. "The Issues and Needs of a Local Library Consortium." *Journal of Library Administration* 8, no. 3/4 (Fall–Winter 1987): 15–29.

Weber, David C. "A Century of Cooperative Programs among Academic Libraries." *College and Research Libraries* 37, no. 3 (May 1976): 205–21.

Weingand, Darlene E. *Administration of the Small Public Library.* Chicago: American Library Association, 2001.

———. *Marketing/Planning Library and Information Services.* 2nd ed. Englewood, CO: Libraries Unlimited, 1999.

Welsch, Erwin K. "A Collection Development Model for Foreign Literatures." *Collection Management* 7, no. 1 (Spring 1985): 1–11.

Wetherbee, Louella V. "Multistate Library Networks: A Model for Lay Representation on Library Network Boards." *Journal of Library Administration* 8, no. 3/4 (Fall–Winter 1987): 31–49.

Williams, Pauline, and Rosemary Arneson. "Using the Automated OCLC/ WLN Conspectus at a Small University." *Against the Grain* 13, no. 2 (April 2001): 1–26.

Wolf, Milton T. "Cooperative Collection Management: Online Discussion." *Collection Management* 23, no. 4 (1998): 59–93.

Wolf, Milton T. and Marjorie E. Bloss. "The Whole Is Greater than the Sum of Its Parts." *Collection Management* 24, no. 1/2 (2000): 105–18.

Wolfe, Lisa A. *Library Public Relations, Promotions and Communications: A How-to-Do-It Manual.* New York: Neal-Shuman, 1997.

Woolls, Blanche. "Public Library-School Library Cooperation; a View from the Past with a Prediction for the Future." *Journal of Youth Services in Libraries* 14, no. 3 (Spring 2001): 8–10.

INDEX

The letter "f" following a page reference indicates a figure.

James Burgett is Collection Development Coordinator and Team Leader of Collection Services for the University of Kentucky (UK) Libraries. He allocates state and endowment collection resources, oversees the acquisition of systemwide resources, monitors the collection development activities of subject teams, supervises the Gifts and Exchange section, and serves as bibliographer for the German and French collections. Burgett represents UK on the Collections Committee of KYVL, Kentucky's statewide virtual library, and chairs the State-Assisted Academic Libraries Council of Kentucky (SAALCK) CD group. Author of several articles, he is co-editor of the print and online annual *Reference Reviews Europe*. He holds a Ph.D. in German language and literature from the University of Minnesota and an M.L.S. from the University of Kentucky.

John Haar is Associate University Librarian and Director of the Central Library at Vanderbilt University. He has specialized in academic library collection development since 1977. Haar recently chaired a working group sponsored by the Center for Research Libraries that created an international "map" of cooperative collection development projects. The author of numerous publications, including a *Guide to Collection Development and Management Administration, Organization, and Staffing,* he chaired the Collection Development and Management Section of the Association for Library Collections and Technical Services 2003–2004. Haar holds a doctorate in history from the University of Georgia and a master's degree in library science from Emory University.

Linda L. Phillips is Alumni Distinguished Service Professor and Head, Collection Development and Management at the University of Tennessee Libraries. A leader in the development of Tennessee's statewide resource-sharing network, TENN-SHARE, she received the Tennessee Library Association Honor Award for 2000 in recognition of her contributions to the formation of the Tennessee Electronic Library. Phillips has published numerous articles about state and local library collaboration. She has served on the ACRL Board of Directors and as member-at-large to the ALCTS Collection Management and Development Section and is a member of the *Library Resources and Technical Services (LRTS)* editorial board. Phillips holds a master of library service degree from Rutgers University.